Crossroads in Psychoanalysis, Buddhism, and Mindfulness

Crossroads in Psychoanalysis, Buddhism, and Mindfulness

The Word and the Breath

Edited by Anthony Molino
with Roberto Carnevali
and Alessandro Giannandrea

JASON ARONSON
Lanham • Boulder • New York • Toronto • Plymouth, UK

Published by Jason Aronson
A wholly owned subsidiary of Rowman & Littlefield
4501 Forbes Boulevard, Suite 200, Lanham, Maryland 20706
www.rowman.com

10 Thornbury Road, Plymouth PL6 7PP, United Kingdom

British Library Cataloguing in Publication Information Available

Library of Congress Cataloging-in-Publication Data

Crossroads in psychoanalysis, Buddhism, and mindfulness : the word and the breath / edited by Anthony Molino, with Roberto Carnevali and Alessandro Giannandrea.
pages cm
Includes bibliographical references and index.
ISBN 978-0-7657-0937-0 (cloth : alk. paper) -- ISBN 978-0-7657-0938-7 (electronic)
1. Buddhism--Psychology. 2. Psychoanalysis and religion. I. Molino, Anthony, 1957-
BQ4570.P76C76 2014
294.3'36150195--dc23
2013041818

™ The paper used in this publication meets the minimum requirements of American National Standard for Information Sciences Permanence of Paper for Printed Library Materials, ANSI/NISO Z39.48-1992.

Printed in the United States of America

In memory of

Nina Coltart and Richard De Martino

Contents

Foreword

Jeff Shore

The enthusiastic reception of Buddhism among psychoanalysts and psychotherapists is nothing new. Several generations have grown up inspired by the volume *Zen Buddhism and Psychoanalysis* (published in 1960 and containing essays by D. T. Suzuki, Erich Fromm, and Richard De Martino). Already in 1936, C. G. Jung had written what would become his Foreword to Suzuki's *Introduction to Zen Buddhism.* (Jung's foreword was published in English in 1949).

It is a different world today. Buddhism has hit the main line, big time. The 1989 Nobel Peace Prize was awarded to a Buddhist leader (the fourteenth Dalai Lama). In 1991 the Nobel Peace Prize went to a Burmese Buddhist laywoman (Aung San Suu Kyi). Renowned Buddhist teachers such as the Vietnamese Thich Nhat Hanh, one of the authors in this volume, have a fair following of therapists and patients. For decades now, research studies have been showing the positive effects of meditation. The recent interest is becoming more firmly grounded in therapists who not only read and discuss Buddhism, but seriously practice Buddhist meditation—and let it inform their lives and their therapy. Likewise, people practicing Buddhism are coming to see the value of psychotherapy in their lives. This book is one encouraging and courageous result.

Buddhism has a long history. Buddhist practice in the West is still in its infancy. Witness the many scandals over sex, power, and money that have come to light, caused by troubled people posing as Buddhist teachers—with or without credentials. Unfortunately, some of those most in need of therapy delude themselves into thinking they are beyond it. Buddhism has much to learn from psychotherapy, and this is not limited to issues of transference and counter-transference. Psychotherapy can help provide insight and alleviate the pain and turmoil caused by such abuse. While the onus for abuse lies squarely with the people posing as teachers, students need to face their naïve notions about their teacher's "enlightenment." Psychotherapy can help here as well.

Therapists and others the world over are coming to appreciate the insight that Buddhism offers into our emotional and intellectual life. It is also finally becoming clear that Buddhism is not found in mind-states, states of consciousness, or awareness. Nor is it found in other ways of being, including being present, not to mention the "oceanic feeling." But where then is it to be found? Buddhism begins—not ends—with the first noble truth, which can be rendered as the distress or dis-ease of being and having a self. Although clearly manifest in greed, anger, hatred, and ignorance, it is the fundamental uneasiness of birth-death, of life-death, the very being of the self—whatever our mind-state or station.

According to the *Dona Sutta* (AN 4.36), Gotama was asked what kind of being he was: a heavenly being, a demon, or a human. He denied all of them and finally stated that he was simply to be remembered as one who is "awake." This is the meaning of a "Buddha." Note that he even denied being human, at least in the terms that the question was put. Commentaries mention that someone who has cut off the root of self-delusion (the delusion-of-self) cannot be identified or defined as anything at all. This may sound inhuman. But what if this is to really be human?

A metaphor may help. Consider the life of the self as our experience in cyberspace. Virtually every site/sight and sound is literally at our fingertips. But are we satisfied with that; can we come to rest in it? The aim of Buddhist meditation is not to replace the screensaver with a zenistic one or provide a soothing *shakuhachi* soundtrack. It is to unplug the machine. This can be unsettling at first, especially if our self-identity and our world are tightly wrapped up in the sights and sounds that are now gone.

But the point is to awaken to what really is. Released from our self-reflections in cyberspace, we suddenly realize who and what we really are. Finally off the agonizing treadmill of self, we are no longer beings endlessly chasing desires that cannot be satisfied. The root-delusion has come undone. Now we look freely out of our own eye, directly encounter the other, and really see the sun in the sky, rather than its distorted image reflected on the screen of self. Realizing "my" true nature, the inviolable dignity, the sacred reality, of each and every thing is manifest: weaknesses, problems, and all. This is a fine place to continue the healing process. Gotama was a doctor of the human soul, par excellence. (How different this is from dangerous religious cults that assume enlightenment solves all problems and makes perfect "beings," or the equally naïve and dangerous delusion of assuming that there is no self and no being, so problems are unreal and can be ignored.)

This is not some state of mind, or a way of being, nor even an experience or event in the self-confining world of cyberspace. These terms no longer apply. For lack of better ones: it is waking up to supreme happiness and contentment, and then bringing this to life with real wisdom and compassion. This is the heart of Buddhism and of Buddhist meditation. It is by no means a monopoly of Buddhism, however. It is the heart of every human. It is the "inconceivable" mentioned by one author in this volume; in the words of another, it inheres not merely in giving up the idea of self, but in giving up the very "burden" that is self.

Genuine stability and mental health are the common goals of Buddhists and psychotherapists alike. The editors and contributors to this volume provide an engaging account of the joint efforts to achieve and promote those goals. May the book also serve as a springboard for us to work ever more closely, continuing to mutually nourish and inspire each other along the Way.

Kyoto
June 1, 2013

Introduction

Anthony Molino

On the dining room wall of the Freud Museum in London, by the veranda door, hangs a print of Mount Fuji. Dated 1929, it is by Kiyoshi Yoshida (1876–1956), and was a gift to Freud in 1932 from the Japanese psychologist Heisaku Kosawa. On February 20, 1932, two days after receiving the gift, Freud wrote to his faraway friend thanking him "for the beautiful picture which presents to my eyes what I have read so much about and a sight which I myself have not been granted." At about the same time, and with more than a hint of regret, Freud wrote to his dear friend Marie Bonaparte, on the eve of a trip of hers to the Orient, that he was now "paralyzed with regards to travelling." One can imagine him penning these words, at his desk, in the company of the countless antiquities that swarmed the area behind the first couch. There, standing in a relatively privileged position, was a small statue of the Buddha.

As Janine Burke recounts in her book *The Gods of Freud* (Knopf, 2006), Freud had purchased the sculpture in New York in 1909, at Tiffany's, while on his famous stateside trip in the company of Jones, Ferenczi, and Jung, following a visit of his to the Metropolitan Museum of Art. Years later, in the 1930s, Freud's interest in Oriental art grew, and several Chinese pieces made their way into his noteworthy collection. Among these one in particular stood out, a little bronze statue dating back to the Ming dynasty, that Freud affectionately dubbed "the smiling priest." The likely evocation of a Taoist demigod, I like to think that from behind the couch the figurine tells a story of its own. Of an imaginary voyage, an impossible trip eastward that Freud, the Jewish iconoclast, yearned to take but could only manage in fantasy, in the company of the complicit gods that guarded his space and with whom, at the start of every day, knowing, loving glances were exchanged.

***

Ever since, many years ago, I published *The Couch and the Tree: Dialogues in Psychoanalysis and Buddhism* (1998), I've often thought that I was the wrong person to compile such a book. This sense of mine, over time, grew into a conviction, especially as the book got translated into other languages and I'd get routinely invited to conferences or give interviews on the relationship between psychoanalysis and Buddhism. In point of fact, these occasions, while exceedingly gratifying, invariably put me in the position of having to apologize for not being a practicing Buddhist or meditator. Needless to say, this disclosure would often leave my audience or interlocutors perplexed, if not altogether disappointed. I could understand, of course, how their enthusiasm and genuine curiosity at meeting me was thus sometimes dampened in short order. Anyway, it came as no surprise when, after the translation of my book into Italian, an Italian publisher approached me to put together a new collection on the topic. By now I had been typecast, and totally albeit unwittingly identified as the "expert" in the field. And to some extent this identification persists, undoubtedly not without some degree of collusion on my part, fifteen years after *The Couch and the Tree*, even as the book published in Italy now serves as the backbone for this third collection of mine on the "crossroads" between psychoanalysis and Buddhism.

There are analysts who maintain that it is only at the end of an analysis that a patient comes to fathom fully his or her motivations for seeking out treatment in the first place. Similarly, it is only now, as this third book comes to a close, that I sense why I ever agreed to the project. In *The Couch and the Tree*, there's a paper of mine comparing aspects of Zen Buddhism with Jacques Lacan's theory and practice of psychoanalysis. In it I noted how both Zen and Lacan systematically indict prevailing notions of the ego, of that monumental "I" to which all of us, all-too-often, remain fiercely loyal or sadly attached. In his writings, regarding the transference, Lacan talks of the analyst as "the subject supposed to know" (though I prefer speaking of "the presumed subject of knowing"). At this point, the reader may begin to intuit how these last two books—and in particular the space of this introduction—have offered me the paradoxical opportunity to shake off the identification in which I've been caged for too long. A chance, I'd say, to shed the emperor's old, sticky clothes. I write these words knowing, of course that, at one and the same time, my readers have every reason to suppose, or presume, that I must know what I'm talking about. But as Antonio Porta, an Italian poet whom I've translated extensively into English, once wrote:

> I can only laugh and answer: my name is No-one
> And I don't know where I live or what I'm saying.[1]

***

In the brief period of one hundred years during which psychoanalysis has become the core introspective philosophy of the West, how do we understand its intriguing *unconscious* integration of Eastern and Western frames of mind? . . . (I)s it possible that growing commerce between East and West will de-repress the maternal order and challenge the hermeneutically-bound, causal-inclined paternal focus that has so dominated psychoanalytic discourse?

—Christopher Bollas

This book looks to inhabit the interstices of that "growing commerce" of which Christopher Bollas writes in *China on the Mind*, his masterful exploration of what we may broadly term the differences between Western and Eastern thinking. In aiming, therefore, to promote the ongoing integration of their respective "frames of mind" (I hesitate here, in such a volitional project, to use a word like "unconscious"), *Crossroads in Psychoanalysis, Buddhism and Mindfulness* will, by necessity, document just some of the challenges, conflicts, pitfalls and "wow" moments that inhere in today's historical and cultural intersections of theory, practice and experience. These crossroads are rich beyond belief in integrative potential, as baffling as they are fertile, capable of inspiring just as readily—at opposite ends of a volatile spectrum of human emotions and attitudes—squinty suspicion or facile devotion. My intent in compiling the book, its guiding principle, has always been to offer a window onto aspects of the commerce of which Bollas writes. Onto the practices of analytically-oriented psychotherapists, themselves of different "climates" and cultures, who break out of the seclusion of the consulting room to think, translate, meditate on and *mediate* their experiences (generated via the maternal order) in such a way as to make those experiences *thinkable* (via the necessary filters of the paternal order of language). In this light, the book's subtitle, *The Word and the Breath*—the privileged "instruments," respectively, of psychoanalysis and meditation—should come as no surprise.

What may, however, prove surprising is another intent of mine: namely, to escape in writing these notes the confines of the genre otherwise known as "*the introduction.*" Custom would have it that I take time here to encapsulate, in a few lines for each of the fourteen chapters that make up this book, just what each chapter is about. With a degree of brazen respect, I will not set out to do so. To navigate the pages of such a collection does not, in my opinion, warrant a compass of the traditional kind. I prefer that that the subjective constellation of each reader's momentary, or perhaps fixed, inclinations guide him or her through the waters of the text. Perhaps the section titles ("Elusive Bridges"; "Being in Practice"; "Psychoanalysis and Meditation"; "Parallel Convergences") will prove sufficiently intriguing to orient the reader. Or perhaps the authors' names will suffice: either because they're established and well-known in the literature (Safran, Young-Eisendrath, Bobrow, Phillips, Thich Nhat Hanh), or foreign and exotic-sounding (Yang, Morgana, Graziani, Munthe). Then again, maybe the buzzword of a given chapter will entice: "consciousness," "mindfulness," *karma*, *dharma*. Whatever the case,

I trust that the collection and the generosity of its contributors—the astral and psychic connections from which this book originates, and the future ones which every reader in turn will spur—will invigorate and intensify this specific form of contemporary commerce at the crossroads of East and West.

***

While most of these chapters appear for the first time in English, a few have been previously published. My thanks go to Joseph Bobrow, Ben Yarling and Elizabeth Clementson (W.W. Norton) for permission to excerpt Joe's "The Bliss Body and the Unconscious," first published in his *Zen and Psychotherapy: Partners in Liberation* (2010); to Jeremy Safran, Lydia Anderson and Josh Bartok (Wisdom Publications) for permission to reprint Jeremy's "Psychoanalysis and Buddhism as Cultural Institutions," from his *Psychoanalysis and Buddhism: An Unfolding Dialogue* (2003); and to Adam Phillips, for his "Reflections on Buddhism and Psychoanalysis," taken from *The Couch and the Tree* (1998). Getting permission to reprint Thich Nhat Hahn's "The Correlation between Psychotherapy and Buddhism" proved instead to be an ordeal. It was my collaborator Alessandro Giannandrea who discovered it on the web, where it is cited as being excerpted from a longer, unidentified essay published by the now-defunct journal *Common Boundary* (sponsor of the November 1990 "Spirituality and Psychotherapy" conference, held in Washington, DC, where the paper was first delivered). Zen Master Dario Doshin Girolami in Rome was instrumental in securing the permission, which ended up involving people scattered across meditation centers in at least three countries: the Avalokita Center in Castelli (Italy); Deer Park Monastery in Escondido (California); and the Plum Village Center in France. To our unnamed facilitators (they know who they are!) go the editors' heartfelt appreciation for helping to bring Thich Nhat Hahn's gem to a wider and deserving reading audience.

The chapters by my co-editors Roberto Carnevali and Alessandro Giannandrea (whom I thank for their collaboration and enduring friendship), as well as those by Graziano Graziani and Gherardo Amadei, are here offered in English for the first time courtesy of Società Editoriale Arpanet, publishers of *Tra Sogni del Budda e Risvegli* di Freud (2010), the Italian book of mine referred to earlier. I am doubly grateful to Arpanet's publisher, Paco Simone, for his kind permission to translate Michela Morgana's "Psychoanalysis, Transgenerational Psychotherapy and Karma," excerpted from her book *Il fango e il loto*, also published by the press. Where publishers are concerned, Jason Aronson's Amy King and Julie Kirsch believed in *Crossroads* from the get-go, and Amy especially has been fundamental in seeing it through to publication. I am grateful to them both. Special thanks go to Sean Mark for his excellent translations from the Italian of the chapters by Amadei, Graziani, Morgana and Carnevali (the latter in collaboration with Elizabeth Breiner); and to Katie Ferrell for her invaluable assistance in preparing the manuscript for publication. Finally, I would like to acknowledge a few good friends: Vanni Macchiagodena, for his generous gift of the book's cover image; Mike Eigen in New York, who graciously put me in touch with Pilar Jennings and Dorothy Yang, two of the book's stateside contributors; Jeff Shore in Kyoto, like myself an expatriate from Philadelphia and former student of Richard De Martino, whose life has crossed paths with mine in happy and serendipitous ways; an old friend I've not seen in decades, Polly Young-Eisendrath, and a new one, Nigel Wellings, whom I hope to meet soon for the first time; and Anna Zambon and Luis Ramos, who together host me every August amid the wondrous colors and spellbinding scenery of Anna's hillside estate in Tuscany. Oddly enough, every year there, the sweltering Mediterranean heat makes for the most reliably placid conditions in which to write. It is from that glorious, sun-drenched corner of the earth that these words issue and these pages begin to breathe. And it is there that Porta's evocation of Odysseus—and the play on words that masks the identity of our Greek forefather, for him to flee Polyphemos—gives way to a dream of a No-one from Elsewhere.

La Ventaia, Tuscany
August 2013

NOTES

1. *Kisses, Dreams, and Other Infidelities*, by Antonio Porta (translated by Anthony Molino) (Riverside, CA: Xenos Books, 2004), 45.

I

Elusive Bridges

Chapter One

The Correlation between Psychotherapy and Buddhism and How Buddhist Psychology Can Be Applied to Life

Thich Nhat Hanh[1]

Buddhism is usually described as a philosophy, a religion. But it is also a kind of psychotherapy, which Buddhists who are not sick practice so that they don't become sick. Those who are ill practice to be healed. The first practice is easier. When you do not suffer much, it's easy to get in touch with the wonderful things in life. I believe that Buddhism and psychotherapy can learn from and help each other. Sometimes Buddhists practicing in a *zendo* deal with remote issues such as enlightenment. They think you should deal with jealousy, anger and hatred before you practice meditation. This is wrong. Buddhist practice has to do with daily problems that psychotherapy can help address. On the other hand, psychotherapists can learn from Buddhist psychology, which is 2,500 years old. Buddhism is based on how the mind works. In Buddhism, we have a treasure of literature called the *Abhidharma* and a sophisticated teaching on mind called *Vijnanavada* (The School That Teaches Knowing). *Vijnana* means consciousness. A deep level of consciousness is called *alaya-vijnana*, the storehouse. Feelings, perceptions, suffering and happiness exist in two forms. The first form is that of a seed. Suppose you learned to smile when you were five years old. You may not have smiled in the last twenty years, but the seed of smiling is still there. Because you have not manifested this seed on the conscious level, *mano-vijnana*, your seed of smiling becomes weak. When someone says something to you, it enters your *mano-vijnana*. Everything manifested here engenders a similar seed in *alaya-vijnana*, which makes the original seed stronger. If you allow the seeds of sorrow to monopolize your *mano-vijnana*, you continue to plant new seeds of the same nature in your *alaya-vijnana*. Seeds influence and transform each other. Practice allows the seeds of peace, joy and happiness to come up and be strong.

One day, I lost a close friend, who was gracious and gave me a lot of joy. He had a heart attack and died during the night. I could not sleep the following night because the loss was so painful. So I practiced breathing. I lay on my bed visualizing the beautiful cedar trees I had planted in our yard. During walking meditation, I used to stop and bow to these cedars. I hugged them, breathing in and out. It seemed that these cedars always responded to my hugging and breathing. That night I invited these images up. I just breathed in and out. I became only the trees and the breath. It was very helpful. Each of us has moments of difficulty. When we are not able to deal with them, we have to ask our seeds of joy to come up. In this way, we counterbalance the suffering.

When I was in Vietnam, the war was intense. People outside the country did not know the war's true nature. I accepted an invitation to speak about the war at Cornell University in the United States and then made a tour of North America, Europe and Asia, telling people that the Vietnamese didn't want the war. Sometimes our voices were lost in the sound of bombs and mortar, and we had to burn ourselves alive to draw attention. But people thought our actions were political. After the tour, I was not allowed to go back to Vietnam. I was not popular with either the anti-communist or the communist government. During that first year of exile, I frequently dreamt of going home. The image I have of my childhood is a beautiful green hill with trees, flowers and small cottages. I dreamt of going back, but as soon as I arrived at the foot of the hill, some obstacle was there and I could not climb up. Then I would wake up. At that time, I was also practicing mindful living, recognizing what is beautiful, peaceful and good in Europe and America. There were trees, flowers, and fruits that do not exist in Vietnam, and I practiced being in touch with them. After some time, the dream stopped. I did not have to analyze it. The new seeds I had planted took good care of the bad seeds, which were the feeling of being in exile, the feeling of not being with my friends in Vietnam who were in difficulty. Also, as I worked and supported the peace work back home, I planted seeds that helped transform the seeds of suffering. Most of us ask the question: "What is wrong?" We forget to ask: "What is right?" Many things are not wrong. When you focus your attention only on what is wrong, you can make the situation worse. It is wise to meditate on your capacity to enjoy peace, happiness and joy, your capacity to be in touch with what is refreshing, healing and wonderful in the present moment. During the war, we were so busy helping the wounded that we sometimes forgot to smell the flowers. Night has a pleasant smell, especially in the country. But we would forget the smells of mint, coriander, thyme and sage. I would mention these herbs to the peace workers so they could be in touch with them. Southeast Asian refugees have a lot of pain within themselves. Many have lost their fathers, mothers or children. But when they come to Plum Village, our monastery near Paris, they don't show any of this. They are advised to practice breathing, smiling, looking at children. We tell people to make the children happy. By doing so, they get happiness. Last year, a sixteen-year-old girl came from England. We did not know she was mentally disturbed, that she had been seeing a therapist. In Plum Village, she lived among other young people without any special attention. After a month, she went back to England where she was staying with other children cared for by British social workers. In their view she was transformed. She showed no signs of maladaptation and also tried to help the other children around her.

COMMUNITY IS THE KEY

The existence of healthy, joyful communities is important, and psychotherapists need to take the lead in organizing such communities. Then we can send people who need help there. Community members will become helpers. First, they will help without knowing about it. That's the best kind of help. Then you can identify people who need special care and select people to help them. The people who need care will not know they are being helped. They will suddenly find that someone is spending time caring for them. That's the way we do it in Plum Village. This model is deeply rooted in the Buddhist tradition. The Buddha is important because he is the teacher. The dharma is the way shown by the Buddha, but without the *sangha* (community) it is difficult to practice. It might be a Catholic or Jewish *sangha*, but it must be a mindful and happy one. In Buddhist circles, there are teachers and students of the dharma. But the dharma is not just a theory. One cannot give students a theory. One has to give them the fruit of one's practice and experience. Therefore, teachers have to practice. The same is true of western psychotherapy. If therapists do not practice what they are trying to achieve for their clients, their therapy is not good. A therapist's practice should be directed to herself first because if she's not happy, she cannot help people. If I needed therapy, I would look for a therapist who is happy. As a teacher, I have to practice. That means I am also a student. This illustrates the principle of non-duality. By looking deeply, I can see the student in the teacher and vice versa. If there is no teacher within the student, the student has no future. A good teacher tries her best to give birth to the teacher in the student. In this way, the student is not dependent on the teacher. We have to practice in such a way that the person we help can soon be on his own. The way to do this is to give birth to the therapist in the client. A therapist should be able to share everything with her clients because if something has worked for the therapist, it will work for her clients. Some therapists say they have learned a lot by practicing meditation, but hate to share it with their clients. I don't understand that. If you cannot use your insights to help your clients, it means you have not been able to integrate those insights into your life and understanding.

INTERBEING

I hear from Buddhist psychotherapists that the Buddhist teachings about non-self cannot be applied in therapy. They think that for people to recover their mental health, they have to recover their healthy self. Talking about non-self will confuse them. Some people think that psychotherapy deals with the "self" and Buddhist practices dissolve it. Others say before we can dissolve the self, we have to have a healthy self. I don't think that is so. You cannot dissolve something that is not there. What have to be dissolved are our wrong views concerning the self. It's important that when we look at a person, we know that he or she does not exist alone. No self exists independently of other beings. Buddhists, in their practice, are working for a healthy self, a true self, understanding that this self is made only of non-self elements. Suppose we look at a leaf. There are many leaves on a tree, but each leaf is individual. When we look deeper, we see the leaf cannot exist without non-leaf elements like sunshine, earth, roots, trunk, branches and so on. Non-leaf elements maintain the leaf. In the *Prajnaparamita Heart Sutra*, there's a term I translate as interbeing. Interbeing means that you cannot be a separate entity. You can only interbe with other people and elements. You could also call it true self, the awareness that you are made wholly of non-self elements. When we look at a flower deeply enough, we see non-flower elements in it, like sunshine. Sunshine is not a flower, but you cannot have a flower without it. Another non-flower element is garbage. Those who do not practice meditation look at the flower but don't see the garbage. If they wait five or seven days they'll see the flower become garbage. Those who look deeply see it right away. When we look at garbage, we also see the non-garbage. We see the flower there. When good organic gardeners look at a garbage heap, they see cucumbers and lettuce. That is why they do not throw garbage away. They keep it to transform it back. If a flower is on her way to the garbage, the garbage is on his way to the flower. To me, this is the most important Buddhist teaching: non-duality. The flower does not consider garbage her enemy. The garbage does not get depressed and look at the flower as his enemy. They realize the nature of interbeing. In Buddhist therapy, we preserve the garbage in ourselves. We don't throw it out because if we do, we have nothing left to make our flowers grow.

DEALING WITH ANGER

Western therapists tend to take what they don't want out of their bodies and minds. Some behave like surgeons, cutting out the negative and throwing it out. Peace activists in the West think of peace that way. They think that throwing out atomic bombs will end war. They don't realize that the roots of our bombs are within us. We must deal with these roots. Anger is energy; it is garbage. We must preserve and transform it. During the war, I wrote a poem on my anger after American bombers had, for the fourth time, destroyed a village we rebuilt: I hold my face in my two hands. No, I'm not crying. I hold my face in my two hands in order to keep my loneliness warm. Two hands to nourish, two hands to protect. Two hands to keep my soul. From leaving me in anger. I held my anger; I did not express it. I took good care of my anger because I knew I had to transform it into the kind of energy that was needed for the peace of my country. There is a naïve belief that every time you get angry, you must express it in order to feel better. If you say something angry to someone, he will get hurt and say something stronger to you. So you will get more hurt. Similarly, if you are not very angry, but express anger, you may find yourself becoming angry because you have invited the seeds of anger up. You may feel that you want to express your anger to throw it out of your system. But by doing so, you only practice your anger, rehearse it. The more you express your anger, the angrier you become. When you close the door and hit a pillow, you think you are getting in touch with your anger. But you are only transforming the energy of your anger into the energy of pounding and hitting. You feel better because you have spent much energy hitting the pillow. But the seeds and roots of your anger are still there. I don't think you are in touch with your anger as you hit the pillow. You are dominated by your anger and are practicing it. You are planting more seeds of anger within. The Buddhist attitude is to take care of anger. We don't suppress it. We don't run away from it. We just breathe and hold our anger in our arms with utmost tenderness. Becoming angry at your anger only doubles it and makes you suffer more. The important thing is to bring out the awareness of your anger to protect and sponsor it. Then the anger is no longer alone, it is with your mindfulness. Anger is like a closed flower in the morning. As the bright sun shines on the flower, the flower will bloom because the sunlight penetrates deep into the flower. Mindfulness is like that. If you keep breathing and sponsoring your anger, mindfulness particles will infiltrate the anger. When sunshine penetrates a flower, the flower cannot resist. It is bound to open itself and reveal its heart to the sun. If you keep breathing on your anger, shining your compassion and understanding on it, your anger will soon crack and you will be able to look into its depths and see its roots.

A fourteen-year-old boy in Plum Village who practices mindfulness told me this story. When he was eleven years old, he was angry with his father.

Every time he fell down and got hurt, his father would shout at him. The boy told himself that when he grew up, he would be different. Just a year ago, his sister was playing with another little girl on a hammock. Suddenly they fell off and his sister was hurt. The boy got very angry. He wanted to shout at her: "Stupid! Why did you do that?" Fortunately, he controlled himself. Because he had practiced breathing and mindfulness in Plum Village. While other people were taking care of his wounded sister, he turned away and practiced breathing on his anger. "Suddenly I saw that I was exactly like my father," he told me. "I realized that if I didn't do something about the anger in me, I was going to transmit it to my children. Yet I saw something important. I saw that my father might have been a victim like me. The seeds of his anger might have been transmitted by my grandfather. I told myself to practice in order to transform my anger into something else. After a few months I was able to look at my father without anger. I brought the fruit of my practice back to my father and told him that I used to get angry at him, but now I understood its roots and wished that he would also practice like me in order to transform his seeds of anger."

In Buddhism, we talk about suchness. It is the nature of a person or a thing. When we understand a person's suchness, we can begin to love and help him. A person has flowers and garbage within. When we love, we accept both. It's like a cylinder of gas. We know that gas is dangerous, but it cooks a good meal. We can live peacefully with it because we know the suchness of it. So it is with your wife or husband and children. They, too, have their suchness, they too have their flower and the garbage. If you know their suchness, you will be able to live with them happily and peacefully. You will know how to turn to the flower in them and you'll profit from that. If you are ignorant, you will turn to the garbage in them. Therefore, you must understand a person if you want to help him and therefore help yourself. Meditation is the practice of nourishing the flower and transforming the garbage to flowers again. It is a continual process. You have to practice it your whole life. Basic peace work is learning to develop the capacity to enjoy the peace that is already available, like breathing and enjoying fresh, clean air. If you enjoy clean air, you know that it is precious and you will do something to prevent it from becoming unclean. Those of us who look at the state of the world feel that everyone should become a peace worker, including therapists. Psychotherapists should not deal only with sick people, but with the roots of that sickness in nature, the environment, society and the family. I urge psychotherapists to apply their own principles to their lives, to spend more and more time healing themselves and their families. In the past, we lived in houses surrounded by trees. It was pleasant to sit among the trees and play with our children, with our grandfathers and grandmothers. The family at that time was big. Now, most of us are in cities where we live in high boxes close to the sky. We don't have trees up there, we are surrounded by concrete worlds. In the past, we touched the earth; we planted our vegetables; we played with the soil. Now, children don't play with the soil. They are not in touch with trees or rivers. That is why we become mentally sick. Therapists, like others, have to try to bring us back to Mother Earth. If we touch our mother every day, we will be all right.

NOTES

1. The text excerpted from Thich Nhat Hanh's "The Correlation between Psychotherapy and Buddhism and How Buddhist Psychology Can Be Applied to Life," permission for which is covered by due diligence, is available at www.lifepositive.com/mind/psychology/psychotherapy/buddhist-psychology.asp. *Common Boundary* magazine.

Chapter Two

With Buddha in Mind

Mindfulness-Based Psychotherapy in Practice

Nigel Wellings

Soon after I started my first analysis I painted a triptych of three selves that I had become particularly aware of. The first I painted naturalistically—an image of myself as others saw me—a young man at that time. The second I painted in reds, oranges and browns. A devilish man with little horns and a wicked glint in his eyes, a self I knew too well. The last, however, was unfamiliar and very painful to admit. In dull blues and greys a third man emerged, small, crushed and very sad. He was the pain I had only just realized was inside of me. An image of my own unacknowledged suffering.

This should not have been such a surprise given my interest in Buddhism. Two and a half thousand years ago the Buddha was approached by a woman, Kisa Gotami, whose son had just died, asking that he be brought back to life. The Buddha replied that she must gather a mustard seed from every house that had not known death but as she travelled from house to house she quickly found that everyone, without exception, had lost "a child, husband, parent or friend." Finally at twilight she sat sadly by the side of the road and realized that as the lights in the valley twinkled on and off, so all life comes and goes, and that no one is free of the grief and anguish this causes. The Buddha, an expert on suffering, had known that her experience was universal—not one of us escapes the suffering of loss.

As counselors, psychotherapists, and analysts we too have people who bring their suffering to us in the hope that we can find a way to help them feel better. If I think about my own clinical practice I have been brought the experiences of:

- being valueless
- being lost within an imaginal world
- being with an absence of feeling
- being expected to be clever
- being with abusive alcoholic and violent parents
- being with self-destructive unexpressed rage
- being the renegade child
- being the victim of sexual abuse
- being made always wrong and humiliated
- being crushed
- being abandoned
- being terrified of emotional vulnerability
- being fearful of emotional expression
- being ignored, emotionally undernourished and shamed
- being in fear of father's unpredictable moods
- being special
- being annihilated by one's own goodness

Buddhism tells us that the Buddha, before he became enlightened as the nobleman Siddartha, had his own wake-up call when he first became conscious of suffering. Discovering his intoxicating pleasures to be distractions, he went out onto the streets and saw all around him illness, old age, and something mostly hidden from us nowadays—death. This deeply disturbed him. He thought if this happened to other people it would surely happen to him as well. He too would know insecurity, being sick, being infirm and dying.

The Buddha's response to his shocking discovery was to become immediately curious. Rather than retreating back into what had become a meaningless life, he looked even closer at the unhappiness he saw all around him and tried to understand its different expressions and where each came from. Early Buddhism says that the fruit of this investigation was taught by the Buddha during his first discourse, in which he talks about taking a realistic look at what is happening and how to do something about it. It is interesting to look at this in detail and see how precise it is. He starts by describing suffering as an inseparable element of human experience, and he sees this as falling into three distinct categories. The first he called the *suffering of suffering*. That is to say, the unavoidable and universal suffering that comes from the round of biological life: having children, ageing, physical and psychological ill health, old age, decrepitude and death. The second he called the *suffering of change*. Coming to grips with the ephemeral and transitory nature of human existence, the Buddha came to understand that life could only frustrate and distress us: especially as we grasp, ineffectually, onto precious but transient things while being compelled to accept life's often unwanted impositions. He saw that our wanting and not wanting, so deeply part of our human psyche, was nonetheless in conflict with an ever-changing universe over which we had no control. The third category he called the *suffering of conditioned existence*. This is both the most profound and also easily missed of the three. It describes a low-grade, pervasive dissatisfaction that comes from things never being quite right, never measuring up or fulfilling our expectations, always leaving us wanting something more or different. Think, for example, of shopping and how quickly the pleasure of a purchase decays. Sigmund Freud may have put his finger on it when he said that the ego is the seat of anxiety. That there is something just about being a person that creates a deep uneasiness and uncertainty. We could also see this as the suffering that arises from not knowing who we are.

The Buddha's word that we translate here as suffering is *dukkha*, and as we have seen, it is rich in its variety and spread of meaning. Originally it referred to an ill-fitting axle hole on a cart which made for a bumpy ride; by extension the concept ranges between the pervasive unsatisfactoriness of everything that mars our happiness, the feeling that nothing is ever quite right, to experiences of anxiety, stress, anguish, deep despair and emotional chaos. It also includes the rubbing uneasiness that there is something more to life, the discomfort and perhaps longing of an unanswered spiritual hunger. This last element can also build into yet another category of suffering, the awareness of the suffering of others.

This makes me think of C. G. Jung, who'd found that in a long analysis the suffering of the broader world came to replace the suffering of the individual. Jung noted, in fact, that after a patient had gone through his or her own pain, the pain of the world and how *to be* with it often took center stage. Pema Chödrön, a wonderfully compassionate American Buddhist nun says much the same thing, suggesting that as we open our hearts we begin to feel the pain of the world around us. A pain more difficult and challenging than our own because it seems there is nothing we can do to really help it.

I think many of us will have felt this—it is hard not to when we have daily news updates on the unimaginable suffering of the world. As I write I am aware that whenever I have spoken of this shared suffering there have always been natural disasters, calamities or wars afflicting our planet. I think of how, unexpectedly, an ordinary airplane flight has sometimes put me among people who have had homes, parents, grandparents, aunts and uncles, brothers and sisters, cousins, friends, children, or tiny babies snatched away from them. People dispossessed, violated, killed. In the face of such suffering I can see myself escape defensively into distraction, into indifference, looking at the next news item. An earthquake, nuclear leaks, the latest Middle East uprising. . . . And then the football scores.

The Buddha as Health Professional

Some of us may find all this focusing on suffering a source of suffering itself. It is indeed depressing and frightening to confront what hurts us and others. The Buddha in his time was also criticized for focusing on suffering. His answer to this criticism—and we as counselors and psychotherapists may borrow it—was to describe three types of doctors. The first is a reckless optimist. Called to the patient he declares there is nothing wrong. The second is a defeated pessimist. Called to the patient he says the patient is truly ill but there is nothing that may be done. The third is a realist. Called to the patient he sees there is a problem but can also see its cause, knows it cure, and the medicine it will take to promote the cure. This cause, cure and medicine are what we shall next consider.

THE CAUSE

If suffering is the illness then what is it that makes us susceptible to it? The Buddha's diagnosis of the root cause of suffering was not something social or political outside of us but a personal and insatiable "craving" driven by a deep spiritual ignorance—*tanha.* Christina Feldman, an accomplished insight meditation teacher, gets to the heart of this when she says that suffering arises in the gap between how things are and how we want them to be. It is our craving that is the problem ultimately, not really the circumstance. Buddhism, with its love of lists, spells this out systematically.

What causes suffering is our craving for sensual pleasure, craving for existence and craving for non-existence. The first, craving for sensual pleasures, is clear: it's to do with that endless drive to seek pleasurable sensory (and, I would add, psychological) experiences while defending against anything unpleasant, repugnant or threatening. This style of craving is particularly displayed in addiction. There the darker side of its nature is fully revealed—a nightmarish compulsion that is without any hope of full or lasting satisfaction. Thinking about this I am reminded of Freud's rather bleak belief that there is something inside each of us that he called the "it": a form of agency, an insatiable appetite, that simply wants what it wants. An unreflective mouth that gobbles up everything but knows no satisfaction. The experience of wandering around our house wanting something without knowing what. Buying more superfluous stuff off the Internet, turning on the TV when there is nothing on, looking in the fridge when it is empty. The fruitless compulsion to consume . . .

The second and third forms of craving, for existence and non-existence, take us deep into the psychoanalytic territory of the formation of the self. Here, questions arise concerning how we become addicted to a sense of personal identity dependent on continuity, stability, and agency. An identity capable of prevailing against and dominating ourselves, those around us and the world we all inhabit. And yet, at the same time, this self also yearns for rest and oblivion, to feel nothing, to dissociate and be free of the conflicting emotions and tormenting thoughts that comprise much of its experience. Again, severity reveals its interior. These two cravings show themselves particularly in the existential crises that psychoanalysis has come to recognize as narcissism—a pandemic psychological disorder in our Western world. Narcissism is the hurt we feel when we do not know who we are, a "disorder" that takes its name from the Greek myth of a beautiful young man called Narcissus. In the myth, the nymph Echo dies from the grief of unrequited love because Narcissus cannot love anyone but himself. The god Nemesis, as a punishment for this, causes Narcissus to fall in love with his own beautiful image reflected in a pool of water. At the water's edge, captivated by his own face, Narcissus remains trapped until he too pines away and dies.

When wounded narcissistically we may present to the world a highly successful mask, an accomplished and pleasing persona. Tough, generous, charming and seductive. But beneath this facade, barely acknowledged by ourselves and greatly feared, is another set of emotions, equally distorted by grandiosity, where we feel desperately impoverished, shame soaked, depressed, worthless, and inferior. Longing for a love through which to come to know ourselves, we remain incapable of receiving or giving any. Acknowledging the emotions behind the mask is extraordinarily painful because it feels humiliating, even annihilating, and the vulnerability this threatens is the very thing we all want to avoid.

I offer here an example of a narcissistic wound in someone attracted to Buddhism. Carl had been interested in spirituality since his early teens. He had read many books about meditation and transpersonal psychology. He also took lots of hallucinogenic drugs and believed that the meditative states of non-ordinary consciousness he had read about he had experientially achieved. Inhabiting what he believed to be an exalted state, he tried to join a spiritual group under the guidance of a teacher. This experience however brought some problems. First, his relationships with the other students was made difficult by his need for them to recognize his spiritual superiority, cloaked in a persona of caring and seeming detachment. Several of the younger women within the group had been seduced by this and then had been badly hurt by his inability to appropriately meet their emotional needs. Second, his relationship with the teacher was marred by deep ambivalence. Initially he had listened attentively, keen to be seen as a central and important student, but once the teacher recognized his presence and began to invite him into a student teacher relationship, he immediately drew back feeling angry and defensive. Carl was incapable of the relationship that the spiritual teaching demanded. While he wanted the teacher to acknowledge his spiritual insights, stolen through drugs, he was not prepared to actually undergo any real initiation that might entail a surrender of his narcissistic self.

Carl's story closely mirrors the Narcissus myth. Driven by a mixture of omnipotence and escapism, he is drawn into searching for a relationship with something other and perhaps greater than himself. However he does not yet have the capacity to love. Incapable of either giving or surrendering, and thus incapable of relationship, he ends up as he always has been, alone. His legitimate psychological needs for the existence of a healthy, robust ego are sabotaged by his narcissistic craving for acknowledgment of his empty grandiose persona. Fearful of intimacy he retreats, still armored against his vulnerability. Ultimately the issue of narcissism is one of identity. The story offers one last twist that strangely links its insight to that of the Buddha. The reflection that Narcissus becomes mesmerized by is actually nothing but an illusion. While it appears that Narcissus looks at himself there is really no one there. This strangely mirrors Buddhism's insight that behind all our experiences there is no experiencer, no single person who is having the experience. There is only the experience itself, part of which is the feeling of an enduring yet illusionary self that it happens to.

Buddhism links this absence of a discrete and lasting self to its understanding of *shūnyatā*, the emptiness or absence of an enduring and separate self that is discovered under close analysis. The insight meditation teacher Joseph Goldstein says that one way of understanding emptiness is to think of it as an absence of self-centeredness. This reveals a deeper understanding of narcissism. Narcissism is more than believing the universe revolves around us. It is the mistaken belief that there is an enduring self around which the universe revolves. The craving for pleasurable experiences, for existence and non-existence, creates suffering because it insists on a control that is impossible to achieve, by a self that was never really there in the first place! A self that is no more than a fearful contraction that we cannot let go of. Observation confirms the value of this insight. All of us experience flow states—when engaged, say, in or by music, the arts, or sports—without having to be aware of our sense of self while engaged in them. When we stop fearfully grasping at our deep desire for a brittle identity, things become more spacious, easier, more nourishing—and fun.

THE CURE

What are our images of "cure" in psychotherapy? Freud offers "ordinary unhappiness" instead of a neurotic unhappiness. Something more manageable and less unrelated to the consensus reality. Jung offers "individuation," an image of psychological wholeness that includes all those parts of the self-repressed. A kind of superman who has a life full of meaning. Object relations therapists value object relations—the ability to become related to another, to love and be loved. Humanistic psychotherapy wants us to realize our human potential, to express a full spectrum of emotional experience. Buddhism imagines something more that it calls *nirvana*: the irreversible burning away of craving which brings all suffering to an end forever.

My sense is that the goals articulated by different modalities of analysis, psychotherapy and counseling all reflect ideal states. They involve complex narratives that easily obscure where we actually are and who we actually are at any given moment. Do any of us really ever learn how to express our "self" fully, love sanely, become whole, let alone become enlightened? In practice are we not all more muddled, even as we subscribe to an ideal, which, though never realized, nonetheless acts as a valuable beacon on a horizon we may never reach?

Buddhism is certainly also prone to such idealism. What could be more idealistic than the goal to bring all suffering to an end forever? But it also has another face, one closer to the ground: one that simply invites us to stay with "what simply is," consciously, mindfully. That invites us not to rush on wishing to be what we are not. Seeing in such rushing a subtle form of self-abuse. A non-acceptance of who we are, a narcissistic grasping at being something more or other. It invites us, ultimately, to be *mindful* of the fact that all the rushing and grasping for ideals, or for narratives of identity—including Buddhist ones—is in itself a source of suffering.

What Buddhism values, in contrast, is something plainer and simpler. Its cure consists of being able to stay with our experience fully, without needing the protection of defensive closure. This is not the same as Freud's ordinary unhappiness because it is the source of real happiness. It is not Jung's individuation, for the creation of individual meaning is much less important than developing a genuinely kind quality of awareness. And it is not just about human love or emotional expression in any ordinary sense because while it values these qualities, it also mindfully discriminates their often hidden, obscure and feral motivations.

The Buddha's cure, though a narrative itself, is something that begins where we are, with who we are, in the emotions we have. It is the ability to be with ourselves without fear and to dissolve the grasping of our narcissism so that we dare to experience our sameness with the world around us. Recognizing that we are all constantly changing, and that we all suffer when we protectively contract around the idea of who we are; that inside of each of us is a limitless expanse of compassionate well-being, our Buddha Nature. Knowing this, directly, nakedly, right here and now is the Buddha's cure. A cure psychotherapy can comfortably share in.

THE MEDICINE

The Buddha's medicine that affects this cure comes in three parts: an ethical relationship with one's self and the world, meditation, and the cultivation of wisdom. In my experience as a psychotherapist, while it may be necessary to be wary of spiritual ideals—particularly when they threaten to invade the consulting room—we need not fear this medicine as its therapeutic qualities are immediately apparent and are widely applicable within and without an explicitly Buddhist context. Let's look at each of them.

Ethics

Buddhist ethics are governed by the belief that all our thoughts and actions have repercussions and therefore it is important to create good causes and this is best done by wishing to do good and actively avoiding doing harm. From this come two central values: unconditional friendliness and compassion, *maitrī* and *karunā*. D. W. Winnicott says something similar when he speaks of the "facilitating environment": we flourish in an atmosphere of kindness and generosity, and we may exemplify and encourage this in our psychotherapeutic practice. This becomes particularly pertinent when we begin to see clearly the depth of our self-criticism, self-rejection and sometimes self-loathing.

Here is an example. Jane was menopausal. Each night she awoke overheated and bombarded with self-critical thoughts which left her shattered and with no sense of her very real qualities and talents. At times her thinking was plainly paranoid and quite unrelated to reality. However she was also a practitioner of mindfulness, and she found that frequently her practice—done in the early morning hours next to her sleeping husband—enabled her to disidentify with what she recognized as the internalized voice of her viciously critical father and, consequently, to find a place of rest. Although this was difficult to achieve and not always possible, it gradually became clear that this phase represented an initiatory threshold wherein Jane was meeting her own destructive self each night. Her ability to allow herself to stay with and experience the fullness of her nocturnal struggles was the fruit of her mindfulness. And the care and kindness she brought to the struggle, not making herself wrong or bad for having it, was an expression of the unconditional friendliness and compassion Jane was slowly learning to extend to herself.

Jane's story, in principle, is one I have come across again and again. It seems that a common component in much of the suffering that comes into the consulting room is self-criticism and self-loathing. A young woman arrives and tells me of a lifetime of depression, loneliness, and self-recrimination. Why does she blame herself? She blames herself for having her depressive moods and thoughts. It is not enough to be bleak and leaden; she is wrong and stupid as well. She says to herself, "You are a fuck wit, a loser." The Buddhist notion of unconditional friendliness, *maitrī*, fiercely challenges this. It asks we bring an intelligent kindness to our woundedness because only once a wound is accepted can the process of healing begin. Furthermore, as the contemplative psychotherapist John Welwood points out, a psychotherapy that is always pushing for change is in itself subtly harmful, if it is colluding with the abusive inner voice of the patient that says, "to be loved I must be different." As Henry James once said: "There are three important things in the world. The first is kindness. The second is kindness. And the third is kindness." I believe a psychotherapy that can embrace this authentically, and not as mere sentiment, is an ethical psychotherapy.

Mindfulness Meditation

To be mindful is to be consciously aware of what is happening inside of us and around us in each consecutive moment. This conscious awareness focuses on the sensory facts of the situation, returning from distracting thoughts, each time they are noticed, to the object of our mindfulness. If I choose to focus my mindfulness on the sounds around me, I just hear the sounds and let go, for instance, of thoughts about the wind and the damage it may be doing to my garden. If I choose my breath, I just stay with the sensations within each breath, intentionally not engaging with any thought processes and when I do, non-judgmentally stopping and returning to the breath. If I choose my emotions—a common choice in psychotherapy—I just stay with the felt sense of the emotion located within my body. I don't immediately go off into the history of the emotion nor speculate where it might lead.

In mindfulness-based psychotherapy kindness and curiosity are central. Mindfulness does not observe with a cold eye dispassionately, but with a gentle interest. Whatever it finds is entirely accepted, what is important is the awareness. This mindful position is always the position of the therapist and, when appropriate, also the position of the one who sits in the opposite chair. Nina Coltart, a psychoanalyst and Buddhist describes her experience of this:

> As regards my own practice, and how Buddhism has affected my clinical work with patients, one of the earliest things I noticed was the deepening of attention. I'd written a chapter on attention in my first book, where I refer to "bare attention," which is a very Buddhist phrase. Bare attention has a sort of purity about it. It's not a cluttered concept. It's that you simply become better, as any good analyst knows, at concentrating more and more directly, more purely, on what's going on in a session. You come to concentrate more and more fully on this person who is with you, here and now, and on what it is they experience with you: to the point that many sessions become similar to meditations. When this happens, I usually don't say very much, but am very, very closely attend-

> ing to the patient, with my thought processes in suspension, moving toward what Bion called *O*: a state which I see as being "unthought-out," involving a quality of intuitive apperception of another person's evolving truth.[1]

To this I would add that a mindfulness-based therapy must include the body and our ability to access our inner sensory world. This provides a bridge between the reflective work of psychotherapy and the capacity to be present with what arises as it arises: namely, with the experience of being mindful. Methods such as focusing, first formalized by Eugene Gendlin, invite us to be present with our emotional experience in our body, the felt sense. They invite us to find words, phrases or images that express the felt sense and remain attentive to any changes without attachment to change. All this while privileging the ability to "stay with" rather than descend into long stories "about" what is felt.

Another example: Ted described his lifelong fear of depression. He had realized that whenever he had a leaden feeling in his guts and limbs and a sense of hopelessness and indifference, he would immediately look to busy himself. When he started practicing mindfulness he became aware of this defensive maneuver and instead decided, simply and bravely, to remain mindfully present with the basic feeling. By doing this it became plain to him that the basic feeling, leaden guts and legs, feelings of hopelessness and lethargy, generated secondary emotions of fear and alarm, causing him to do anything but stay with his actual experience. In time his ability to reverse this process grew. Initially he began to consciously notice the depression and his defensive avoidance of it when it occurred. Then gradually he was able to stay present with the feelings and allow himself to have them without any desire to articulate, change or understand them in any way. Just leaving what was, as it was. Learning to stay with a sensation and a feeling, and remaining present with it until it finally passed of its own accord. Staying with, rather than stories about.

Wisdom

Talking about wisdom in psychotherapy is difficult. I observe in myself a shying away, a fear that I may get too inflated and fall into the fascism of ideals, the unhelpful and obscuring narratives we've just considered. In Buddhism, however, wisdom is equated with knowing how things really are, not just how they appear, and the way to do this is simply by being present with what is happening as it happens, without adding any of our own reactive thoughts and emotions to the experience. In short, the ongoing act of mindfulness already described. A way of being with ourselves that some forms of psychotherapy specifically concerned with trauma are beginning to recognize as extremely valuable.

Where Buddhism and psychotherapy do not meet is on how deep this process can go. At its worst psychotherapy can be satisfied with a general understanding of how wounded patterns of being were created, somehow trusting that a rational view of our neurosis will suffice. In my experience however, such knowledge is never enough. What is required is the ability to remain consciously present with the thoughts and emotions that arise out of our patterns of hurt, our complexes, *while they are being constellated.* Being mindful in this way is to take the middle way between acting out or repression, a position that neither hides defensively nor generates further cascades of the initially traumatizing emotions. When we are repeatedly with ourselves in this way we gradually gain the possibility of making a choice between automatic ways of thinking, feeling and behaving and something different, something more generous, kind and sane.

The Buddhist take on this is to see the personality and all its woundedness as a narrative, a story of who we are, that we tell ourselves all the time. A story we defend when any threat to it comes near. Most analysts, psychotherapists, and counselors will reconize a particularly obvious manifestation of this in those patients or clients that steadfastly cling to their material, actively resisting change. Their fear is probably of the unknown that would emerge if they were to let go. However it is the Buddhist belief that we are all doing this all the time—it's just that most of us do it less obviously. Thus, in a mindfulness-based psychotherapy, the narrative is less important than an awareness of how the narrative is used. The belief that being with our experience openly is more important than knowing how we became so closed. Of course to be human is to spin our own tale and the meaning that comes from this is an important element in keeping happy and sane. However the narrative can be and is frequently used defensively: a closed story about who we are, what we like and don't like and how far we can travel. Becoming aware of our narrative, and not just its content or storylines but of how we use it to defend our "self" against the fullness of experience, is central to the work.

A POSTSCRIPT OF SORTS

Recently I asked someone I have been working with for a long time what wisdom had arisen from their practice of receiving and giving psychotherapy, and their involvement with Buddhism. Their initial response was to laugh—what wisdom!—and then reflecting more seriously on the question they replied. First came the realization that they were not alone in their madness. That all of us suffer in our own way with our own stuff. This discovery made for enormous relief. Second, that telling one's story to another person helps. Relationships, intimacy, are made much better, deeper, richer and more authentic when we really talk to each other. Third, that everything changes. However bad, this too will pass—nothing has the choice to last forever. And finally that the story of "myself" is made up of thoughts, emotions and body sensations which on close examination are not as solid, not as non-negotiable as they initially seem. It really is, after all, a story, and the realization of this brings immense and unexpected freedom.

NOTES

1. This quote is taken from Anthony Molino's conversation with Nina Coltart in his book *Freely Associated: Encounters in Psychoanalysis with C. Bollas, J. McDougall, M. Eigen, A. Phillips and N. Coltart.* While the excerpt is found on pages 203–204, a significant portion of the conversation highlights Dr. Coltart's relationship with Buddhism, surely a pioneering one among psychoanalysts.

REFERENCES

Chödrön, P. 2002. *The Places That Scare You.* Boston & London: Shambhala.
Feldman, C. 2012. Private communication regarding Feldman's manuscript *Why Can't I Meditate: Befriending Your Obstacles to Mindfulness.*
Gendlin, E. 1996. *Focusing Oriented Psychotherapy.* London: Rider.
Goldstein, J. 2002. *One Dharma.* San Francisco: Harper.
Molino, A. 1997. *Freely Associated: Encounters in Psychoanalysis.* London: Free Association Books.
Welwood, J. 2000. *Towards a Psychology of Awakening.* Boston & London: Shambhala.
Winnicott, D. W. 1965. *Maturational Processes and the Facilitating Environment.* London: Hogarth Press.

Chapter Three

The Bliss Body and the Unconscious

Joseph Bobrow[1]

Freud (1918) thinks that we have been dealt "severe blows to human self-love" by three revolutions in human thought. First, Copernicus discovered that the earth is not the center of the universe, and neither is man. Then, Darwin showed that humans are subject to the same laws as microorganisms, so we are not so special after all. Finally, Freud's (1915) elaboration of the unconscious added insult to injury by demonstrating that we are not in control of even our own self-experience. "The ego," he writes, "is not master in its own house." And what about the Buddha? He invites us to discover that our house is not what we thought, that what and whom we take as real may be a case of mistaken identity. We may be more vast and more interconnected than we ever imagined—and less substantial.

Buddhists tend to cringe when they hear about the unconscious. I ran the possible title of this chapter by a longtime friend, Buddhist teacher, and psychotherapist whom I respect deeply. Her response was, "I like the bliss body part." It made me laugh, and when she asked why I was laughing—her question reinforced why I was writing the book. Perhaps, it confirmed Freud's "not master in our own house" hypothesis. Another Buddhist teacher friend, a fellow basketball fan, finds it easy to speak about Michael Jordan or other superstars being "unconscious" or "in the zone" during a game, but he also refers to moments of being unreflective as being "unconscious." On the other hand, psychoanalysts have been known to speak of "getting unconscious together" when describing a supervision group in which the dynamics of a case are explored in the context of the shared reverie of group members. Grotstein (2007) suggests that we "cast a ray of darkness" into perplexing clinical material because attempts to consciously understand sometimes yield only predictable formulations of limited value. Both not-knowing and becoming aware of not-knowing have value. Bion (1970) urges clinicians to listen without memory, desire, or attachment, to welcome the selected fact of a session in a way that lets it rise to the surface. Of course, there is an interplay between not knowing and knowing, translating the fruits of reverie into metaphor and usable, eventually verbal, form. In common parlance, we speak of becoming more "conscious" or aware about a particular automatic behavior or habit, and Freud (1916) writes about making the unconscious conscious.

I have come to believe that Buddhist meditators tend to overprivilege conscious introspection, and for that matter consciousness. They think the unconscious is still just the *Id*, the repository of forbidden sexual and aggressive wishes that reduces humans to a bundle of blind impulses. It gets under their skin. I do not think most appreciate just how far the unconscious has come. That is not to say that Buddhists do not repress sexual and aggressive urges—of course we do. Ideally, we sublimate and channel these urges, and when we do give them expression, we try to do so in a creative and life-giving way, rather than inducing misery in ourselves or others. But, then again, we are human, and thoughts of sexuality and aggression can frequently engross and sometimes capture us as we practice attentiveness on the cushion or when we reveal ourselves in the course of psychotherapy. But, in recent decades, a great deal more has come to light about what the unconscious is and how it works. I briefly summarize a few ways to think about unconscious experience, describe what I mean by "the Bliss body," and then explore how their alchemy might lead us toward a more integrated view of human experience.

UNCONSCIOUS EXPERIENCE

Freud's (1915) dynamic unconscious is characterized by sexual and aggressive bodily based drives, primary process thinking, and conflict and repression. The therapeutic focus of many in the United States who ascribe to this view is on interpreting defenses, resistances, and wishes. Klein's (1952) view is anchored in bodily based fantasies that drive a series of intersecting internalized object relations. Splitting, rather than repression, is privileged, and the analyst focuses on the patient's leading anxiety about these internalized object relations and interprets it in the transference in order to develop the patient's awareness of split-off parts of the personality and foster reparation and reintegration so healthy parts of the personality can grow. Bion's view (1984) is radical within psychoanalysis and in some ways akin to Zen. For him, the basic ground of psychoanalytic therapy is not the unconscious at all but rather infinity. Instead of focusing on repressed or split-off content, he emphasizes containing and metabolizing function necessary to transform raw sensory input into materials to be stored and worked over so they could be thought, felt, and dreamed. The therapeutic task is not to listen for derivatives of unconscious conflict or split off parts of the personality but to listen unsnagged by memory or desire or theory.

The Chilean psychoanalyst Ignacio Matte Blanco is concerned that psychoanalysis is "wandering away from itself" and tries, through his innovative formulations about an unconscious not founded on repression, to recover the essentials of Freud's contribution and extend them. Building on Freud's primary and secondary processes, Matte Blanco (1998) describes an unrepressed unconscious characterized by two kinds of propositions or types of logic: asymmetric and symmetric. Later, he (1988) writes of these modes as thinking and feeling and adds a third—being. Here, Matte Blanco uses an allegory to describe the ubiquitous activity of the unconscious. He remembers the story of a man who enters a bar and begins to walk up the vertical wall, arriving at the ceiling. He walks along it, head down, and asks for a whisky mixed with beer. People are astonished. When he finishes drinking, he pays and repeats the same journey in the opposite direction. When he leaves and closes the door, someone observes, "What a strange man, to drink whiskey mixed with beer!" Unconscious activity is so much a part of our life, we tend to miss it. It is like a fish asking what water is or where the sea is. As Matte Blanco expanded his view of the unrepressed unconscious to include our very *being*, Rodney Bomford (1999), retired Anglican canon, mathematician, and Matte Blanco scholar, makes a case in his book, *The Symmetry of God*, for the unconscious itself being a close equivalent of what we consider the sacred.

Bollas (1989) describes an unrepressed unconscious that he calls the "unthought known" and an emotional field so interconnected that it is the analyst who sometimes receives the patient's free associations before the patient is aware of them. His notion of self-experience, most of it unconscious, is intrinsically interactive with "objects" in the outside world. We each, he writes, have our own distinctive idiom, a personal and aesthetic signature that pre-dates the environmental influences in our upbringing. We seek, again unconsciously, external objects and interactions that will release this personal idiom. A simple example might be how one child is drawn early on to sounds and then to musical instruments and conducting, while another cannot get enough of throwing balls, then street games, and goes on to professional sports. Building on the Freudian concepts of condensation and displacement, Bollas describes how unconscious experience collects and comes together not only in our sleeping dreams, but also in our waking life in powerful moments of psychic intensity, powerful felt senses that are multiply determined and full of possible meanings. By freely associating to these experienced intensities, we crack them up, and their meanings are disseminated into the interpersonal and cultural commons to seed further condensing and dreaming. More recently, Bollas (1998) has spoken about how, when he listens to the unconscious, certain words or phrases or intonations may strike him while he is in a receptive state. Those moments can indicate unconscious emotional communication between him and his patient. Simply "echoing" the word or phrase can often spark a fruitful exchange if what struck a chord in Bollas did indeed represent unconscious communication.

Psychoanalysis has evolved from a one-person psychology to a two-person psychology; today, some at the frontier of research and practice find that a living systems perspective best describes the psychotherapeutic process. So, in addition to the differences between the repressed unconscious and the unrepressed unconscious, there are differences in perspective between an individually oriented unconscious that describes the singular psyche and an intersubjective unconscious, which has more affinity with unconscious emotional experience in the relational field.

Psychoanalytic thinkers describe unconscious emotional communication differently depending on their working theory about basic human connectedness and separateness. I remember a seasoned psychoanalyst I liked who supervised a group of supervisors. He had an ego psychological orientation, and he would speak about externalization rather than projection and projective identification; it blurred the boundaries of the self too much for his taste. Others like Green (1975) and Ogden (1994) write about a third area of experience created between patient and analyst, in which we can "catch the drift" of cocreated unconscious experience. This concept builds on and extends D. W. Winnicott's (1971) notion of a transitional or intermediate area of experience as well as Freud's preconscious. Freud (1912) wrote early in his career that we do indeed communicate unconsciously, and directly, without conscious mediation, but he did not follow up on this idea. Schore (2003), with his groundbreaking neuroanalytic research documenting the extensive work on right-brain-to-right-brain communication and regulation of affective states, intriguingly develops, extends, and perhaps confirms Freud's idea. From another angle, Lisby Mayer's (2007) book, *Extraordinary Knowing*, also pursues this idea and explores how much we know, often quite accurately, about people, places, and things without knowing how we know it. The book *Blink* (Gladwell, 2005) popularizes just how much of our daily information processing and decision making is accomplished outside awareness, often with uncanny efficiency and insight. And, from cognitive neuroscience (Gazzaniga and Bizzi, 2000) and other fields has come the idea of implicit or procedural experience and memory. These terms refer to both nonconscious and nonverbal experiences of repeated and mutually engaged interactional patterns. In the final phase of writing this book, a colleague, reading the manuscript, found herself associating to an intriguing formulation of Ferro (2009), an Italian psychoanalyst. Ferro views the unconscious that emerges in an analytic session as a continually transforming, co-created holographic field consisting of "characters" whose cultivation by the analytic pair grows the capacities to think, feel, and dream. Developing these capacities takes precedence over focusing on dynamic content. Each statement, each action of the patient or psychotherapist is heard as an expression of the shifting resonances of the emotional field, which itself seeks representation. I am in turn reminded of the *gatha*, or verse, we recite when we put on the *okesa*, the biblike garment that represents the Buddha's robe, which we sew ourselves as we study and prepare to accept the sixteen precepts[2] in our lineage in the ceremony called *Jukai*: I wear the robe of liberation/ the formless field of benefaction/ the Tathagatha's true teaching/ Save the many beings (Aitken, 1984, 1993).

This rather dry summary of course does not include all the approaches to the unconscious or convey the excitement in this multidisciplinary endeavor to plumb our psychic depths. I was once wondering why I liked the Bourne film series. Then, one day I slowly pronounced the protagonist's name, Jason Bourne. This time, "J Son Born" is what I heard, and it had great impact. Although language is only one way the unconscious expresses itself, here is another similar example, involving two people: A patient was speaking about someone and could not remember if the person's name was Irene or Ilene. She went back and forth about it. I listened for some time. Then, a light went off, and I slowly said to my occasionally rather concrete patient (not to resolve her dilemma), "Ilene." *I lean* surfaced for us both to see, with all the overtones about frightening yet desired dependence. The unconscious surprises, informs, and amuses; it also shocks and destabilizes. It throws us off our (conscious) game and—although it is an element of our own psyche whose feedback we do well to attend to and integrate—it is, at the same time, "other." Unconscious experience is a force to be reckoned with. One moment, it can be a source of creativity, even wisdom, and in the next feel like a persecutor. Psychoanalysis did not invent the unconscious any more than the Buddha invented essential nature. They are two deep overlapping streams that cannot be grasped but are lived every moment.

Personally, I have come to view communications in analysis as a process of unconscious interactive resonance. I think we are always impacting one another emotionally, moment to moment, in a shifting series of interpersonal configurations. Sometimes, we experience not only a fantasy about what the other's experience is but also a direct imprint of it. We may not know if it is ours or theirs, and we may interpret or ascribe our own incorrect meaning to it, but I believe emotional states can be transmitted directly, outside conscious awareness. Such intimacy is not always comfortable or beneficial. Bion (1994) writes that when we meet someone there is an emotional storm. Stern (1993) spoke at a recent conference about initial connections involving being "captured" by the new emotional configuration, and Symington (1983) wrote earlier in his career about a kind of corporation that is formed when two people meet. His article, "The Analyst's Act of Freedom," describes how he became aware of these forces in a therapeutic relationship and how his struggle to internally free himself had a liberating effect on the clinical work and eventually on his patient. I recalled recently that in 1983 in Plum Village Thich Nhat Hanh spoke about how important it was to keep our mind from being colonized by external elements such as hyperconsumerism as well as certain internal states of mind. I thought his choice of words was dramatic: "colonized." I was confident of meeting anything and tackling it head-on. Now, I appreciate the word and the teaching.

Part of psychotherapy involves coming to accept and appreciate and play in the fertile connectedness—conscious and unconscious—that links us and to use it to examine and remove obstacles to full aliveness. Many, however, find it difficult to accept that unconscious processes even exist, and only with great difficulty come to let them in, not to mention welcome them, as both resource and ally.

Here is an imaginative description by Edelman and Tononi (2001) that captures something of what happens when unconscious emotional communication in the relational field is working in an organizing and mutually enriching, rather than in a dysregulating, way:

> Imagine a peculiar string quartet in which each player responds by improvisation to ideas and cues of his or her own, as well as to all kinds of sensory cues in the environment. Since there is no score, each player would provide his or her characteristic tunes, but initially these various tunes would not be coordinated with those of the other players. Now imagine that the bodies of the players are connected to each other by myriad fine threads so their actions and movements are conveyed back and forth through signals of changing thread tensions that act simultaneously to time each player's actions. Signals that instantaneously connect the four players would lead to a correlation of the sounds; thus new, more cohesive, and more integrated sounds would emerge out of the otherwise independent efforts of each player. (p. 49)

Such intricate coordination, with no conductor, is quite akin to Buddhism. Physicist Michio Kaku (2005) speaks about resonance on another register:

> Matter is like tiny notes on tiny little vibrational strings. The laws of physics are the laws of harmony. When the strings bump into each other they create chemistry. Chemistry is the melodies played out on these strings. The universe is a symphony of strings. The mind of God that Einstein wrote about is cosmic music or resonance. (p. 162)

When dysregulated, the result is not sweet, spontaneous, harmonious communication (music) but rather more a painful cacophony or perhaps deadening silence. Notice how Edelman and Tononi's (2001) and Kaku's (2005) language fleshes out and adds dynamism to the metaphor of the Jeweled Net of Indra.

THE BLISS BODY

> Chao-chu asked Nan-ch'uan, "What is the Tao?"
> Nan-ch'uan said, "Ordinary Mind is the Tao."
> Chao-chu asked, "Should I try to direct myself toward it?"
> Nan-ch'uan said, "If you try to direct yourself you betray your own practice."
> Chao-chu asked, "How can I know the Tao if I don't direct myself?"
> Nan-ch'uan said, "The Tao is not subject to knowing or not knowing. Knowing is delusion; not knowing is blankness. If you truly reach the genuine Tao, you will find it as vast and boundless as outer space. How can this be discussed at the level of affirmation or negation?"
> With these words, Chao-chu had sudden realization.
>
> —Aitken, 1990, p. 126

> What did Chao-chu realize?
> Bright, bright, clear, clear, naked and splendid.
> The great earth, mountains and rivers, the uncovered womb.
> There are flowers and the moon—who is the Master!
> Spring, Autumn, Winter and Summer compete with new garb.
>
> —Yasutani Rōshi, 1973

Here is the Bliss Body—suchness, the way things are, beyond dualistic construction. Intrinsic to it is the Jeweled Net of Indra, the seamlessness of singularity and interconnectedness that emerges vividly as we slough off and relinquish self-preoccupation through focused meditation. If mutual affective resonance describes a central element of psychoanalytic intersubjectivity, the Jeweled Net of Indra conveys our fundamental existential interdependence. Emotions make us human and are the stuff of human communication. Unconscious communication in the relational field puts human flesh on the filaments of Indra's Net. In the psychotherapeutic register of connectedness, emotions are the catalyst, the glue, and simultaneously the transmitter, the receiver, and the "stuff" that is transmitted and received. The process is much faster and more seamless than this unwieldy language conveys. Buddhists do well to learn about how instantaneous this process is for it can help us make sense of what otherwise seem like disconnected events: eruptions of interpersonal anguish that tear asunder the *sangha*, out of apparently peaceful circumstances.

For psychotherapists, patients, and others, the connections here are not only emotional ones—which rise and fall, come and go—but also fundamental representations of a container more vast than interpersonal relations, and without circumference, center, or diameter. In 1984, during the last of his fourteen two-week yearly visits to Maui, our Japanese teacher, Yamada Roshi, called senior students in one at a time for *dokusan*. He had usually been rather grandmotherly in dokusan with us, but on this occasion it was a classical Zen "examination in the room." He asked each of us, "What is the mind?" I responded, he challenged my response, I responded again. We went back and forth, and I could not gauge "where we were." Then, he asked me to ask him the same question, "What is the Mind?" I asked and waited. He gathered himself and responded, "The mountains, the river and the great earth, the moon, the sun, and the stars." Now, these were the words that served as the catalyst for his own enlightenment experience decades earlier and had been written up in *Three Pillars of Zen* (Kapleau, 1980) as the Japanese businessman. But, as he spoke, there was no there and then or here and now. There was no right and wrong response, good or bad student, or master for that matter, no feeling of confidence or inadequacy. He was presenting what we would call the bare essential fact of existence, and it echoed with a vastness that was palpable.

Thich Nhat Hanh is from Vietnam, the only country where Theravada and Mahayana traditions developed seamlessly in concert. As we have seen, he likes to speak about a piece of paper and how it owes its very being, its "paperness" to all things nonpaper: the sun, the earth, the rain, the lumberjack, the truck driver, and the paper factory employees. He looks at the piece of paper and sees that fundamentally there is no such thing as paper apart from its constituents. It is void of self-identity, yet we know and use it and its qualities. It is literally made up of nonpaper elements. An experience such as the late Flora Courtois's awakening, for instance, documented in her book *An Experience of Enlightenment* (1986), is not adequately captured on the interpersonal affectively embedded register alone.

EMOTIONS IN CONTEXT

Emotions are one constituent element of what makes us human. In Zen, we speak about the five *skandhas*, or bundles: form (body and breath), feeling (sensation), perception, mental reaction (formation), and consciousness. They interact and, moment to moment, come together in clustered arrangements to give us the experience that there is a "there there"—a solid person. Yet, moment to moment they are dissolving and rearranging themselves.

As with identity, emotions too can be deceiving. A Buddhist-inspired bumper sticker reads: "Don't believe everything you think." We could say the same for emotions: be discerning with what you feel—you may be deluding yourself. We know how compelling feelings can become and how convincing the truth value of our perceptions can be when colored by powerful emotion. We just know, say, that we are on the right side of an argument because the feeling of being wronged tells us that our perceptions are correct. We feel we *know* that the driver in front of us is purposely making us late for a most important appointment—until, that is, we are able to see that two cars ahead of him, traffic is stopped because a driver who wants to turn right is waiting for a mother, toddler in hand, walking in the crosswalk on the way to preschool. Emotion, like all experience, can deceive and awaken, depending on how we use of it. "At the service of what?" is a question we would all do well to ask regarding our experience. Once I told my analyst that I was unsure whether what I was talking about was defending against some other feeling or was an authentic experience. I "knew" of course that it could be both and could switch from one moment to another. I enjoy remembering his response, "Let's see." We don't know, we need to listen to the context, the harmonics, the impacts that ripple and radiate in multiple directions. We await the voice of, and consultation from, our resonating unconscious—the other and the intersubjective echo—and, of course, we stay alert to the behavioral harvest. This tracking is a critical element in an integrated narrative or archetype of liberation. No matter the number of enlightenment experiences we have had; the koans we have passed, our status as teacher, therapist, or guide; or the years of therapy or analysis—we must understand that there are impacts we are creating, and energies and qualities we are actually conveying and about which we don't have a clue. Our pets and our loved ones may actually have a better seat. It is not for want of interest or practicing awareness, but rather in large part because that is the way unconscious emotional communication in the relational field works. Bollas (1992) provides a wonderful metaphor for thinking about the impacts we generate. He suggests we imagine watching someone moving through space in a room full of people, then imagine that we cannot see the person's body but only the effects of his actions. It is as if the person is a ghost. It is like the old TV show *Topper*. What impacts do we leave in our wake?

I now develop a series of interconnected ideas that bring together the Buddhist notion of cause and effect with unconscious motivation, intention, presence, the Bliss Body, the nature of reality, the act of perception, and an integrative myth, ideal, or "dream." I gather together these and other strands we have been exploring into a narrative or praxis of liberation. But, first, some personal stories, which may help illustrate and connect the integrative "model" I want to convey.

THE UNCONSCIOUS AND THE BLISS BODY IN ACTION

In the recent past, I worked for several years with teenagers and young adults in the juvenile justice system in San Mateo County, California. I was asked to supervise second-year graduate students who were providing individual and group mental health services to high-risk youth in a variety of settings—from residential camps, to jails, to community-based schools within a school—within the context of a private nonprofit agency. At the time, I was busy starting up Deep Streams Institute and teaching Zen and psychoanalysis and practicing both, and I agreed only because of a long-time connection with the person who asked. However, this work turned out to be extremely compelling. I decided to sit in with my supervisee in group therapy sessions. In short order, we realized that traditional psychodynamic group process would not work, and that we needed to be more interactive and become more "real objects" than traditional therapists to these people whose lives were in such a state of chronic crisis. After a few meetings, I happened to ask the group what mattered most to them in their lives. This thought generated much discussion as few adults had ever asked them such a question with real interest. What really matters, why do you think it matters, how do you know it matters, and how did it come to matter so much? As the students came to trust us, they began to lay it out: conquering girls, "bling," lots of money, their "moms," how many guys they could beat up, hanging with the coolest guys, and so on. As time passed, they began to include other things, like happiness, making a difference in someone's life—more altruistic and even existential matters. One of the questions I asked that facilitated reflection was what happened when they acted out of what mattered to them. It began to dawn on me that I was asking about motivation, intention, core values, internal working models, and philosophies of living, although I did not use these words. When you are driven by having to have lots of bling and wanting to be the top dog, or belonging to and being taken care of by the top dog, where does that lead you? What are the results? What fuel are you using to power your "ride," and what are the effects? We would discuss it, without moral lessons or judgments. I recalled Freud's (1895) early energic model and wondered about psychic fuels and energies, not simply unconscious wishes, dynamics, and conflicts. What emotional fuel is driving your behavior? What these students valued and held most dear sponsored certain emotional qualities that drove and informed their behavior and then led to certain results. Mostly, it worked unconsciously—meaning, here, without reflection.

I began to see that we were also discussing cause and effect, the law of *karma*, or action, a key teaching in classical Buddhism but relatively underprivileged in Zen and generally not considered directly at all in psychotherapy. It is not only our outer behaviors but also our inner intentions that determine what unfolds from a certain state of mind, action, or interaction. The impacts from our intentions radiate far and wide in visible and invisible ways that last a long time. But, how can we truly determine an intention given that motivations are multiple and unconscious? The road to hell is paved with good intentions. I was initially skeptical of practices such as *metta*, or loving kindness meditation, that sought to consciously generate particular beneficent spiritual qualities of mind and heart. My concern was that such practices could obscure a possible conflicting unconscious inner motivation or affective state. Within the history of Zen Buddhism, however, the critique may have been that, when these practices were used to generate merit, they reinforced dualistic thinking and even ego aggrandizement. Zen may thus have tended historically to deemphasize these classic practices.

By way of example, the emperor of China is reputed to have asked Bodhidharma, the fierce legendary Zen monk, what the first principle of Buddhism was. "Vast emptiness, nothing holy," Bodhidharma replied. (Notice the difference from the earlier Dhammapada, "We are what we think, having become what we thought.") The emperor asked, "I have built many temples and sponsored many monks, what is my merit?" Bodhidharma said, "No merit at all." "Who is this standing before me?" the emperor asked. Bodhidharma's reply, "I don't know," was not the response of someone in an identity crisis. He was speaking, we could say, from the essential, absolute, or dharmic perspective, where the process of becoming does not arise, not to mention operate as a focus. In this book, I also explore what we call the phenomenal, relative, or karmic dimensions. I also want to illuminate their interpenetration, and what gets "lost in translation" between realization (in which the universal and particular are inextricably interwoven) and personalization (by which we bring to life and apply that realization in the particulars of our daily living).

In my work with the high-risk youth, I began to see that the energies driving these young men and woman were in turn determining their fates: scores of their homeboys and homegirls injured or dead, family members caught up in gang violence, pregnancies that brought children they could not care for, fine minds wasted. The cause-and-effect relationships were clear. I developed the notion of psychic fuels (similar but not reducible to unconscious motivation and intention)—energies outside our awareness that inform, drive, and infuse our behavior. They are also transmitted (communicated) through our interactions, no matter what we said, meant, or felt. They have resonating impacts that ripple across the filaments of Indra's Net and continue reverberating in unpredictable ways for a long time. Insight here was less crucial than fundamental presence.

Emotional and personal growth continue throughout life, at least they had better, for spiritual teachers and psychotherapists. Some think that those who are truly spiritually adept achieve a state that is permanently resistant to affliction. But, the people to whom they ascribe this state, such as the Dalai Lama, categorically deny it and are the first to discuss their human afflictive emotions such as anger, frustration, or a sense of failure. I do not think that such a person is happy when their strategy for their country's liberation does not work. It saddens them deeply. They do not take it personally, but they do take responsibility, as H. H. has done for "the failure" of his policy of nonviolence. Rather, whatever emerges, a spiritually evolved person is able to fully experience its impacts and meet them with equanimity. His or her response is generally a skillful and compassionate one that prevents further harm and creates a good chance of results that benefit all. The long view, based on understanding the impermanence of all things, also helps. I was struck by H. H.'s response to a question about the state of Tibet. After acknowledging his grief and upset and concern, someone asked why he did not advocate taking up arms. Wasn't this making the plight of his people worse? "When I feel most despairing," he responded, "I think, let's see what evolves in one hundred years." I have heard it said that certain spiritually evolved people *say* they experience the full range of human emotions, but those who know them well know otherwise: They are permanently in another register of existence, and afflictive states do not even visit such individuals. Perhaps, but this view might also reflect a persistent clinging to an ideal of how such an evolved individual should be.

THE ALCHEMY OF ZEN AND PSYCHOTHERAPY

So, what is the upshot? What is the alchemy that these "golds" of Zen and psychotherapy, the Bliss Body and the unconscious, generate? In the film *What the Bleep Do We Know* (2004; directed by Arntz and Chasse), a quantum physicist makes two statements: One, from the beginning, essentially there is nothing; two, we create reality as we know it by how we connect the dots of the data we receive on multiple channels. In Zen, we call it *shunyata*, the fertile void. It is not something called "nothing." D. W. Winnicott's (1971) phrase, "potential space," is perhaps a better term. The basic ground is vast, boundless, timeless, measureless potential space. I think we have little control over our emotions. Likewise, I think pain is part of life, but anguish is optional. How we respond to our emotions and our pain and to afflictive situations and life circumstances is where we have a measure of control. But, these two statements in the film jolted me into awareness of a new possibility. It is that, prior to responding, in our very act of apprehension—how we construe a certain situation by connecting the dots of sensory and affective data—there may be some play in determining how and what we experience. Our uptake in turn has impacts on the others involved and perceived and so "constructed." We know that the brain is actively constructing models of reality moment to moment and readjusting these based on new data. It is not that we "choose" or "dial up" whatever reality we want, carte blanche. Rather, our assimilated internalized and personalized insights develop, through ongoing attentional "practice," a kind of *dhyana*. They shape our very perceptions (not solely our responses to perceptions and affective experience) and so have influence over what realities, both psychical and material, emerge.

We see this in terms of expectations. Students who are expected (and perceived) to be capable of success are more likely to succeed. Experiencing a drug addict sprawled out on the street as a child of God, a Buddha, a human being with basic dignity, rather than a bum will not only affect our response to that person but also affect and *create* that person. A documentary about hunger and homelessness, *You Call Me By My Name* (Robert Jones, Sylvia Hirsch Jones, and Deborah Stern, 2000), asks, "Does our own internal sense of desperation or psychic hunger causes us to blind ourselves to what confronts us in the street? In protecting ourselves, do we deny the personhood of those truly in need?" The film's title is taken from a statement of a homeless person, who said: "You saw me, you called me by my name." Jean Sanville thinks that a self (or we might say a mind) is "born of illusion because mother and father believe that a self is there and call it into being by their own responsiveness" (1991). Fonagy (2000) likewise found that developing a mind of one's own depends on being perceived and understood as someone with thoughts, feeling, intentions—in brief, personhood and a mind. We could say that as we connect the dots of our sensory visual and other experience and bring forth a person (or other being) with dignity, we help liberate that "other" from "other" status so he, she, or it can realize and share intrinsic awakening or liberation.

Many in Buddhism and psychotherapy focus on seeing things as they "really are." But perhaps our perceptions, on the one hand, and "what is," on the other, co-arise: We awaken to what is as we perceive and create it. Our perceptions are infused and informed by a guiding myth, a dream, a philosophy of living. In Zen, no matter our *kensho*, no matter the "transmission outside of words and letters," no matter our presentation of koans, the proof of the pudding is in the eating. How does insight manifest? How is it cultivated and disseminated into the world of action? Some may counter, "Why these are dualistic categories; it is one movement, not 'even one.'" Since words can be put at the service of different functions, this may be so, and it may also be so much hot air. "By their fruits ye shall know them." We need to track those fruits, understand that they often differ from what we think, realize that it takes other skills to do this tracking, and keep learning.

In accord with what understanding, motives, psychic fuels, energies, spiritual qualities, are we connecting the dots, making links, deriving meanings, acting on them, perceiving? Aitken Roshi (1992) says that we live Buddha's dream. We live it out and create it moment to moment. It is the same with the psychotherapeutic dream of fully welcoming the disparate and disowned parts and experiences, making space for them as we widen our tent of the self, the space of the heart. Dylan (1963) writes: "You can be in my dream if I can be in yours." We are The Bliss Body and the Unconscious 173 by nature in one another's dream; we are moment to moment dreaming one another. It behooves us to cultivate a mutually beneficial dream.

Nanao Sasaki (1987) has a poem:

I sit down quietly in lotus position,
Meditating, meditating for nothing
Suddenly a voice comes to me:
"To stay young
To save the world
Break the mirror" (p. 47).

Can we break the self-absorbed mirror and painful storyline that we construct and sustain? Currently, many say, "It's just your story, let it go." But it is our story, our dream—what drives us, what we live and stand by, what actually gets communicated in our moment-to-moment interactions, no matter what our conscious intention, how we connect the dots—that makes all the difference in the world. This story is not ego aggrandizement; it is what we live by, how we live, and what we leave in our wake.

DREAM

Ideals cut different ways. They can inspire, and they can tyrannize. Each path, Zen and psychotherapy, has them: archetypes, myths—stated and unarticulated. They are the dreams that animate the practice. They work behind the scenes as guides to live by. No matter how useful, however, it is important to stay open to revising them and to learning from experience. How would a fully functioning human being live? In *Mahayana* Buddhism (great vehicle), it is the *Bodhisattva*, in *Theravada* Buddhism (school of the elders), the *Arhant*. Mahayanists used to refer to Theravadins as the *Hinayana* (lesser vehicle) school. But, all vehicles shall be towed, at owner's expense. Since alignment and integrity are important to me, I have thought of suggesting the mensch as a possibility.

When I was a young adult, before I began to practice Zen, I had the experience of wondering what it would be like if thought no longer shaped our perceptions of the world. A space opened. Later, I read the following line from the *Dhammapada* (1974): "We are what we think, having become what we thought" (p. 22). One question opened the universal dimension. The other helped me appreciate how things work in the karmic or relative dimension. (Please remember—they are not two, not even one!) The first speaks to "letting go," realization, *prajna*; the second, I believe, more to "coming forth," to personalization. Both questions, both dimensions are crucial.

Here is a dream: In baseball, the ideal is a five-tool player: The player can hit for average, hit for power, throw, field, and run. Some have deep insight, some highly focused *zazen*, some follow the precepts and understand them deeply. But, can we be three-tool players? Can we develop and integrate dhyana, prajna, and sila so that they are in alignment and naturally potentiate one another? There is the experience of the Bliss Body and the insight it provides into our essential nature and that of all beings (prajna). There is strong attentional practice on the cushion (dhyana), turning toward truth, opening, not just to the pure suchness of the birds and clouds, but to what comes forward from unconscious emotional communication, from intimate and other relationships. We continue to refine the jewel, both through zazen and koans that refine the enlightened eye (prajna) and by refining our personal and interpersonal being-in-the world. When we ask, "At the service of what?" and "How and to what ends am I using the treasure?" we are acknowledging that we do not know, and we are open to using data from interactions and relationships to shine a ray of darkness into the matter. We consult not only with the unconscious impacts of our actions and the psychic fuels they convey, data that can be sometimes available in somatic experience, we also check in with our pets, our intimates, and track the *après coup* fruits, the traces we have left in our wake. *Sila*— enlightened activity, ethical conduct, goodness, mutual benefit—is both a result and an engine of this activity. As psychotherapists, we can imagine the analogues in our practices and lives.

Here is Zen master Dogen:

> To be enlightened by the 10,000 things is to free one's body and mind
> and those of others.
> No trace remains
> and this traceless enlightenment
> is continued forever. (Maezumi, 1978)

Do not suppose that his amounts to riding off into the sunset in perpetual liberation. This notrace that is continued forever needs maintenance and refinement. There is a risk that "arriving," described as a relief in the introduction, can calcify and lull us into thinking "we're there" and there is literally nothing to do. Is genuine curiosity and learning by experience operating? Or, has realization become a stale, lifeless artifact? Suzuki Roshi once responded to a questioner, "Yes, we are perfect just as we are. And we all can use a little improvement" (Suzuki, 2006). This speaks to what we call the essential and the training levels in Zen.

I believe that the continuing education of both the Zen and spiritual practitioner, and the psychotherapist and patient, should ideally include the kind of "tracking the traces" that I am describing, which requires an understanding and appreciation of unconscious emotional communication in the relational field. Even though psychotherapists may understand unconscious emotional communication, and Zen practitioners may have experienced the Bliss Body, each element operates only as it is activated and expressed moment to moment. Since the universal and the personal "interare," opening to the unconscious relational field of emotions enriches our enlightened eye, makes us more discerning, and brings us into alignment. It opens the gate of wisdom, for right conduct is the living expression of emptiness, completely in accord with our insight into our fundamental insubstantial and intimately interconnected true nature.

Although many emphasize the "mind training" element of Buddhist meditation, our practice, Zen or psychotherapy, is not just a technique, a means to an end—it expresses the universe, and it calls it into being. We are responsible for our impacts in the world, intentional and unintentional. At the end of the film *Black Orpheus* (1959; directed by Camus), two young boys call up the sun with their guitar playing. Like them, we are bringing forth the universe in every act, every perception. Is this myth, or is it realty? Can we trust that what we call up, name, perceive, and thereby bring forward into the universe will be of benefit to all as well as to ourselves? Nyogen Senzaki (1973), whom we heard from earlier, has left us words of instruction: "Trust your own head/Do not put on any false heads above your own/Then moment after moment follow your steps closely/These are my last words to you."

In Zen, we sometimes use the term *person of no-rank*. Such a person responds freely, in accord with circumstances, unfettered by concepts such as gain and loss, enlightened and deluded, subject and object. His or her actions do not come from a formula, a cookie cutter, and they may therefore seem contradictory. But, this spontaneity ideally is not random or chaotic but infused with prajna—thorough-going, internalized understanding of our empty and interconnected nature—and responds in accord with the situation at hand. This wisdom must be lived and personalized in the crucible of daily relational living, through practice, or dhyana. How is Zen, as Yamada Roshi (1973) said, "the perfection of character"? The Bliss Body is a direct, unmediated experience, part and parcel of a narrative of liberation. From the beginning, things just as they are—standing up, sitting down, laughing, weeping—nothing is missing and nothing left over. How does this penetrate into our everyday conduct, our relationships? The upwelling of compassion that comes with realization wanes as we resume everyday life. Continued clarification of enlightenment through koan study and mindfulness in everyday moments can help. But, mindfulness needs to be complemented, not only by awareness of emotional and social intelligence or by new ways of thinking about trauma in the body but also by unconscious emotional communication in the relational field, awareness of how we are using our experience, what "fuel" we are utilizing and conveying, and what unconscious rippling impacts we are generating.

In Zen, there is a purification chant in which we acknowledge the harmful effects our actions have had on others, effects wrought by greed, ill-will, and delusion. In some traditions, we develop ways to work with the precepts and with the paramitas[3] to bring home their relevance in daily living. But, chanting and working on a conscious level with ethical guidelines go only so far. I want to say that the process of purification, refining what Aitken Roshi calls the "agent of compassion," can stand to benefit from awareness of unconscious emotional communication in the relational field. The person of no-rank trusts his or her own mind, head, heart, and realization. But, we need to "trust and verify." Why? Because unconscious experience happens, and all of us are, as Sylvia Boorstien says (2004), "just a moment away from a meltdown," from delusion.

As these understandings and practices become more integrated within us and in our behavior, a "new normal" develops. We observe how things work, the impacts of our actions—inner and outer, conscious and unconscious—on our own well-being as well as on others. If we are "turning toward truth," we learn from experience. There is another question that can arise: How much "truth" can we take? It is one thing, in circumscribed settings, such as the consulting room or the dojo or the dokusan room, to feel "together," to welcome all manner of experience in a more accepting way, and to act in an integrated way. It is quite another to come face to face with ourselves and our impacts in daily relational living in real time, or après coup. Sometimes, it can be more than we can handle. But, this capacity can grow, and with it we can have many moment-to-moment awakenings to what is really happening. "Just this" moments characterized by deep suffering require contact with something that is "not suffering" in order to metabolize the pain and awaken to the moment's immanence. The Bliss Body is not always blissful. It has no permanent absolute substance and cannot be bought or sold. It is not respectable, and has no meaning and no particular "use." Yet, its "marvelous functioning"—eating, sleeping, falling down, getting up, laughing, weeping, grieving, rejoicing, being born, dying—never ceases.

Flora Courtois and I were each gazing, she at a desk and I at a photo on a book cover. Gazing freely, as the painter Bonnard describes it, reflects and generates liberated attention. We open ourselves to learning from the depths, now the universal, now the personal. There are moments when both dissolve, others when they interpenetrate. We cultivate openness to the impacts of living. Neville Symington (1994) says that personality organizes around the "beestings" of relational living. They hurt; it is pointless to pretend that they feel good. The capacity and the ongoing, freshly generated willingness to bear and transform them is crucial. This is the "standing" we spoke about that coarises with understanding.

With the ever-renewing "new normal"—physical, emotional, or spiritual—we become more resilient, less subject to insults and injuries, more naturally restoring and self-righting. We can "trust our own heads" (and hearts and minds and bodies) not only because we follow the precepts, not only because we have internalized a sense of ethics, but also because we are, moment to moment, experiencing, tracking, and refining our "impact in the world"—and feeling the sting as we wake up to things that unsettle and trouble us. We also wake up to the other side: how certain fuels and actions generate mutual benefit in their wake. This entire movement, this entire function requires us to be multilingual. The two paths not only contain and hold us as we change, they also restrain and temper us with their respective vernacular and their discipline.

We live more freely, peacefully, and ethically, creating in an unforced way more buoyancy, aliveness, and true contentment and less pain and harm for all. As an emotional samurai who prided himself on nondualistically meeting whatever emerges head-on, I once found this hard to accept. But, we can also practice selectively focused attention (without being Pollyannas and Goody Two-shoes) so that we "water" and amplify those tendencies that lead to mutual benefit and restrain ourselves from acting on afflictive psychic fuels, greed, ill-will, and delusion. We stop, look, and listen; reflect on our experience; pick up cues when things are awry and out of alignment; stay open to unconscious emotional communication in the relational field; ask "at the service of what?" and become aware of how we are "turning toward truth"—until it becomes second nature. Then, we again take a sounding of the entire field and keep "following (the impacts and ripples of) our steps." A prelude, in a way, to refraining from neglecting, minimizing, overriding, disavowing, rejecting, or simply denying the realm of the personal and its transformative and integrative possibilities.

NOTES

1. From *Zen and Psychotherapy: Partners in Liberation*, by Joseph Bobrow. Copyright 2010 by Joseph Bobrow. Used by permission of W.W. Norton & Company, Inc.

2. These are the Ten Grave Precepts: not killing, not stealing, not misusing sex, not lying, not giving or taking intoxicants; not discussing faults of others, not praising yourself while abusing others, not sparing the dharma assets, not indulging in anger, not defaming the three treasures. The following are the Three Refuges: I take refuge in the Buddha; I take refuge in the Dharma; I take refuge in the sangha. The Three Pure Precepts are as follows: Renounce all evil; practice all good; keep your mind pure—thus all the Buddhas taught. The Mahayana version drops the final line and rewrites the third: Renounce all evil; practice all good; save the many beings.

3. In Mahayana Buddhism, the Lotus Sutra lists the Six Perfections as (original terms in Sanskrit): *Dana paramita*: generosity, giving of oneself; *Sıla paramita*: virtue, morality, discipline, proper conduct. *Ksanti* (*kshanti*) *paramita*: patience, tolerance, forbearance, acceptance, endurance; *Vırya paramita*: energy, diligence, vigor, effort; *Dhyana paramita*: one-pointed concentration, contemplation; *Prajña paramita*: wisdom, insight. In the Ten Stages (*Dasabhumika*) Sutra, four more paramitas are listed: *Upaya paramita*: skillful means; *Pranidhana* (*pranidhana*) *paramita*: vow, resolution, aspiration, determination; *Bala paramita*: spiritual power; *Jñana paramita*: knowledge.

REFERENCES

Aitken, R. 1984. *Mind of clover*. San Francisco: North Point Press.

———. (Ed. and Trans.) 1990. *The gateless barrier (Wu-men Kuan)*. San Francisco: North Point Press.

———. 1992. *Zen talks, essays and prefaces*. Honolulu, HI: Honolulu Diamond Sangha.
———. 1993. *Encouraging words*. New York: Pantheon.
Bion, W. R. 1970. *Attention and interpretation*. London: Tavistock.
———. 1984. *Learning from experience.* London: Karnac Books. (Original work published 1962)
———. 1994. "Making the best of a bad job." In *Clinical seminars and other works*. London: Karnac Books.
Bollas, C. 1989. *The shadow of the object.* New York: Columbia University Press.
———. 1992. *Being a character*. New York: Hill and Wang.
———. 1998. *Differences between classical and Kleinian technique*. Presentation at Herrick Hospital, Berkeley, CA.
Bomford, R. 1999. *The symmetry of God*. London: Free Association Books.
Boorstein, S. 2004. *Dharma talk.* Presented at Buddhism and Psychotherapy Retreat, Deep Streams Institute, Santa Rosa, CA.
Courtois, F. 1986. *An Experience of Enlightenment*. Wheaton, IL: Quest Books.
Dhammapada. (P. Lal, Trans.). 1974. London: Noonday Press.
Dylan, B. 1963. *The talking WW III blues. On The freewheelin' Bob Dylan*. Columbia Records.
Edelman, G., and Tononi, G. 2001. *A universe of consciousness: How matter becomes imagination.* New York: Basic Books.
Ferro, A. 2009. "Transformations in dreaming and characters in the psychoanalytic field." *The International Journal of Psychoanalysis*, 90:2, 209–230.
Fonagy, P. 2000. "Attachment and borderline personality disorder." *Journal of the American Psychoanalytic Association*, 48:4, 1129–1146.
Freud, S. 1895. "Project for a scientific psychology." In *The standard edition of the complete psychological works of Sigmund Freud*, edited by J. Strachey, vol. 1. London: Hogarth Press, 295–397.
———. 1912. "Recommendations to physicians practicing psychoanalysis." In *The standard edition of the complete psychological works of Sigmund Freud*, edited by J. Strachey, vol. 12. London: Hogarth Press, 109–120.
———. 1915. "The unconscious." In *The standard edition of the complete psychological works of Sigmund Freud*, edited by J. Strachey, vol. 14. London: Hogarth Press, 161–204.
———. 1916. "Introductory lectures on psychoanalysis." In *The standard edition of the complete psychological works of Sigmund Freud*, edited by J. Strachey, vol. 6, part 3. London: Hogarth Press.
———. 1918. "A difficulty in the path of psychoanalysis." In *The standard edition of the complete psychological works of Sigmund Freud*, edited by J. Strachey, vol. 17. London: Hogarth Press, 140–143.
Gazzaniga, M., and Bizzi, E. 2000. *The new cognitive neurosciences* (2nd ed.). Cambridge, MA: MIT Press.
Gladwell, M. 2005. Blink: *The power of thinking without thinking.* New York: Little, Brown.
Green, A. 1975. "The analyst, symbolization and absence in the psychoanalytic setting." *International Journal of Psycho-Analysis*, 56, 1–22.
Grotstein, J. 2007. *A beam of intense darkness—Wilfred Bion's legacy to psychoanalysis.* London: Karnac Books.
Kaku, M. 2005. *Parallel worlds: The science of alternative universes and our future in the cosmos*. New York: Allen Lane.
Kapleau, P. 1980. *Three pillars of Zen.* New York: Rider.
Klein, M. 1975. "The origins of transference." In *The writings of Melanie Klein. Volume 3: Envy and gratitude*. London: Hogarth, 48–56 (Original work written in 1952).
Maezumi, H. T. 1978. *The way of everyday life*. Los Angeles: Zen Center of Los Angeles.
Matte Blanco, I. 1988. *Thinking, feeling and being*. London: Routledge.
———. 1998. *The unconscious as infinite sets: An essay in bi-logic*. London: Karnac Books.
Mayer, E. L. 2007. *Extraordinary knowing*. New York: Random House.
Ogden, T. 1994. *Subjects of analysis.* Northvale, NJ: Aronson.
Sanville, J. 1991. *The playground of psychoanalytic psychotherapy*. Northvale, NJ: Analytic Press.

Sasaki, N. 1987. *Break the mirror*. San Francisco: North Point Press.
Schore, A. 2003. *Affect regulation and the repair of the self*. New York: Norton.
Stern, D. 1993. *Psychoanalysis: Diversity and integration*. Panel discussion at American Psychological Association, Division 39 annual meetings, New York City.
Suzuki, S. 2006. In P. Chödrön, *Practicing peace in times of war*. Boston: Shambhala.
Symington, N. 1983. "The analyst's act of freedom as agent of therapeutic change." *International Review of Psycho-Analysis*, 10, 283–291.
———. 1994. *Emotion and spirit*. New York: St. Martin's Press.
Winnicott, D. W. 1971. *Playing and reality*. London: Tavistock.
Yamada, K. 1973. *Zen teisho*. Talk given at Maui Zendo, Maui, HI.
Yasutani Roshi. 1973. "Last poem" (Aitken Roshi, Trans.). *Journal of the Diamond Sangha*, no. 2.

II

Being in Practice

Chapter Four

The Role of No-Self in Creativity

Expanding Our Sense of Interdependent Engagement

Polly Young-Eisendrath

In preparing for this chapter, I decided to turn back to my marked and tattered paperback version of Harry Stack Sullivan's *The Interpersonal Theory of Psychiatry* to remember specifically why I had a vague sense that Sullivan had something important to say about my topic. Having always felt a deep resonance with Sullivan's work and life, I looked up his concept of "self-system" and saw that it's essentially a definition of something that's not there: the system involved in maintaining interpersonal security, or the systematic ways in which we learn to protect ourselves against anxiety. Of course, I don't need to remind you that the personifications of this system are good-me, bad-me and not-me. What I am about to say about self and no-self shares little with these personifications; specifically, the "not-me" of Sullivan shares nothing with the concept of the no-self from Buddhism. And yet, Sullivan's not-me seems congruent with what I have come to call "non-self," as I will describe below. All that said, it seems significant that Sullivan's view of the self as a dynamic system is congenial with what I'll be saying here about a Buddhist-Jungian account of self.

In Buddhist practice, we eventually come to experience the self as empty as the sound of a bell. The self has no essence, no substance, and when we experience it this way, we don't separate ourselves out from the flow of experience; there's no gap between in-here and out-there; there's no self. When this view is in our viewfinder, we can actually see how we arise together with everything else, moment by moment, context by context, with nothing left out. This manner of seeing introduces new possibilities into our way of being which open up fresh encounters with, and descriptions of, our human phenomenology. Even though the original Buddhist teachings on interbeing—another word for no-self—are more than a couple thousand years old, they bring groundbreaking contributions to our contemporary refinement of a relational theory of psychoanalysis. In this chapter, I will argue that embracing a Buddhist phenomenology of emptiness adds to our ability to be creative in therapy, and enhances our ability to be creative in any context, in all forms of expression.

My own training to become a Jungian psychoanalyst began in 1979, eight years after I had formally become a student of Zen Buddhism. For past ten years, I have also practiced Vipassana, another approach to mindfulness. I came to my study of psychology in general, and to Jung's psychology in particular, with a background in Buddhist practice and thought. The blending of Buddhism with psychoanalysis has formed a core aspect of my development as a human being, writer and psychotherapist throughout most of my adult life.

While this perspective has been extraordinarily useful, it hasn't always been easy or clear. Considerable perplexity has arisen for anyone interested in the dialogue between Buddhism and psychoanalysis over the past five decades, as Buddhism has taken hold in the West. Perhaps most troubling has been confusion about language and terms—especially concepts such as ego, self, consciousness, unconsciousness, and no-self—and distortions in history or fact. Both traditions have subtle and complex theories about conscious and unconscious subjective and intersubjective life; it has been very difficult to determine where they overlap and depart from each other. Most difficulties come from their long and complex histories; whereas the history of psychoanalysis is about one hundred years, the history of Buddhism is about twenty-six hundred years. There are many diverse forms of Buddhism and no central office adjudicating the differences—making diversity within Buddhism similar to diversity within psychoanalysis, but over a much longer period of time. What I am presenting tonight comes from my own efforts to blend what I have learned from Zen, Vipassana and psychoanalysis (especially Jung's approach) into a new model for describing relational psychoanalysis, with a pragmatic view from the no-self.

TWO ILLUSTRATIONS

Perhaps you're beginning to sense how impossible my task is. But instead of allowing that sensation to turn into overwhelm or despair, let's engage with a couple of Zen parables or stories that may help us step closer to the practical issues at hand. These stories are traditional, but I will tell them in my own words.

The first one: Please try to picture yourself crossing a lake in a rowboat, rowing hard with a goal in mind—perhaps to have lunch with a friend on the far side of the lake. You're hungry and looking forward to seeing your friend, when suddenly, Bang! Crunch! Your boat collides with another boat! Furious, you spin around on your seat to confront the oaf who has broadsided you. Turning, you see that the other boat is empty. It's drifted into you. Relieved, you sigh and smile and go on rowing. There's no one to blame.

This relief of no-blame is a fundamental therapeutic benefit when no-self is fully embraced with its implications of contextuality and interbeing. But in order to appreciate this more fully, I need to take a short detour into basic Buddhism. According to Buddhist teachings, there are three primary marks or characteristics of our existence or reality. In Pali, the language that is closest to what the Buddha spoke, these are called Dukkha, Anicca, and Anatta.

The first, Dukkha, is often translated as "suffering," but its meaning is closer to unsatisfactoriness or discontent. The quality that Dukkha refers to is being off-center or out of whack—like a wheel riding slightly off the axle or a bone riding off the socket. Human life is shot-through with this kind of unsatisfactoriness, in large part because of our impermanence and limitations. Everything that comes into existence will decline and decay and eventually disappear; we will lose everything that we have and all of the people we know; we will all get ill (or have an accident), grow old and die. By the same light, whatever solutions we apply to our problems will eventually become problems themselves because everything is always changing. Even our best ideals are frustrating to put into practice because they always depend on others who will tend to see things differently and disagree with us, giving rise to negative emotions and enactments of troubling dynamics. Many times a day, we get thrown off-center when things don't go the way we'd like, inwardly or outwardly.

The second mark of our existence, Anicca or impermanence, was originally understood as a negative factor—guaranteeing a great deal of Dukkha. But over the centuries of teachings and practices, impermanence has been gradually re-visioned as ultimately liberating, although it certainly brings with it the experience of loss. And yet, to experience impermanence directly, and mindfully, is to feel the flow of moment-to-moment change—a soothing and supporting force—break down the ways in which we cling to what we like, and disparage or reject what we don't like. From a contemporary Buddhist perspective, impermanence has both positive and negative valences or meanings.

Psychoanalysis—as a theory and practice—seems to have an easy fit with the first two categories of Buddhist phenomenology: unsatisfactoriness and change. Freud's vision of human life was fundamentally tragic because he saw that Dukkha is built in to our existence. Change, impermanence, loss, grief and conflict are touchstones of all psychoanalytic theories. Analytic treatment sensitizes us to these aspects of ourselves and our lives. But when it comes to the third mark of existence from Buddhism—Anatta—psychoanalysis and Buddhism appear to part ways, although an aspect of Jungian phenomenology is a notable exception, as I'll soon explain.

The third mark of existence, Anatta, means that there is no essential self or thingness in our world. Nothing exists apart from everything else. This quality, which is sometimes translated as "emptiness" and sometimes as "no-self" points to the fact that everything is conditioned by, and connected to, something other than itself. Jung recognized this quality, which he called *unus mundus* (one world), but he tended not to understand how it logically contradicts any form of teleology or essentialism. Freud, as is widely known, did not appreciate the "oceanic feeling" that sometimes comes along with insight into no-self. In this discussion, I will use the terms no-self, interbeing, emptiness and Anatta interchangeably in an effort to provide a Buddhist epistemology that is useful in psychotherapy and understandable in everyday language.

When we see deeply into Anatta, we know that we don't exist as separate selves, but that we arise and pass away repeatedly, moment by moment, always changing if only subtly. As in the Zen parable of the empty rowboat, this insight promotes a no-blame attitude about our condition because we see that our fate and context are beyond our individual control.

In my view, two kinds of experience in psychotherapy may open a door to insights about no-self: one is the union of the therapeutic dyad and its mutuality in the creative process of the discovery of meaning. Sometimes, in reflecting upon what is emerging in the room—especially when communications may be only through emotional dynamics without words or gestures—patient and therapist follow a line of inquiry and understanding that clearly belongs to no "one." Insights and understandings come spontaneously and effortlessly and both partners are delighted by the experience which feels expansive.

The second type of no-self opportunity is the opposite because it feels contractive, as though the possibilities for making meaning or acting have collapsed. This negative opportunity arises from a rupture that impinges on the therapeutic frame or alliance, either from within the dyad or from outside. An enactment or impingement threatens to destroy the therapy because the patient no longer trusts the therapist, or the therapist no longer trusts the relationship (for example, because of outside intrusions from gossip, legal problems or something else). To illustrate the emotional tone of such a rupture, I will draw on a second Zen story.

This is a well-known Zen koan or puzzle about an old woman. The old woman of Zen stories often symbolizes a wisdom figure who, because she is marginalized in the social order, must resort to unique means to teach her valuable insights. In this story, an old woman has, for twenty years, been supporting a head monk by sending him food (through her servant girls) and providing him the means to lodge solo at a hermitage. One day she decides to test his spiritual acuity. And so, she instructs her beautiful sixteen-year-old servant girl to walk through the door of the monk's hut and embrace him warmly when she next delivers his food. In the midst of the embrace, the girl is to ask him, "How do you feel this very moment?" The girl does exactly as she is told and the monk immediately steps back from her embrace and says, "I feel like an old withered tree during the three coldest months of the winter, leaning against the rocks with no warmth." When the girl returns to her mistress and describes what has happened, reciting the monk's short poem, the old woman exclaims, "This monk is worthless! He's attained nothing! For twenty years I have been feeding and housing him and he does not even tell the truth!" She then goes straight to his hermitage, puts him out and burns the place down. What is the meaning of her actions? What was wrong with the monk's response? What would you do if, after twenty years of celibate practice, a very attractive person unexpectedly gave you a surprisingly warm embrace?

Of course, psychotherapists and psychoanalysts repeatedly face such moments when our patients passionately express their erotic desires, devastating critiques, imperious rages or destructive threats. For instance, when a patient says "I am in love with you. I'm sorry, but it's just the way it is. I think about you all the time and can't get excited by anyone else," it can be a regrettable error to recite a monkish verse from psychoanalytic theory, trying to make an interpretation. Your patient might throw you out and burn down your hut. On the other hand, if you were to take advantage of your patient's vulnerability at such a moment, and say something like "Well, it just so happens that I've had romantic fantasies about you, too," your patient might run away like a frightened servant girl, not trusting your commitment to her safety. And still, on another hand, if you just sit there silently without offering any kind of response, you're also likely to have your hut burned down.

The hermitage koan presents us with a relational dilemma. When the no-self enters, like the servant girl who's unannounced and unexpected, what can we do? There are no rules to play by, and we can't rely on our habitual identity, and still, we must access our fundamental humanity and deepest honesty in making a visceral expression of our interdependence. We have to turn away from the self with its catalogue of habits.

SELF AND NO-SELF

And so, what is self? Perhaps you think that the concept refers to something obvious. But, I wager if I were to ask ten colleagues, I would get ten different answers. As the Buddha taught, when we look for evidence of the self, we can't readily find any. We cannot see, hear, smell, taste, touch or cognize it clearly because it is not a thing. Even those psychoanalysts who have spent decades writing about it, rarely agree about what it is.

While the self is hard to define, most Buddhists regard the no-self as spiritually dangerous to define. Even to speak about our experiences of no-self will threaten to reify emptiness and distorts its truth. The well-known Zen scholar and social activist, Professor Masao Abe claims "No-self represents nothing but the true nature or true Self of humanity which cannot be conceptualized at all and is beyond the self and no-self." (See Abe, in Molino, 1998: 186.) Richard Payne, another Buddhist scholar and professor of Religious Studies, disagrees with Abe's humanistic tone, but lays bare the problem of no-self, saying, "There is no such thing as emptiness which may itself be experienced. One cannot experience an absence of something." (See Payne, in Young-Eisendrath and Muramoto, 2002: 182.) Drawing on the Buddhist patriarch and philosopher, Nagarjuna, the founder of the Madhyamika School that specializes in the epistemology of emptiness, Professor Payne comments, "It is in its rejection of essences that Buddhism makes a radical break from the rest of the religious culture of India, and continues to offer a radical challenge to our own conceptions of the world. Despite much confusion about the matter, emptiness of the self does not refer to the non-existence of the personality, but rather to the absence of any essence from each and every thing that exists. In other words, it means exactly the same thing as the teachings of impermanence and interdependence" (Payne, in Young-Eisendrath and Muramoto, 2002: 182). The Madhyamika School insists that emptiness is itself empty. It cannot be theorized or prepared for. And so, whenever our circumstances challenge us with no-self, we cannot draw on a particular form or context in which to respond. And yet, there are certainly ways to think and speak about no-self—or I wouldn't be up here trying—even if they are existentially and spiritually treacherous.

Because it's my intention to describe no-self in relation to creativity both within and outside of psychotherapy, I will take the advice of the philosopher Nagarjuna and begin by describing the human "self," and then negate it. The human self is an action: it's something we do to unify our subjectivity in space and time, separating it out from the flow of experience and creating a boundary around it. Sometimes we do this self-consciously, but mostly we do it unselfconsciously in micro-movements in our perceptions that create a mental impression that we are "in here" while something else is "out there." Aspects of every language and culture reinforce the tendency to make this separation. But we are not born with a separate self, but with a rudimentary beginning of it. In Jungian language, I'd call it an "archetype of self." This archetype gradually unfolds and develops through a biopsychosocial environment of relationships and physical maturation.

All human beings develop and sustain an experience and image of being an individual subject, although the degree and style of individuality vary by culture and situation. The universal characteristics of the archetype of self—no matter the language or culture—can be described as (1) coherence: a sense of being contained in a single body; (2) continuity: a going-on-being over time that eventually becomes a life story; (3) agency: the experience of being an intentional actor who causes things to happen; and (4) dependence on attachment relationships in order to develop the first three. Around eighteen months of age, a normal human infant begins to be motivated by self-conscious emotions—that are secondary to primary emotions present at birth. These emotions—such as pride, shame, jealousy, envy, guilt, embarrassment, and self-pity—naturally motivate us to perceive ourselves as separate and to have feelings of comparison with others.

The toddler comes to master this separation of self and other, and announces its nascent ego with shouts of "me!" "mine!" and "no!" From this beginning, the growing child eventually organizes an "ego complex" that produces images, body sensations, verbal thought and actions which promote a personal, gendered, particular life story that is unified and highly motivating. As I said earlier, the self is something we do, not something we are. Early in his career Jung demonstrated, through his association experiment, that the ego complex is only one among many autonomous complexes that are naturally dissociated and discontinuous, organized by disparate emotional dynamics that compete for the stage of action. But the ego is the most conscious complex (and now we would link it to frontal lobe functions) and tends produce an emotional conviction of our separateness and distinctness from others.

All complexes contain within them distinct "subject" and "object" poles, essentially an inner theater in which emotional scripts can be unconsciously acted out with others. Even the ego has an identity and a shadow pole, inviting others to play an alien or opposite role to the self—say, to play the aggressive, ambitious other to my self-deprecating, polite self.

Within this wide array of competing roles and complexes, the archetype of self motivates us to perceive and imagine ourselves as individual subjects. When this archetype is not impacting our experience, we don't "do" the self and there is an absence of coherence, continuity, agency, and separation of inside-outside. Many pathological states—as well as shock and dissociation—involve the disintegration of self. They occur without mindfulness and are often accompanied by fear. I want to call these "non-self" states (perhaps similar to not-me, in Sullivan's language) rather than no-self. I would then reserve the traditional "no-self" of Buddhism for those events in which a person is conscious and centered without a self. In such circumstances, the knower-known or observer-observed barrier drops away and there is complete unity between inside and outside. Buddhism encourages us to become familiar with such states for what they teach us. Having direct conscious awareness of Anatta allows us to experience directly our interbeing, as well as to see how and why we create the separateness of an embodied self. Because of our strong habits of doing a separate self, we often fail to perceive the quality of Anatta in our walking-around lives, even though it is ubiquitous.

NO-SELF AND CREATIVITY IN PSYCHOTHERAPY AND ELSEWHERE

So, why pay attention to, or become familiar with, Anatta? Well, first because it's an aspect of reality that's affecting us all the time and second, because we can live more harmoniously if we can directly perceive our interbeing. In fact, our most refined sciences, especially sub-atomic physics and submolecular biology, are struggling now to find symbolism and language that allow us to jettison our old templates of in-here and out-there, even of time and space, so that we can attend more fully to the characteristics of interbeing. As you noticed in the parable of the row boat and the story of burning down the hermitage, there are immediate relational rewards—even perhaps survival advantages—to becoming conscious and flexible in our interbeing. I'll return to a discussion of these factors in regard to psychotherapy in a moment, but I want to turn first to creativity per se.

As we have more access to no-self in our perceptions and experience, we discover a powerful and profound wisdom that comes naturally, effortlessly. As with our dreams, this wisdom is ready-made and delivered in immediate insights, solutions, images, words and teachings that come from a non-personal intuitive source. Eventually we come to trust that creative solutions to any kind of problem will emerge if we can tune into this interbeing in relation to whatever is arising.

Because Buddhist teachings parse reality into all sorts of lists—of, for instance, three, four, six, eight, ten items—I need to bother you with just one more list. This is a list of three qualities that will expand our discussion of the endless creative outpouring of no-self. The three major qualities are cultivated in all Buddhist practices; they are called Sila, Samadhi, and Prajna in Sanskrit (Shila, Samadhi, and Panna in Pali).

The first, Sila, refers to good character and ethical guidelines. Like the ground rules for a good therapeutic set-up or alliance, these guidelines help you stay mindful of your interdependence by sustaining the welfare of self and other together (four or five basic rules: cherish life; don't take what's not given to you; speak the truth; don't use your sexuality in a manner that harms others; don't take intoxicants that would cloud your mind).

The second quality, Samadhi, refers to the concentration and equanimity that develop from practicing meditation. This quality refers to a range of awareness from tuning in mindfully to what you're doing to having continuous clear perceptions of impermanence and no-self as they arise in your experience. Meditation practices cultivate and develop a mindfulness muscle so that a relaxed concentration becomes less and less effortful.

If we develop a certain degree of Sila and Samadhi, then Prajna—the third quality—is guaranteed. Once prajna can be accessed, then it strengthens the other two as well. Prajna is usually translated as "wisdom," but the Sanskrit word is cognate with the Latin "gnosis" and the English "knowledge" and actually means something more like "knowing forth" or "prognosis." When you can connect to your natural Prajna, you have a constant stream of insight and creativity that pulls you along, generated from no-self and responding to the immediate concerns of interbeing—yourself and your context.

Many creative artists and writers stumble upon Prajna early in their lives and recognize that if they can just get the ego out of the way, they will commune with the muse or the mystery or however they conceptualize this streaming inspiration. In my own case, I discovered early in my life that I could write easily and effortlessly if I could just get out of my own way. I've often felt shy about taking credit for "my creativity" because it can seem like I am channeling the material from an impersonal source (however, I do have to make the effort to put it on paper and revise it within a more conscious state). And so, one of the tremendous benefits of many years of meditation is this access to a streaming creativity, if you can witness it without pushing and pulling on it too much. Its source is Anatta—an emergent insight and knowledge—that is available through our ordinary being.

So, how is Anatta relevant to psychotherapy? In a number of ways that fit remarkably well with contemporary relational theory. First, the Buddha taught no-self as a practical way of getting around, even before it can be accessed directly through awareness. He urged us to deflect judgments of good and bad away from the self and only toward our actions and their effects. Instructing even his seven-year-old son on this principle, the Buddha said that shame, guilt, envy, embarrassment, and jealousy only lead to negative self-absorption and confusion. We should let our self-consciousness fade and always return only to our actions and their effects. This leads to a new perspective, described as follows by a contemporary Buddhist scholar:

> First and foremost, it forces you to be honest about your intentions and about the effects of your actions. Honesty here is a simple principle: you don't add any after-the-fact rationalizations to cover up what you actually did nor do you try to subtract from the actual facts through denial. (Thanissaro, 2006, p. 44)

By focusing on our actions and intentions, rather than ourselves, we develop a moral integrity and a calm ability to be alert and mindful witnesses of our so-called subjective and objective experiences. It is our nature, according to the Buddha, to be perpetually dissatisfied, annoyed, and irritated that the world or others do not go the way we believe they should. When we are thrown off our center and out of our comfort zone in Dukkha, we want to blame someone—ourselves or others. As the empty rowboat story suggests, we can also arrive at a no-blame view that the complexity of our lives often arises in circumstances beyond our control, even though we are responsible for our actions and our speech.

Sometimes in therapy we come upon an empty rowboat. For example, a client, now in her mid-forties, recently discovered that her birth mother, who was judged incompetent to raise her when she was two years old, was herself born during the holocaust. My client's mother's first two years were lived in camps and wilderness, fleeing the Nazis, always terrified. Naturally, when she gave birth to her first child, the terrors returned. Who's to blame? The Nazis? The mother? The conditions that spawned the Nazis? There is enormous relief in recognizing that a whole context, rather than an individual one, is at the roots of our misery. We can begin to see the nature of interbeing.

In addition to this kind of spontaneous insight, as analysts we can cultivate a deep mindfulness of our subjective states, sitting with our patients and tuning into Anatta in the therapeutic relationship. Usually we talk about this as "countertransference," but that seems to be a strangely constrained term for this kind of knowing. In a mindful state of equanimity and concentration, I watch my body sensations, feelings, thoughts, and images as they arise and pass away, while I'm listening or just sitting with my patients. In the midst of a highly charged emotional enactment, I continue to watch with as much mindfulness as I can muster and I trust that—as long as we are both contained within a safe therapeutic set-up which has its reliable ground rules—together we will discover meanings and insights from any enactment (whether it's my patient's or mine). I don't think. I just watch what is arising. When I speak, I offer my words, images, views tentatively, inviting my patient to join me. There is no expression of interbeing unless we can both participate in it, no matter how apprehensively.

CONFIDENCE IN NO-SELF

Ultimately, my position as analyst can be seen in any or all of the roles in the hermitage story. Like the old monk, I have been sitting in my consulting room for more than twenty years, attempting to become more and more mindful. Like him, I'm hampered by theories and ideas, even by the theories of getting rid of theories and ideas. Like the servant girl, occasionally I come on strongly and say or do something that is very disturbing and disruptive, often because I am making a challenge or a test that I've put myself up to.

And like the old woman, I have the power to wholly revise what I am doing from a place of deepest wisdom.

When I am faced with a dangerous test of my ability to express or embody something from no-self—to tune into a source that is entirely spontaneous and emergent—I feel confident only in mindfulness as a technique: paying close and careful attention to what's arising. When it works, my patient and I freely enter into a not-knowing what comes next, but feeling confident that it will be interesting. When it doesn't work, I need to put my attention into not having my hut burned down. While I could give several specific examples of just how I've done this, I will only say in general that I strongly believe in admitting to mistakes, sometimes even if my habitual self cannot figure out how what I did was truly a "mistake." All the same, like the old monk I sometimes find myself turning to theory (developmental, Jungian, Oedipal, self-psychological) to justify why I did what I did. Usually, not always, this creates still another level of challenge to my hut.

Most of the time, though, when I am sitting for my thirty-five to forty clinical hours with patients and supervisees each week, I draw primarily on prajna and interbeing. I rarely think. Instead, I am watching my subjective experience, modestly with an awareness of my limited view. When I say something, I express it tentatively because I recognize that it might not make sense, and I have seen it only from my own angle, and I need to hear from the patient in order to flesh it out. Humor and modesty are extremely helpful in this endeavor, and ultimately so is the self if I take it lightly. By this, I mean that I also consult what I know about my own emotional history, as well as my patient's history, as I watch the configurations that arise in my subjectivity. And yet, after treatment gets underway, I don't consult that kind of knowledge very frequently or make it into a strong formulation unless it comes to me already packaged.

Through these comments, I hope you can see how I believe the aspect of Anatta is relevant to relational psychotherapy and to creative work. It seems to me that my patients—through the process of mutual inquiry and discovery in our work—become more sensitive to experiences of interbeing in their walking-around lives and gain confidence in the no-self, although I never call it that. Consequently, they become alert to no-blame when the complexity of experience makes it impossible to fault anyone for what is arising. They also embrace the value of staying interested in what is arising from moment to moment. They come to see that what arises—especially when we're in pain, desire, grief or negative emotional states—needs to be looked at with mindfulness in order to discover solutions and insights. And they also come to believe that they can tap into a creative source that refreshes them by witnessing their own subjectivity before they act. Perhaps we could say they have increased what Jung called the "transcendent function" and what Winnicott called "potential space." From a Buddhist perspective, they have made a connection with Anatta and prajna. But I'd better stop before you burn down my hut.

REFERENCES

Abe, Masao 1998. "The Self in Jung and Zen." In *The Couch and the Tree: Dialogues in Psychoanalysis and Buddhism*, edited by Anthony Molino, 183–194. New York: North Point Press.

Bhikku, Thanissaro. "The Integrity of Emptiness." www.accesstoinsight.org/lib/authors/thanissaro/integrityofemptiness.html.

Payne, Richard K. 2002, "Locating Buddhism, Locating Psychology." In *Awakening and Insight: Zen Buddhism and Psychotherapy*, edited by P. Young-Eisendrath and S. Muramoto. New York: Taylor and Francis.

Sullivan, H. S. 1953. *The Interpersonal Theory of Psychiatry*. New York: W.W. Norton & Co.

Chapter Five

What the Emotions Ask of Us

Psychoanalysis and Dharma Psychology

Gherardo Amadei

In the Beginning Were Emotions

In his 1993 paper "Playing into Reality," Colwyn Trevarthen, biologist and internationally renowned expert on child development, writes that his research has led to the conclusion that the emotional system is complete, by and large, before birth and directs consciousness, action and learning henceforth (1993, pp. 67–84). Indeed, the emotions of a newborn baby, much like those of an adult, may be of a transient nature but may also create stable emotional conditions that last over time. These observations are consistent with the work of Bowlby (1979), Stern (1985), Emde (1995), Sroufe (1995), Greenspan (1997), Siegel (1999), Fogel (2001), Shore (2001), and Louis Sander (2006).

The data collected in infant research studies performed by these authors and some of their colleagues has enabled us to establish, unequivocally, the importance of emotions, so that—with the additional support of the results provided by visualizing brain activation—we can now maintain that emotions structure the anatomical architecture of the brain and, therefore, mental functioning.

The opinions of two clinical experts like Safran and Muran (2000, pp. 53–56) fit well in this context of overlapping views, as they affirm that often very different research traditions consistently converge in considering the role played by the emotional system in guiding feeling and action a primary one, compared to the motivational systems that are usually considered.

If a harmonious connection between feelings, desires and action is the basis of good mental functioning (Greenspan, op. cit., p. 18), we may argue that a difficulty in establishing such a connection is the basis of psychological malaise, caused by a lack of competence in dealing with emotions and desires. This malaise would originate not so much in a repressed desire but in a desire lost as a result of emotional incompetence.

> Therapist (bringing to an end the silence that has descended on the session after an initial, brief and very formal exchange): How are you feeling?
>
> Patient: Well, it's been a very difficult year, so many things have changed and . . . I don't know; it's difficult to dig up past feelings . . .
>
> Therapist: Naturally—but I mean how are you feeling now?
>
> Patient: Oh, now. Well, in these past months I've got used to not really knowing what problems I'll be facing . . .
>
> Therapist: No, look, I was asking how you're feeling, how you are, right here, right now . . .
>
> Patient: Ah, that's what you meant . . . Well, a lot of things happened to me this past week that were difficult to understand . . .
>
> Therapist: I'm not referring to how you've been during the past year, months or weeks, but how you're feeling right now, here with me . . .
>
> Patient: Well, I've spent the whole day, you know, running around, without really knowing what to do today . . .
>
> Therapist: Not today, but now, here, as we're sitting here . . . Right in this moment . . . How are you? What do you feel?
>
> Patient: Ah . . . I see, I see . . . Well, I don't really have anything to say about how I'm feeling . . .

The strategy adopted by the patient to avoid my question consists, first and foremost, in taking refuge in the past in an attempt to discover something more about himself; however, the subject's lack of emotional competence is so profound that he can find nothing to say about the past or the present, that is, when the emotions, of which he seems unaware, are effectively being determined. The subject appears entirely oblivious to his "own" set of emotional reactions to sensory experiences he carries within him. According to

Greenspan (op. cit., p. 24), each and every one of us builds up and stably possesses such a "set," without wanting or knowing so; indeed, through individual[1] and relational[2] variants, sensory experiences tend to lead to emotional reactions that are specific to each individual.

The "set of reactions" guides the development of logical and rational qualities in both a precise and unconscious way. In this way, we come to possess "an extraordinarily sensitive 'meter' on which to gauge our reactions"; "in a certain sense, however, it almost possesses us," precisely because we are unaware of it (p. 22). That is to say, we remain unaware to the extent that we are not present, in mind and body, to witness this reaction in the moment in which it is determined. This meter (or set of reactions, pattern, internal operating model or however we may choose to define this memory of experience) is therefore of an unconscious nature, and remains implicit, certainly not as a result of repression but, rather, a lack of training in feeling what there is to be felt.

Many psychoanalysts find it difficult to accept such insight deriving from extra-clinical studies and research, as to do so would mean pledging loyalty to the essence of Freud's revolutionary endeavor rather than to a set of theories that wax and wane in popularity (e.g., the Oedipus theory; schizo-paranoid, depressive and autistic-contiguous positions; the death impulse; primitive intrapsychic fantasies; the succession of psychosexual stages; primary narcissism; beta-elements that must be worked upon by the alpha-function, and other fanciful metapsychological hypotheses). This revolutionary endeavor resides not so much in the discovery of unconscious determinants in our lives, but rather in the possibility of a scientific study of these determinants that is able to transform them. Ultimately, this is the difference between Arthur Schnitzler, for example, and Freud. Research into regaining competence of the "meter that possesses us" has stressed the need for clinical work in which analyst and analyzed work together to construct the emotional experiences required to attain mastery of the particular abilities that are missing, seeing as, in Greenspan's words (op. cit., p. 200), "Genuine mental growth can result only from experiences, whether through skilled therapy or life circumstances, that meet each individual's developmental needs."

EMOTIONAL INCOMPETENCE

Alongside traditional hypotheses linking the causes of mental illness (i.e., when the subject reaches emotional incompetence) to trauma, conflict or deficit, a fourth hypothesis has been formulated based on misattunement. This hypothesis is a point of convergence between infant research studies (in particular, Louis Sander's work on "living systems") and the clinical practice of therapists, prevalently of a psychodynamic, but also cognitive, orientation, who endorse an interpersonal, experiential approach.[3]

With his mid-1980s publication, *The Interpersonal World of the Infant* (1985), Daniel Stern picks up where Sander left off, placing particular emphasis on the concept of affect attunement, intended as "the performance of behaviors that express the quality of feeling of a shared affect state without imitating the exact behavioral expression."[4] Stern speaks of cross-modal attunement processes not only in terms of widely recognized affects, which are organized by traditional categories (happiness, fear, anger, sadness, etc.), but specifically in relation to what he defines "vitality affects": in particular, almost elusive manifestations of affect. In fact, these intricate forms[5] have a decisive impact and "impinge on the organism most of the time": the child is constantly immersed in these vital affects or emotions, as his or her parents have "a thousand smiles, a thousand getting-out-of-chairs, a thousand variations of performance of any and all behaviors, and each one presents a different vitality affect" (op. cit., p. 56).

According to Stern (op. cit., p. 164), the child's experience of the social world is prevalently determined by these vitality affects[6]—what Sander (2006) calls "states," that is, a configuration of biological and emotional variables that can be seen as a single gestalt, characterized by exclusive functional qualities. Attunement would thus appear to be a potentially continuous process, as it may be addressed to the vital affect—the "state"—that any form of behavior conveys. According to both these authors, that which allows one human being to "be with" another is precisely the ability to recognize the vitality affects that are present at any given time, and attune to them. Greenspan, too, believes that to the degree that caregivers understand the child's communications and elaborate on them in the direction the child is moving, the child's "internal world keeps expanding, forming an ever more logical and refined network of thoughts and images that gives structure and meaning to his inner life" (op. cit., p. 99). On the other hand, if the caregiver attributes erroneous and critical meaning to the child's affects, emotions and intentions, the child will find it difficult to explore and "expand his emotional space" (ibid.).

The process that leads to this sharing of inner experiences—whether they are affects, "vitality affects," emotions, intentions—is therefore articulated over two stages. To reach the second stage, in which attunement occurs, a first step must have taken place: a step in which subjects identify their vitality affects, emotions, and intentions (which are present moment after moment). This is the recognition phase,[7] a process that thus precedes and permits possible attunement.

Having thus established the temporal priority of the recognition process, any possible (and multiple) recognitions or disavowals therefore constitute fundamental micro-events that can lead the individual through a sequence of stages, the first of which—attunement or misattunement—is followed by the subsequent normal or pathological development. Psycho-pathogenic events[8] are found in acts of disavowal[9] that result in various degrees of misattunement, which should thus be regarded as an experience that is real (not a product of fantasy), relational (arising from a non-intrapsychic situation involving two people), not experienced passively by the subject (who, it must be said, always plays a "primary role," regardless of the relational context) and applied on the micro level. Regarding this latter point, Kohut writes (1977, p. 31) that "the psychoanalyst's attentiveness shift(s) from the investigation of macrostructures (the agencies of the mind) and macrorelationships with objects (the Oedipus complex) to the investigation of molecular units of psychic structure." As a result, experiences of disavowal-misattunement are the events responsible for reducing (to the point of disappearance) the individual's ability to know his emotions, and thus himself, which leads in turn to the "emotional incompetence" that underlies various disorders, primarily those involving interpersonal relations.[10]

RESTORING EMOTIONAL COMPETENCE

At this point, we may therefore affirm that re-establishing contact with emotions is the first task to curing an ill mind and thus regaining lost vitality. Generalizing some of Marsha Linehan's clinical observations, we may argue that a central issue for many patients with relational disorders is "whether they can indeed trust their own perceptions, judgments and decisions" (1993, p. 147)—and, we may of course add, their feelings and sensations. Indeed, the self is built on emotions, sensations and perceptions ("I sense this"; "I feel that"); the environment, however, may or may not recognize the "this" and "that," and "may insist that the individual feels what she says she does not ("You are angry, but you just won't admit it"), likes or prefers what she says she does not (the proverbial "When she says no, she means yes"), or has done what she said she did not. . . . In any case, the individual's private experiences and emotional expressions are not viewed as valid responses to events" (op. cit., p. 50). To restore the authentic self, which has thus been tarnished, it is imperative that the subject's trust in his or her emotional competence and perceptual adequacy is restored. Daniel Goleman (1995) cites a number of studies that suggest the existence of a magical quarter of a second in which our emotions are linked to the experience of the moment; after this time lapse, they are once again ensnared in the usual emotional and perceptive habits that underlie maladaptive behavioral patterns: "To reach the immediacy of the experience allows us to regain our centre, to once again be the person who, in essence, we have never really ceased to be" (Amadei, 2005, p. 201; 204–205, translated from the Italian). The state of the recovered self is therefore that of a self harmoniously engaged in a constant process of integration and supported by awareness.

For this reason, it is crucial to understand how emotions are felt, heard and perceived during psychoanalytic treatment: in particular unexpected, unforeseen, embarrassing emotions, whether negative or positive. This is because individuals often find it difficult to tolerate unexpected feelings of distance from, or proximity to, another person. These feelings are difficult to deal with because they are ill-mannered, unguarded, brash, overwhelming, shameless, indecent, spring-like in autumn, autumnal in spring, unexpected, excessive, unhoped-for, angry, sly, dangerous, unseemly, "inadmissible for a respectable person such as I" . . . These emotions resist a pattern of thought that does not wish to admit them, and which the individual must learn to integrate.[11] During psychoanalytic treatment,[12] this is essentially achieved by witnessing how the therapist—the other significant presence in the therapeutic context—is able to perform this integration. Still, the question remains: do the concepts that classical psychoanalysis continues to revere allow for this potential integration?

PROJECTIVE IDENTIFICATION: THE WRONG ANSWER TO THE RIGHT PROBLEM

In this chapter, I do not wish to address the concept of projective identification thoroughly, but rather to stress the startling metamorphosis that has taken it from being initially seen as a means of control (exerted on the analyst's mind by the primitive part of the patient's)—and thus possessing destructive connotations[13]—to subsequently being considered by other authors as an archaic mode of communication—and thus possessing constructive connotations[14]—adopted by the subject so that the other (in this case, the therapist) may share in his or her emotional world. Whether we choose to consider it in one way or another, projective identification ultimately allows the analyst to return certain emotions—which he or she is unable to accept and recognize as his or her own—to the presumed sender: "these are the patient's projections inside me, and therefore they do not belong to me."

Only in the psychoanalytical universe—in which, unfortunately, the same word is often used to indicate different concepts (I am thinking, for example, of the term narcissism)—could one term unexpectedly shift from describing one thing to describing its opposite, without anyone feeling entitled to change it. Indeed, in any other field of study, a new term would have been coined to describe a different phenomenon. To some extent, the original sin of psychoanalysis is that it is founded on inaccurate definitions of invariably elusive realities. It is precisely for this reason that the discipline deserves a greater effort toward descriptive accuracy—which has been virtually unattempted,[15] and even looked upon with a degree of arrogance by the psychoanalytic establishment. After all, it was Winnicott (1989, p. 508) who remarked how Freud himself uses "ego" and "self" as synonyms. Such open-endedness has, in fact, never been uncommon in psychoanalysis: we may recall, for example, Freud's indiscriminate use of the terms "ideal ego" and "ego ideal," and the resulting abstruse theoretical digressions that this provoked among his devotees.

In Finnell's words (1986, p. 106): "The ultimate value of a clinical concept lies in the degree to which it fosters accurate understanding and analytical skill. Projective identification runs the risk of shutting down rather than opening up the therapist's attitude to the patient and the clinical material." The assertion is quoted in an article by Karen Maroda (1996), in which she stresses that several other authors[16] also perceived the dangers of projective identification. Stolorow, Atwood and Orange (1998, p. 724) also show similar views: "The concept allows therapists and analysts to disavow unwanted aspects of their own affectivity, attributing them to unconscious projective mechanisms originating in the mind of the patient."

Indeed, the concept of the patient projectively identifying his or her emotions onto the therapist can be very easily employed "to exonerate the analyst" from an in-depth examination of the countertransference: "To the extent that the patient's affect stimulates existing conflicts or complimentary narcissistic vulnerabilities in the therapist, the situation becomes even more complex and difficult, and certainly requires a willingness on the part of the therapist *to take responsibility for his or her emotional responses*" (Maroda, p. 234, italics added). Safran and Muran express a similar point of view: "There is something intrinsic to the concept that lends itself to being used defensively" (2000, p. 65).

As a consequence of Freud's concern with becoming involved with his patients on a personal level (and a more general desire for the analyst to keep a distance from the experiential level and stay, instead, in the dimension of scientific objectivity—see Orange, 2003, p. 83), the origins of the post-Freudian take on projective identification (i.e., to make sense of the therapist's emotions during the session) show us that this concern has been passed on to subsequent generations, taking on new forms. What has heightened this concern, however, is not the obvious matter of taking no action that might constitute a breach of ethical code; rather, it is an attempt to avoid "being entirely present" with the patient by cultivating a distancing, defensive detachment which may have potentially re-traumatizing effects on the patient. After all, current psychoanalytic training does not truly encourage the individual to pursue full self-awareness, often proving, instead, to be a purely intellectualized experience (something which is also perfectly possible in the analysis of persons not involved in the profession). Indeed, it is paradoxical that those who run this risk most are precisely our young colleagues in training, whose analyses, more so than others, could well reflect the form of psychoanalytic treatment but not the substance. In these cases, treatment could bear more resemblance to a philosophical/existential discussion, or even a sort of "rite of verification" of how much trainees have internalized the dominant theories of their psychoanalytic society or analyst. Hence, they are encouraged not to adhere to "who they are," but rather to a sophisticated "needing to be in a certain way." It is no surprise, then, that when the undertrained therapist faces the fundamental question: "How does this situation make me feel?" he or she will struggle to relinquish a concept that externalizes the origin of unexpected and inconsistent emotion, so ill-fitted to an analyst.

If the most immediate motive leading subjects to projectively identify is to deflect emotions they do not wish to take responsibility for, intrinsic to this would be the assumption that an individual's maturation, development and progress occur only in deficient conditions, and that any direct support would undermine his or her capacity for activation. The problem is, however, that this theoretical framework (which would make the case for rigid analytic abstinence, i.e., giving the patient no real gratification) has proved completely erroneous. Once again, the rule of abstinence has nothing to do with ethical concerns, but rather with the distance between analyst and patient: in such a climate, manifesting an emotion would run the risk of being perceived as giving the patient real gratification. It has, however, been ascertained that not offering the patient this type of gratification means exposing him or her to a new traumatization.

A further problem that arises from resorting to the concept of projective identification is that it exonerates the patient from being attentive, and entitles him or her to strut about in the assumption that to adopt a psychoanalytic attitude is, in itself, a sort of self-indulgent disposition to distraction. In this sense, the "field theory" of M. and W. Baranger (2008)—in arguing that "the temporality of the analytic situation is comparable to time in fairytales or dreams" and that "the space of the analytical situation is similar to the space in dreams" (p. 795) constitutes a dangerous step toward the patient's emotional abandonment. Indeed, to follow these proposals would distance us both from the present (into the "once upon a time" of the past) and from reality (toward an oneiric dimension), once again shielding the analyst from direct involvement in the clinical exchange, which, despite having determinants arising from other times and places, also undoubtedly has some consistency in the phenomenal present. It is, in fact, precisely what the therapist listens to, sees, hears and experiences in the session that determines the patient's experience of being listened to, seen and heard for the first time, unconditionally. For this to happen, and for it to help the patient regain confidence and thus competence in himself, the therapist must assume an attitude that is radically different to the expulsive attitude of projective identification, which, in actual fact, "does to the patient exactly what the theory says the patient is doing to the clinician" (Stolorow, Atwood, Orange, 1998, p. 724). The therapist would therefore have to tolerate encountering unexpected emotions and be able to share this experience with the patient, as "actually expressing the affect experienced in response to the patient is often the most therapeutic intervention possible" (Maroda, op. cit.).

Clearly, classical and post-classical psychoanalysis struggle the most with "handling" emotions. Relational psychoanalysis appears better equipped to deal with unexpected emotions because its means of clinical intervention are neither guided by meta-psychological theory nor by a theory of technique directing the relational responses with which the analyst's sensitivity engages the patient. But how might we further "temper" this diverse relational sensitivity?

MINDFULNESS: TREATING EMOTIONS WITH RESPONSIBILITY AND RESPECT

In recent years, it has not been uncommon for western psychotherapists of psychoanalytic orientation[17] to interpret Eastern texts in a different and idiosyncratic manner, picking up and drawing on their indispensable value in the existential and psychological understanding of man. I am thinking here of well-known figures such as Carl Gustav Jung (1983), Karen Horney (1987), Erich Fromm (1960), Nina Coltart (1993), Mark Epstein (2007), Jeffrey Rubin (1996), Jeremy Safran (2008)—to name but only a few. A number of these authors have reflected specifically on the concept of attention, surprised by how little this crucial issue had been covered by the psychoanalytic literature—with the notable exceptions of Theodor Reik (1948) and, in particular, Wilfred Bion (1970). Indeed, aside from Reik, it may be said that all the authors who've addressed such issues—either without explicit acknowledgement of their sources (Bion) or with precise reference to them (Horney, Coltart, Epstein, Rubin and Safran)—adopt the timeless indications inherent to the practice of awareness, or mindfulness: indications which form the core of the Dharma,[18] the systematic and first-ever formulated practice for the transformation of the mind originating from within the mind itself.

Mindfulness[19] refers to a particular form of awareness, characterized by a mode of being, supported by a non-judgmental, non-selective form of attentiveness toward self and others, one moment after another.[20] The idea being put forward is to bring an attitude of mindfulness to the therapeutic setting, in the way in which sessions are conducted and in the manner in which the relationship is formed; to maintain, during the session, a state of "constant and bare attention" which is to be achieved not through effort, but by "letting go," in the sense of an active rather than a passive attitude. Let me note here that it has become somewhat customary to use the term mindfulness,[21] which is largely taken to signify "mental presence," "full" or "mental" awareness. These expressions do not fully preserve, however, the term's meaning as they refer to an eminently cognitive capacity, that either we possess or do not; to the contrary, mindfulness is, in fact, a way to maintain oneself in a complete and open attentiveness toward the experience as it occurs, moment after moment, in the session as it takes place. An attitude of mindfulness can enhance presence, receptivity, empathy, mutual attunement and communicative resonance. These are all points of reference for relational psychoanalysis, which strives to encounter and recognize the other (while also allowing the other to encounter and recognize us), rather than simply telling the other something about himself, be it in terms of an objective truth or an alphabetizing function.

More than any other author, Nina Coltart has helped to clarify the difference between "paying attention," in the sense of being cognitively alert, and "being attentive." Indeed, the latter occurs when "we try to teach ourselves continuously to observe, and watch, and listen, and feel, in silence," with such diligence that this mode of being becomes second nature (1993b, p. 181) and, by means of a suitable experiential training, we may finally reach willful attention as a kind of love that may be learned (op. cit., p. 119). Coltart believes that the issue of attention is central to the very nature of treatment: "If I'm asked now to select one comprehensive feature as the most constantly and positively therapeutic, what would be my choice? Without doubt, the quality of sustained, unflagging attention. The slow development of this kind of attention reminds us of how paradoxical the analytic attributes need to be; our attention should be both detached and involved, both scanning and focused. . . . Thus we free all our psychic and emotional energies for attending to his here-and-now; blended with a strong curiosity and an unexploitative wish to reduce his suffering, attention forms the constant matrix of a positive therapeutic attitude to our work" (1992, p. 110). It is not, then, so much in an attempt to reconstruct and reconnect elements of the past that we engage with the here-and-now, but to learn to stay in our experiences and thus develop our own emotional competence, as well as our competence in life. We must acquire these competences if we are to encourage the same "existential movement" in the people whom we encounter and who encounter us.

We are here describing a form of psychoanalysis in which an aptitude for relational attention supported by mindfulness leads us to set aside a number of traditional concepts and diktats, such as projective identification and indiscriminate abstinence. Constant, unfluctuating and bare attention certainly satisfies one of the patient's fundamental needs, but not to do so, after all, would mean (re)traumatizing the patient. The therapist using mindful attention (as a mode of being with the patient and with himself in the clinical encounter) is finally able to recognize and respect his own emotions; and, through his presence and listening, the therapist may alert the patient that a similar possibility can exist in relation to his or her own emotions. The mode of listening, in particular, is instrumental for the patient to begin to hear what he or she is destined to be.[22]

In conclusion, I believe that all the contributions[23] cited have enhanced our understanding of how psychoanalysis might increase the effectiveness of its specific way of promoting transformations of the mind originating in the mind itself. After all, what emotions ask of us is that we respect them, and the only way for a patient to learn this in clinical experience is if the therapist first takes responsibility for the emotions that he or she encounters.

NOTES

1. Individuals differ in terms of the emotional quality that they attribute to the same physical property.
2. Relationships differ in terms of the emotional quality that is attributed to the same relational event.
3. Revisiting the work of Greenberg and Mitchell (1983), I use this term to indicate a common area between the interpersonal model (as defined by its founders, Harry Stack Sullivan (1940), Clara Thompson (1950), Erich Fromm (1964), and the contributions made by Frieda Fromm-Reichmann (1950) and, more recently, Philip Bromberg (1998)), Bowlby's attachment theory (1969), the psychology of the self (Kohut, 1977) and its intersubjective approaches (Stolorow, Atwood, and Branchaft, 1994; Orange, 2003), motivational systems theory (Lichtenberg et al., 1996), the relational model in its stricter sense (namely in its theorization by Mitchell, 2000, and others, including Jessica Benjamin, 1988, Aron, 1996, Ghent, 1995) and the systemic-dyadic model (Beebe and Lachmann, 2002). Nowadays, for the most part, these models appear to converge in a single, consistent center of attraction, an "almost common" theoretical domain that encompasses (as mentioned above) data coming from clinical work, both psychoanalytic and not, and data deriving from infant research.
4. Therefore, if "imitation is the predominant way to teach external forms" to the child, attunement is "the predominant way to commune with or indicate sharing of internal states. Imitation renders form; attunement renders feeling. In actuality, however, there does not appear to be a true dichotomy between attunement and imitation; rather, they seem to occupy two ends of a spectrum" (op. cit., p. 142).
5. These may arise both *internally*, from the vital processes of life (such as breathing, getting hungry, falling asleep, feeling emotions, etc.) and *externally*, from a multitude of parental acts (the way in which the mother picks up the baby, feeds the baby or combs its hair, etc.) that do not qualify as "regular" affective acts.
6. Because "on average, expressions of affects that belong to traditional categories occur only occasionally in mother-child interactions . . . if the process of attunement of affects were limited only to these affects it would lack continuity."
7. Rather than in the sense of "becoming aware of something previously perceived," I use the term "recognition" in the sense of the "attribution of identity."
8. With the exception of certain specific situations such as post-traumatic stress disorder.
9. Or, alternatively, when the quality, quantity, timing or reciprocity of the recognition is inadequate.
10. Further clarification of the topics addressed in this paragraph may be found in Amadei (2005), from which some passages have been drawn.

11. Not in the sense of Hegelian synthesis, but rather of Winnicott's "non-integration," understood as a co-presence of radically different elements that do not lose their individuality in their co-existence.

12. And—in an alternative context in which we encounter our emotions—through the practice of meditation to promote *mindfulness*.

13. I am here referring to Melanie Klein's theorization, as present in Fònagy (2005, p. 221).

14. Unable to absorb the intense experiences he or she faces, the child projects them into the mind of the parent, so that they might be metabolized and then returned in a form that has become tolerable (the theory is Bion's, as present in Fònagy, [op. cit.]).

15. Laplanche and Pontalis (1967) come to mind as distinguished exceptions, as well as Thoma and Kachele (1985).

16. Such as Whipple (1986).

17. And of other schools—I am thinking here of innovative and courageous psychotherapists such as Carl Rogers and Fritz Pearls.

18. I am using the term *Dharma,* rather reductively, to indicate the set of the Buddha's teachings.

19. *Mindfulness* is the English translation of *Sati*, from Pali, the language used by *Buddhist psychology* as far back as 2,500 years ago. It refers to states of awareness and compassion implying the intention of constantly (re)directing one's *presence in the experience* that is unfolding, in order to be fully receptive and resist categorizing.

20. This paragraph and the following two have been taken, with slight reworking, from Amadei, Cimma (2008); readers should see this work for a more detailed discussion of the topic.

21. As in Linehann (1993).

22. See Rogers (1980, p. 41).

23. All authors who deserve a more in-depth analysis which, however, exceeds the scope of the present chapter, but is nonetheless warmly recommended.

REFERENCES

Amadei, G. 2005. *Come si ammala la mente*. Bologna: Il Mulino.

Amadei, G. and Cimma, I. 2009. "Mindfulness e psicoterapia psicoanalitica." *Rivista Ordine degli Psicologi della Regione Piemonte*.

Aron, L. 1996. *A meeting of minds: Mutuality in psychoanalysis*. Hillsdale, NJ: The Analytic Press.

Baranger, M. 2008. "The Analytic Situation as a Dynamic Field." *International Journal of Psychoanalysis*, 89.4: 795–826.

Beebe, B. and Lachmann, F. 2002. *Infant research and treatment of adults: Co-constructing interactions*. Hillsdale, NJ: The Analytic Press.

Benjamin, J. 1988. *The bonds of love: Psychoanalysis, femininsm, and the problem of domination*. New York: Pantheon Books.

Bion, W. 1970. *Attention and interpretation*. London: Tavistock Publications.

Bowlby, J. 1979. *The making and breaking of affectional bonds*. London: Tavistock Publications.

Bromberg, P. 1998. *Standing in the Spaces*. Hillsdale, NJ: The Analytic Press.

Coltart, N. 1992. *Slouching towards Bethlehem*. London: Free Association Books.

———. 1993. *How to survive as a psychotherapist*. London: Sheldon Press.

Emde, R. 1995. "Fantasy and Beyond." In *On Freud's Creative Writers and day-dreamers*, E. S. Person et al. New Haven and London: Yale University Press.

Epstein, M. 2007. *Psychotherapy without the self: A Buddhist perspective*. London: Yale University Press.

Finnell, J. 1986. "The merits and problems with the concept of projective identification." *Psychoanalytic Review*, 73: 103–120.

Fogel, A. 2001. *Infancy*. Belmont: Wadsworth/Thompson Learning.

Fonagy, P. 2000. "The place of psychodynamic theory in developmental psychopathology." *Development and Psychopathology*, 12.3: 407–426.

Fromm, E. 1994. *The art of listening*. London: Constable Press.

Fromm, E., Suzuki, D. and De Martino, R. 1960. *Zen Buddhism and Psychoanalysis*. New York: Harper & Bros.

Fromm-Reichmann, F. 1950. *Principles of intensive psychotherapy*. Chicago: University of Chicago Press.

Ghent, E. 1995. "Interaction in the psychoanalytic situation." *Psychoanalytic Dialogue*, 5: 479–491.

Goleman, D. 2004. *Emotional Intelligence*. London: Bloomsbury.

Greenberg, J. and Mitchell, S. 1983. *Object relations in psychoanalytic theory*. London: Harvard University Press.

Greenspan, S. 1997. *The growth of the mind: and the endangered origins of intelligence*. Reading, MA: Addison-Wesley.

Horney, K. 1987. *Final Lectures*. New York and London: Norton & Company.

Jung, C. G. 1969. *The collected works of C G Jung*. London: Routledge.

Kohut, H. 1977. *The Restoration of the Self*. Chicago: The University of Chicago Press

Laplanche, J. and Pontalis, J.B. 1967. *Vocabulaire de la psychanalyse*. Paris.

Lichtenberg, J., Lachmann F., and Fossage J. 1996. *The Clinical Exchange*. Hillsdale, NJ: The Analytic Press.

Linehan, M. 1993. *Cognitive-Behavioral Treatment of Borderline Personality Disorder*. New York: The Guilford Press.

Mitchell, S. 1988. *Relational concepts in psychoanalysis*. Cambridge, MA: Harvard University Press.

Maroda, K. 1995. "Projective identification and countertransference interventions: Since feeling is first." *Psychoanalytic Review*, 82: 229–247.

Orange, D. 2003. "Why language matters in Psychoanalysis." *Psychoanalytic Dialogue*, 13.1: 77–103.

Reik, T. 1948. *Listening with the third ear*. New York: Farrar, Strauss.

Rogers, C. 1980. *Way of being*. Boston: Houghton Mifflin.

Rubin, J. 1996. *Psychoanalysis and Buddhism. Toward an integration*. New York: Plenum Press.

Safran, J. 2006. "Before the ass has gone, the horse has already arrived." *Contemporary Psychoanalysis*, 42.2: 197–212.

Safran, J. and Muran, C. 2000. *Negotiating the therapeutic alliance: A Relational Treatment Guide*. New York: The Guilford Press.

Sander, L. 2008. *Living systems*. London: Routledge.

Shore, A. 2001. "The effect of early relational trauma on right brain development, affect regulation and infant mental health." *Infant Mental Health Journal*, 22: 201–269.

Siegel, D. 1999. *The developing mind*. London, New York: Guilford Press.

Sroufe, A. 1996. *Emotional development: The organization of emotional life in the early years*. Cambridge: Cambridge University Press.

Stern, D. 1985. *The Interpersonal World of the Infant: A View From Psychoanalysis and Developmental Psychology*. London: Karnac.

Stolorow, R., Atwood, G., and Branchaft, B. 1994. *The intersubjective perspective*. London: Aronson.

Stolorow, R., Atwood, G., and Orange, D. 1998. "Projective identification, begone!" *Psychoanalytic Dialogue*. 8: 719–726.

Sullivan, H. S. 1940. *Conceptions of modern psychiatry*. London: Tavistock Publications.

Thoma, H. and Kachele, H. 1987. *Psychoanalytic practice, vol. 1: Principles*. Springer-Verlag.

Thompson, C. 1950. *Psychoanalysis: Evolution and development*. New York: Hermitage House.

Trevarthen, C. 1993. "Playing into reality: Conversation with the infant communicator." *Winnicott Studies*, 7: 67–84.

Whipple, D. 1986. "Discussion of "The merit and problems with the concept of projective identification" by Janet Finell." *Psychoanalytic Rewiew*, 73: 121–128.

Winnicott, D. 1971. *Playing and reality*. London: Tavistock Publications.

———. 1989. *Psychoanalytic explorations*. London: Karnac Books.

Chapter Six

Psychoanalysis, Transgenerational Psychotherapy, and Karma

Michela Morgana

Originating as a branch of clinical psychology, transgenerational psychotherapy expands its application to the psychic life shared by a group—usually (but not exclusively) members of the same family—over a period of time comprising several generations in succession. The duration of the succession may be of some length, even including ancestors from previous centuries. (In so doing, by broadening the temporal scope under consideration, transgenerational psychotherapy has expanded the systemic model of family therapy.) Freud himself speaks of the "collective psyche" in Totem and Taboo (1912) but does not develop the concept in a clinical sense. Breaking with Freud and developing his own theory, Jung contemplates the existence of a "collective unconscious," passed down from generation to generation, which permeates society and allows human experience to sediment. He holds that, in addition to a personal unconscious, every individual may also access a collective unconscious which is shared with others to a varying degree (greater, for example, for people of the same culture with regard to certain events and symbols; total with regard to universal symbols). For Jung, this collective unconscious is innate and exists, therefore, irrespective of an individual's personal experiences and denial. He goes on to underline the existence of synchronicity phenomena, which, after discussion with the physicist Wolfgang Pauli, he describes as: "the meaningful, but not necessarily synchronous, coincidence of an external, material event with the emergence of an inner symbol or psychic event, where these two events are casually unrelated and present no suitable causal connection . . . since the two events are linked only by their meaning" (quoted by M. L. von Franz, translated from the Italian). Obviously, such ideas had an immediate effect on the practice and manner of conducting Jungian analysis. However, although recognizing the collective unconscious, Jung's model did not take into account the subjective specificity of transgenerational psychism, which is only contemplated fully in transgenerational psychotherapy.

When the theoretical disputes subsided, different schools of thought (both psychological and not) were able to come together on the question of transgenerationality, each providing valuable contributions which allowed transgenerational psychotherapy to originate and develop. As its name suggests, transgenerational psychotherapy deals primarily with the generations related to a subject, and tackles his current situations and problems in light of the events that affected those who came before him. The importance of including past generations in clinical work became particularly evident following therapeutic treatment of individuals showing symptoms not ascribable to meanings linked to their own personal lives. The process of understanding and healing had, in such cases, come to a standstill, which could be overcome only by questioning past events in which the subjects were not directly involved. There have been several cases in which the children of concentration camp survivors present symptoms that may be traced back to their parents' traumatic experience, even if it they had never discussed the matter with them before. Indeed, although the atrocities remained veiled in silence, so great was the trauma that it appeared to have been passed down from unconscious to unconscious, from parent to child: an unresolved inheritance (as the trauma had not been worked through) that became manifest in the children's symptoms. Spurred on by a need to understand within the framework of the therapy, the subjects began to question their parents about their past, and the facts and emotions that emerged from these accounts made their own symptoms understandable too, while also granting new perspectives on aspects of the self.

Naturally, adopting a wider temporal scope to consider the concatenation of cause and effect, in relation to problems in current clinical experience, has not only proven effective in the specific treatment of the children of concentration camp survivors—it may, in fact, be of use in all clinical situations and even a necessity when something particularly traumatic has occurred to one of the patient's ancestors. The subject may well be unaware of said serious event, but if particular symptomatic presentations emerge as the treatment progresses—which cannot, strictly speaking, be connected to the subject's history or particular symbolic meanings that are significant to him—we may legitimately ask ourselves whether he has "inherited" an unsolved problem from another family member. This could mean, for example, that a man whose grandfather committed suicide by shooting himself might have an aversion to and a phobic fear of firearms—or a strong passion and fascination for weaponry. Similarly, the female nephew of a man who drowned might suffer from a phobia of water. Such examples abound. And while claims of this sort may seem absurd, I hope to provide sufficient elements to suggest differently.

As with the inheritance of physical features and character traits, where children with the same parents inherit different traits, which they may or may not develop depending (also) on their place in the siblinghood, transgenerational psychic inheritance is also specific to each child, whether it takes the form of unresolved trauma, or individual talents and tasks to pursue. In terms of material inheritance, we may, for example, recall that one of the reasons why the Cavalry originated in the Middle Ages was to avoid the wasting of the family fortune, which the firstborn inherited entirely. Similarly, for centuries many religious "careers" (appropriately dubbed) were determined by order of birth rather than any sort of spiritual vocation, with all the inevitable consequences that this entailed.

Within a strong psychoanalytic tradition, Haydée Faimberg has explored, over the course of her long academic and clinical career, how patients can be influenced by the transmission of unconscious forces and issues deriving from events that occurred before their lifetime and affected people who, often, have already passed away. Through a careful examination of unconscious identifications revealed in transference, Faimberg[1] presents a theoretical formulation of the concept of the "telescoping of generations"—in other words, a condensation of three generations where identifications constitute a "link" between them. Faimberg believes this type of identification to be alienating and opposed to any sort of psychic representation, making it difficult for the analyst to recognize them; indeed, he or she must use interpretative construction to make the passage from identification to representation (as theorized by André Green). For Faimberg, the narcissistic modality discovered in transference may be partly transmitted by the parents too. (I would stress that the author does not use the concept of narcissism in relation to that of self, but solely as a particular mode of libidinal cathexis.) Analysis would thus aim to promote the disidentification that takes place when patient and analyst are able to recognize that the patient's listening to the analyst's interpretations is linked to his internal parents and their narcissistic discourses. The patient can then begin to recognize "otherness"; transference in the analysis changes from narcissistic to Oedipal; and psychic energy breaks free of the tyranny of the past and may be returned to the present and new modes of understanding. While Faimberg's interest in telescoping concerns three generations and originates in transference issues in analysis, transgenerational psychotherapy looks at an even greater period of time, with its investigation of the influence of transgenerational transmission looking several generations into the past, and draws on psychoanalysis as well as its neighboring disciplines in the field of the human sciences.

As biographies have an important role in transgenerational psychotherapy, it may be of interest to acquire the principles of the discipline and revisit its major developments by briefly reconstructing the professional biography of one of its foremost experts, Anne Ancelin Schützenberger. Schützenberger, who trained in different psychological disciplines and had a wide variety of professional experiences, formulated a model of transgenerational psychotherapy which is still widely recognized and admired today for its breadth of vision and clinical effectiveness.

Schützenberger began her studies in psychology at the University of Paris after World War I. In 1951–1952, she observed and studied processes of interaction and group dynamics, taking specialized, post-university courses at the University of Michigan with Kurt Lewin's students at the Research Center for Group Dynamics. That same year, she became acquainted with J. L. Moreno and discovered the concept of psychodrama, and met Carl Rogers, whose work she greatly appreciated. She spent two more years in the United States studying social psychology in an interdisciplinary context involving psychology, sociology, cultural anthropology, communication, and group dynamics. On returning to Paris, Schützenberger began her first analysis with Robert Gessain, a doctor, psychoanalyst, and anthropologist, following it with a second tranche of analysis with Françoise Dolto. It was, in fact, through Dolto that Schützenberger began to develop an interest in the transgenerational, inspired as she was by her analyst's conviction that unconscious and involuntary transmission have an important role in transgenerational bonds: "In a family, children and house dogs know everything, always, and particularly when it's left unsaid" (Dolto).

During the years of her training and professional practice, Schützenberger also developed an interest in the School of Palo Alto, with its emphasis on systemic-strategic and systemic-structural therapy, and psychoanalytic family therapy. Through the work of psychoanalyst Ivan Boszormenyi-Nagy, one of the founders of the transgenerational approach, Schützenberger learned the importance of invisible family loyalties, according to which relationships should take account of how issues related to justice and fairness play out within a family. Schützenberger identifies 1982 as the year in which she could blend her intuitions concerning such loyalties, repetitions and "anniversary syndrome" into a single theoretical vision. Since then, she has devoted herself to transgenerational psychotherapy with enthusiasm, and is now seen as one of the leading experts in the field. Throughout her life, Schützenberger's encounters with people, places and ideas have shown a degree of serendipity, a notion considered fundamental to scientific discovery, which she summarizes thus: "The concept of serendipity is at once a synchronous coincidence that is meaningful and important to the subject, an openness of spirit and a gift for noticing new and unexpected things, reacting to and making use of them to benefit the self or others" (translated from the Italian). With this brief overview, I hope to have suggested that Schützenberger's model of transgenerational psychotherapy is not the recent, fanciful finding of a bizarre-minded therapist, but rather a discipline based on a solid theoretical foundation and substantial clinical experience, which articulates correspondences that today have also received validation of a statistical nature.[2]

Schützenberger was often asked whether she was a Buddhist and this led her to clarify, once and for all, in one of her most famous books[3] that she was not, and knew nothing about the religion. Such a statement confirms that her views are the result of her research and the data she and other scholars collected; indeed, she candidly admits that, though able to confirm the concurrence of much of the data in her possession, she cannot explain how transgenerational transmissions actually occur. However, in her most recent, and strongly autobiographical, book,[4] Schützenberger does not refrain from using the term karma—despite professing her adherence to Protestant Christianity—as an effective synthesis of a set of ideas linked to the clinical realities she knows well.

Indeed, it would be natural for a Buddhist, or anyone with some knowledge of Buddhism, to question Schützenberger's relationship with Buddhism, as her work presents several analogies with the Buddhist conception of karma, although expressed in different terms and used in a (somewhat) different manner. Karma is a Sanskrit term which may be translated as "action" and, also, "condition." It is connected to the principle of cause and effect, and is thus far removed from the notions of destiny or blind, unchangeable fate with which it is sometimes confused (by its very nature, karma is in fact subject to change). The principle of cause and effect holds up the entire Buddhist system of living—concerning every aspect of life, both human and not—and leads to seeing all things as interdependent, albeit through different degrees of spatiotemporal concatenation. Let us take one of the classic examples. Every apple seed has, within it, the potential to become an apple tree and generate apples. This can occur if the seed is planted in the correct soil and receives enough water and light for it to grow. Given the same conditions, if a different kind of seed is planted, another type of tree will grow. If the soil is perfect for an apple seed, which would have grown into a beautiful apple tree, it might not be particularly well suited to the seed that has been planted, and the tree may grow stunted. If, instead, the seed is kept in a drawer, it will not have the chance to germinate. Hence, the seed in itself is not enough for the tree to grow; likewise, however good the soil may be, receiving plenty of water and light, without a seed there will be no tree. Karma works in a similar way (and, in itself, this part of reality linked to vegetation is karma—karma of the apple tree, in our example). In the same way, a human being may perform an action, the seed-condition, which, under certain conditions, will lead to specific effects-fruits. The time element is one of the necessary conditions for the maturation of a cause's effects, and, over an extended period of time, the conditions for the manifestation of these effects will eventually be met.

By basing all ethical reasoning on the law of cause and effect, Buddhism does not consider sin in the same way that the revealed religions do. Translating from one language to another, the word for sin appears in Buddhism too; we must however bear in mind that the word does not possess the same meaning as it does in Christian terms, despite being its equivalent. Buddhist sin denotes every negative action of body, speech, and mind that will give rise to a negative consequence, but does not involve the idea of punishment. In the same way, Buddhist use of the word penance is linked to the practice of purification and does not contemplate atonement through a penalty given as punishment. There is no condemning God; it is the action itself that will bring its author a corresponding dose of suffering. This, however, is not the place for embarking on reflections of a philosophical and theological nature; my intention is simply to draw attention to a more conscious and contextual way of listening to words, "opening them up" to their deeper meaning, especially if they come from a tradition that differs from ours.

On the subject of karma, it is necessary at least to mention the principle of interdependent origination, as conceptualized within the "twelve-link chain of interdependent origination" (which, it is believed, leads to continuous suffering). Without going into detail regarding the twelve links of this chain, I believe it is nevertheless worth referencing, as it maintains that concrete elements come into being by virtue of an uninterrupted series of their complete state of dependence. The Middle Way preached by the Buddha with regard to actions performed, and thus karma, rejects both the idea that the person who experiences the fruit of an action is the same person who initially performed it, as well as its opposite, that is, that the person experiencing the fruit of an action is different than the person who initially performed it.[5] This is, essentially, the crux of several points of reflection (in keeping with other fields of knowledge) and an attempt to forcefully unify and align them here would be neither necessary nor useful, as they can instead be seen in a possible mutual harmony. What we have touched on thus far are, fundamentally, different ways of looking at the same human reality, and identifying comparable meanings expressed in diverse but concordant ways.

Transgenerational psychotherapy maintains that trauma experienced by a parent may have consequences on the life of an offspring; the latter would, according to both Buddhism and Western clinical experience, be reaping the fruits of an action carried out (either actively or passively) by another person. At the same time, what the subject experiences is the fruit of his own karma, and is therefore linked to a personal concatenation of causes and effects, meaning that the subject has determined (and in turn been determined by) his karmic inheritance in his past lives, if not in the current one. In this sense, he who reaps the fruits of an action is he who performed it. For what we have inherited, we are our ancestors; at the same time, however, with our varied inheritance and being masters of our own lives, we are not.

In the opening passage of The Ancestor Syndrome, Schützenberger quotes Saint Augustine: "The dead are invisible beings, they are not absent." Honoring ancestors is of great importance in Buddhism, because they are the roots that we come from and provide the karma we inherit. Indeed, karma is passed down much like genetic inheritance, as we know it in Western science. In the same way that an individual is the product of multiple factors, his karma is equally composite, coming both from his ancestors (of the maternal and paternal lines, as with genetics) and from his past and present lives. All these subjective aspects of karma then come into contact with the (environmental) karma of the places where the subject lives, so that the possibilities of karmic expression of the law of cause and effect result from the alchemy of countless elements. Indeed, we should avoid a superficial approach to karma that implies a crude and immediate consequentiality of cause and effect, and restore its deeper, more worthy meaning. To put it in both clinical and Buddhist terms: psychotherapy deals with the karma that the subject obtains in his present life and that which he receives directly from parents and grandparents (if they are still alive), resulting from his upbringing and the quality of these relationships; transgenerational psychotherapy, on the other hand, also deals with karma inherited from generations predating parents and grandparents in the line of descent. The clinical and Buddhist systems of thought share a substantially consistent view of what contributes to the suffering and well-being of the subject, despite expressing themselves in formally different terms (even acknowledging the importance of formal meanings in relation to further signification).

We may look to the arts for a famous, unintentional example of unresolved transgenerational logic and karma in Turandot, one of Puccini's most famous and admired operas. The story is well-known: the beautiful but cruel princess puts to death her misguided suitors when they fail to solve her puzzles. In scene two of the second act, Turandot herself explains to the audience the reason behind her merciless acts:

> In this royal palace
> a thousand and thousand years ago,
> A desperate cry resounded.
> And that cry has been heard
> from daughter to daughter
> Until here in my soul it has taken refuge!
> Princess Lo-u-ling,
> My serene and sweet ancestor,
> Who ruled in joyful seclusion and silence,
> And who challenged the harsh rule of men
> today lives in me. . . .

And Lo-u-ling,
my sweet ancestor was captured
By a man like you,
Yes, like you, stranger.
That atrocious night she was tortured,
And her fresh voice was stilled forever. . . .

I take revenge on you for that pure one,
For her cry of anguish and for her death!

Thankfully, the opera allows its protagonists to break this negative karmic concatenation (which could be interpreted psychoanalytically as compulsion to repeat): an element of powerful benevolence is introduced and Turandot's age-old suffering resolved.[6] Today, Turandots live among us and we can come across them readily in both consulting rooms and meditation rooms, if we know how to recognize them.

It is written in one of the sutras[7] that we encounter the Teachings because we have the karma to listen to dharma. To paraphrase this passage, we can say that our encounter with clinical tools can also be a good kind of karma. In my personal experience, I believe that my training and clinical practice have contributed heavily to determining my karma to listen to dharma, in the same way that many people have benefitted from psychotherapy thanks to their karma. (The therapeutic alliance, very important in any therapy, is strongly dependent on both the therapist and the patient's ability to form a relationship; and we know full well that we cannot take for granted that those who need help actually seek treatment.) As Buddhism and psychotherapy promote both a more authentic relationship with reality and a greater fullness of living, and operate in a non-contradictory fashion despite expressing themselves differently, it has been natural for me to highlight the harmonic and mutually fruitful connections between them.

NOTES

1. Faimberg, H. 2005. *The telescoping of generations: Listening to the narcissistic links between generations*. London: Routledge.
2. Although he did not collaborate with Schützenberger, I think it is also worth mentioning Bert Hellinger, a therapist who gained notoriety from his (still controversial) therapeutic system linked to family constellations. Hellinger also harks from a background of systemic psychotherapy, and his family constellations share several connections with transgenerational psychotherapy, particularly with regard to the concept of intrafamilial loyalty.
3. Schützenberger, A. A. 1998. *The Ancestor syndrome. Transgenerational psychotherapy and the hidden links in the family tree*. London: Routledge.
4. Schützenberger, A. A. 2010. *Il piacere di vivere* [*The Pleasure of Living*]. Roma: Di Rienzo Editore.
5. For a detailed discussion of this debate, see Panikkar, *The Silence of God: The Answer of the Buddha*.

6. I would like to thank Maestro Daniela Maddalena for the precious thoughts we shared on Turandot, which I unfortunately cannot go into here, but which helped me develop my reflections on issues of the transgenerational and the feminine.

7. *Sutra Mahaparinirvana*, chapter XXII.

REFERENCES

Faimberg, H. 2005. *The telescoping of generations: Listening to the narcissistic links between generations*. London: Routledge.

Panikkar R. 1989. *The Silence of God: The Answer of the Buddha*. Maryknoll, NY: Orbis Books.

Schützenberger, A. A. 1998. *The Ancestor syndrome. Transgenerational psychotherapy and the hidden links in the family tree*. London: Routledge.

———. 2010. *Il piacere di vivere*. Roma: Di Rienzo Editore.

III

Psychoanalysis and Meditation

Chapter Seven

Metamorphoses of Consciousness

Answers in the Light of Awareness

Alessandro Giannandrea, Antonino Raffone, and Katie Ferrell

> To study the Way is to study the Self.
> To study the Self is to forget the Self.
> To forget the Self is to be enlightened by all things of the universe.
>
> —Dogen-zenji, "Shobogenzo" (1231)

> There's an illusion that is taken for granted, but never investigated: there is an I. It's as if there's someone inside me, looking out from behind my eyes.
>
> —Ajahn Chandapalo (2010)[1]

Light and color from the early spring afternoon enter the meditation room where we, a couple of scientists and a group of monks, explore the complexities of consciousness. We were brought together by a shared interest in first-person observation through meditation and a desire to learn from each other. As the seasons changed from spring to summer, fall to winter, and then back to spring, we joined in conversation amid the ever-changing external and internal landscapes. As winter fades, we crack open the windows to let in the sounds and scents of spring, as a breeze fills the room and brushes the golden statue of the Buddha, who has smiled on us during this past year.

In 2010, the monks at Santacittarama Buddhist Monastery honored us, the authors, with a series of meetings throughout the year. The monastery is of the Theravada tradition, more specifically of the Thailand Forest tradition. It is situated in the Sabine mountains close to Rieti in central Italy. This chapter draws on many authors who place Buddhism, psychology, psychoanalysis and neuroscience in conversation. On the basis of such conversations we formulated new questions and searched for answers directly from those who have made the practice of Buddhism a way of life, dedicating their lives to freeing their minds from any illusions of reality. We strove to understand the possible variations of conscious experience in meditative practice, specifically where "self" and "non-self" are concerned. This chapter springs from two strongly interconnected themes that emerged from the conversations at Santacittarama Monastery: the separate self and the nature of conscious experience in the practice of meditation.

According to Buddhist thought, the idea that we each have a core self is an illusion, and our belief in an ever-present and static self leads to suffering through clinging to something that is intrinsically fluid. As Henk Barendregt, a renowned Vipassana teacher, notes, if we try to hold tightly to a moving object, we experience friction between our hand and the object. Suffering, as the Buddha teaches, is that friction. Monks, and others, who work to free their minds from illusion, employ meditation and other processes to undergo a progressive dismantling of the illusion of possessing a solid self, as well as of their experience of individualization. This work, as the Santacittarama monks see and live it, takes years of daily meditation practice.

To the expert meditator, the investigation into the nature of such psychological structures is made clearer by the acquired and consolidated ability to reside in a state of mental calm and concentration. This calm is the ground for the investigation of mental processes through awareness.

A worldwide debate across disciplines is taking place around the question, "How do we study private internal experience?" The field of study dealing with consciousness is so vast as to require extremely heterogeneous and interdisciplinary skills and approaches. These include the contemplative approach, neuroscience, experimental psychology, psychoanalysis, philosophy, poetry, and art. Through this chapter we explore the topic of how to study personal internal experience and awareness itself. We do so primarily through neuroscientific investigations, Buddhist studies and practices, psychology, and our exchanges with the Santacittarama monks.

HOW CAN WE APPROACH SELF AND NON-SELF IN BUDDHISM?

Buddhism is rich in practices that lead to a radical change of perspective regarding one's interior world and sense of "self." For instance, the Buddha would refer to himself not with the pronoun I, but with the epithet Tathagata (translated from the Pali language as "one who has thus come" or as "one who has thus gone"). Through use of the title or pronoun Tathagata, Buddha underlines the ambivalent, or non-solid, nature of the self. Instead of a solid self, this self comes from a movement of closing in on or retreating away from something, either physical or conceptual. The Buddha thus defines himself in relation to the world around him. This differs from the traditional Western way of referring to the self, which, as Westerners, we tend to reify. In other words, we take the abstract (such as "the self") and turn it into something concrete and solid in our thoughts and beliefs. The ambiguity of the Buddha's chosen epithet illustrates the refined care of the Buddhist search into the nature of the self, and how the latter is seen to differ from Western understandings.

While viewing the self as non-solid may seem foreign, reflections and debates on the nature and foundations of inner experience are prominent in Western thinking too. Take, for example, the well-known article by Thomas Nagel (1974)[2] in which he explores the limits of the possibility of the study of consciousness. He opens his discourse with the words, "What Is It Like to Be a Bat? Consciousness is what makes the mind-body problem really intractable," and continues on to explore the question in detail. Some years later, Hofstadter[3] echoed these thoughts by asking, "What is it like to be a Zen master who has attained a satori-like state in which no more subject ("I," ego, self) exists?" He defines this question as, "an orgy of extravagant variations on the theme proposed by Nagel."

From questions on the nature of the self arise questions regarding awareness of the self and our own personal experience. When we look at an object, we experience ourselves looking. Therefore we are conscious of ourselves as subjects of that particular experience. When we look at ourselves, when we reflect on our own experience of the self, we are both subject and object of the experience. It is worthy to note here that no one, perhaps, has made this point more sharply than Richard De Martino and, subsequently, Anthony Molino, in his revisitation of De Martino's work in The Couch and the Tree, where the former's notion of the "structured function of reflective consciousness"—namely, "the once actualized and thereafter reactualizable capacity of the human person to be aware or conscious of his/her own awareness or consciousness"—is examined in depth.[4]

Contemplative Indian Buddhist philosopher Shantideva, who notably influenced Tibetan Buddhism, puts the question in these terms: "Can consciousness thoughtfully observe itself in a particular moment?" According to Shantideva, as the blade of a sword cannot cut itself, or the point of a finger touch itself, so consciousness cannot observe itself in a given moment of the same consciousness. This observation was based on the theory that consciousness unfolds in snapshots or frames, like a movie. He proposed that awareness can only refer to a past, albeit just-lived, subjective experience. In other words, "the consciousness that observes itself" is an epistemological short-circuit. According to Shantideva, to be able to investigate the subjective quality of experiencing an object of the external world, we must first experience and then, only in the immediately successive moment, widen our attention to the dyad composed of subject and object.

Shantideva's analysis and the psychoanalytical point of view share similarities. In fact, according to the psychoanalytic view, human consciousness—or the conscious mind of Freudian tradition—works in a serial way and is only able to take in one object at a time. This seriality, as Ignacio Matte Blanco shows (1975),[5] is not a limit of the unconscious mind, which by its very 'nature' can be said to use non-Aristotelian logic. This last consideration reveals a limit in rationally oriented research. Maybe, a sword cannot cut itself, but "for every gramophone there is a record which that gramophone cannot play," as Hofstadter observes (1979)[6] paraphrasing Gödel's theory of incompleteness. In other words, every self-referential recursive process, such as that of the mind thinking of itself, leads to an infinite regression that can never be short-circuited in a way that is simultaneously coherent and complete. In the words of the abbot of the Santacittarama monastery:

> The eye cannot see itself, therefore anything we come to know is non-self, it is not our true essence. Whether we're concerned with a physical object, or something like a mental object or a thought, we're talking about non-self, something that doesn't belong to us. . . . When the mind becomes serene, all is clearer. There is a simple knowledge of sorts; there is presence as pure presence without the creation of a subject-object dualism. There is no sense of subjectivity. There is only experience. We can say that pure awareness is unitive instead of separative while sensory consciousness, such as the five khandhas,[7] creates a sense of an I in the form of a subject that sees an object.
>
> This holds for the five physical senses and also for the mind, the sixth sense. A mental image or a memory also creates the impression that there is an I, and therefore a subject and an object. But when you withdraw a little from the senses, thus calming their activity, you can live the experience of unification. There is a sense of presence, that one is awake, and it is inclusive instead of separative. Phenomena may emerge, sensations, ideas, memories may emerge, but there is no sense of an observing I. What you have is a field of experience, instead of a subject and an object.

After thirty years of practicing insight meditation (Samatha-Vipassana meditation in Pali), the abbot got to the point where he found it necessary to surrender belief in, and the experience of, an I. In a similar way, William James (1892),[8] one of the pioneers of Western psychology, noted that it was not necessary to postulate a permanent nuclear self to explain how experience gets generated. For James, the basis of the consciousness of the self is a continuous flow of thoughts, experienced, so to speak, in the first person (the implicit "I"). This flow of thoughts, in turn, can refer to aspects of experience lived in the third person, under the explicit and objective form of "Me." We will address this further in the next section.

According to the Santacittarama monks' descriptions of their own contemplative experiences of self and non-self, the sense of I originates from the force of one's relationship with stimuli or objects. To quote one of the monks,

> If, for example, I am attracted by an object, or if an object impacts me emotionally, then we can say that both the object and I exist. But if I remain indifferent towards this object, or if the object doesn't impact me, in effect I become aware of the seeing itself without necessarily entering into a subject-object relationship . . . The experience of an object is a direct experience, as the mind gradually calms and with it all attachments, opinions, ideas . . . you begin to enter into a new perception of consciousness: there is a seeing, there is a hearing, there is a touching but there is no longer a strong identification with oneself as the subject of that experience.
>
> Or, to quote another monk: "through the eye is revealed both the presence of an external object as well as a subject that looks at that object."

Careful introspective analysis of processes that build up the basis of the self ends in a progressive dismantling, a decomposition, of its primary components. This can lead to a profound experience of depersonalization as well as to the perception of union and harmony with the outside world. In the words of one of the monks: "there are moments during meditation in which the sensation of being a distinct entity falls away. The mind is very tranquil and silent, as one becomes present and fully aware. There is no sensation of being distinct from anything else." This radical revolution of the inner world, no longer centered on the idea of a fixed, lasting and distinct I, also brings about a different perception of one's own continuity in time: "a person is somewhat like a river, a continually changing process." In the words of yet another monk:

> The continuity of a "fixed" thing is actually a chain of cause and effect, it is in fact in process and not fixed. Think of a process like a river. We perceive the river to be the same river, but the water is continually changing. Just as the water has a continuity, the water is always new. While the water is always new, the river is not the water. The river is its bed, even though a bed without the water is not a river. However, the river bed is also in continuous change, but slower. We may give the same name to the river but the water is always different. Through the centuries the position of that same river may even change

Alternatively, as another Santacittarama monk puts it: "We are used to hardening reality, considering it stable, but you must realize that reality is a process in movement. You cannot identify something that is fixed and substantial. You begin to understand that what is unfolding corresponds to a law of cause and effect."

Although the self is viewed as insubstantial, the sense of self is not seen as a useless frill to be freed of without a trace. Buddhism does not in fact negate the importance of one's own sense of cohesion, delimitation, and continuity in everyday life, in what the monks define as conventional reality. Buddha himself embodied an excellent example of social and civic functioning by being very skillfully oriented in the lively Indian culture of his time. Indeed, the gradual abandonment of every illusion related to "I" passes through a phase, as the monks suggest:

> In the process of illumination, as per the Buddha's teachings, there is a first phase in which an understanding is reached that there is no fixed personality identifiable in the body or in the other khandas; still, a sense of self remains as an abstract concept . . . Buddha said that this can be compared to that which happens when we wash clothes: the scent of the soap remains, even though no trace of the soap is left. There persists therefore the scent of self, which can still be perceived in relations with others. Even though, at an initial level, there is no longer a belief in an eternal and unchangeable self, it still persists. This sense, of what we might call "self-conceit," is very strongly rooted, quite difficult to uproot.

What remains after the sense of self, the self-conceit, has dissolved? The monks replied: "During meditation experience, the sense of self is diluted. What remains is a field of experience that is not organized into compartments and is not differentiated. There is just a field of experience. . . . There is no need for an 'I' or other such concepts. There is the awareness of one's own activities, there is no longer the sense of a central I,' there is just a field of experience." This experience takes the place of the perception of being a subject that is perceiving an object, and in turn reacts to such objects.

"In this mode of introspection we do not find an I that is within us as if it were a point inside something. Also in science, in the study of consciousness, the center of consciousness is increasingly spoken of as a network rather than as a specific point." That which remains is therefore a thought without a thinker, an awareness without subject and object:

> You lose a little of the idea of a central "you" . . . the idea that inside of us there is a little man who looks out through our eyes and watches the world. . . . At a certain point even this vision is lost, while an idea of consciousness remains, of knowing . . . but you do not find that little man anymore . . . and you begin to feel that this world is not a place that revolves around you . . . while what persists, obviously, is the fact that you live in a world which originates from physical experience. The effect of all this is obviously one of liberation! Why? Because what results is that any idea of "I" is only a useless idea!

SELF IN SCIENTIFIC PSYCHOLOGY AND NEUROSCIENCE

William James (1892)[9] was the first to conceptualize what he called the "floating material" (p. 291) of the "self," intended as "in part known and in part knower, in part object and in part subject" (James, 1892, p. 159).[10] What James described in the correlated phenomenal terms (experiential) of a mentally unified life invites interesting comparisons to the Buddhist approach considered in the previous section.

As James himself noted, reflections on self require a fundamental distinction between an "I" and a "Me." According to James, the "I" is "that requirement that in every moment *is* consciousness, while Me is simply one of those things of *which* one is aware" (p. 175, italics in the original). The I of the "knower" can therefore be characterized as the subject of the experience, in contrast to "Me," understood as the object of the experience and "empirical aggregate of things objectively known" (ibid., p. 191). It must be noted, however, that James did not consider it necessary to postulate a permanent, nuclear self, understood as that "invariant metaphysical entity that generates experience" (ibid., p. 175). Working from the assumption that the thought stream is constantly changing, James did not assume a stable nuclear process forming a self over and above the transient flow of consciousness, or of subjective experience itself. Therefore, given the temporary character of thought streams, the concept of self, as proposed by James, is characterized as a process, rather than a structure. James also observed that the nucleus of "Me" is based on the presence of the physical body in every moment of experience.

Different theories of the self, such as those of Sigmund Freud (1899), Margaret Mead (1934) and Jean Piaget (1954), share similarities with James's theory. All of these authors maintain the same distinction between "I" and "Me." To all of them, "I" corresponds to a subjective sense of self as the subject of thought. It is a causal agent and subject of knowledge. The "Me," on the other hand, is the objective and explicit self.

More recently, in relation to James's perspective, Gallagher (2004)[11] proposed the distinction between a "minimal self," as the pre-reflective aspect of self, corresponding to the personal pronoun "I," and a "narrative self," or autobiographical self, corresponding to the personal pronoun "Me." In this framework, the minimal self corresponds to the sensation of being the immediate subject of experience in the present moment, assuming a perspective in the first person. As such, the minimal self corresponds to the source of thought and action, forming the ecological sensation of belonging to the body, and the awareness of being an agent of active behavior. In contrast, the narrative self regards a perspective in the third person, it is extended in time, creating a subjective sensation of identity and continuity, linking past, present and future. Along these lines, it is interesting to note that the sensation of belonging to a body (minimal self) may be distorted in asomatoagnosia, a neuropsychological syndrome following a selective cerebral lesion. The narrative self, to the contrary, can be altered by amnesia, with effects on the subjective link and past experience.

In the development of consciousness in infants, the sensation of "I" precedes that of "Me" (Damasio, 1999; Zelazo and Frye, 1998).[12] The infant develops an awareness of "I," even though it is nuclear and primitive in the first phase of life. This "I," the subject of all sensations and actions, derives from the sensory feedback gathered through the body and as a result of relationships with the external world. Only later will the first signs of developing an objective "Me" appear. At three months, the baby will start to show interest in his reflection in a mirror; but he will be unable to recognize himself in the reflection until around the age of eighteen months. For example, in a classic experiment, a red spot is applied to an unknowing baby's nose. If he recognizes himself in the mirror's image, he will touch his nose with his hand (Howe, Courage, and Edison, 2003),[13] and this typically happens for the first time when an infant is eighteen months old.

On the basis of neuroimaging evidence, scientists have recently identified the medial cortical structures in the brain as core areas for brain processes related to our experience of self. In particular, various functional magnetic resonance and positron emission tomography studies have shown the activation of the medial prefrontal cortex on occasions in which the subject reflects on his own features in comparison to those of others. The medial prefrontal cortex is also active when people are reflecting or thinking about their own self (see Gillihan and Farah, 2005; Northoff et al., 2006).[14]

Northoff et al (2006), also on the basis of recent neuroimaging studies, propose that self does not exist as a fixed and out-of-context entity. They propose that "self" is, in fact, a process that involves the individual in his relationships with objects in a given context. According to these authors, the self is established on the basis of pre-reflective and affective internal and external stimuli. The establishment of the self is therefore based on the perceived strength of the stimuli and how the individual relates to them. All this, as Varela[15] would have it, occurs of course in a transient and dynamic context of subject-and-object (or environment).

A recent functional magnetic resonance study by Farb and colleagues. (Farb et al., 2007)[16] has highlighted the configuration of cerebral activation associated with two forms of awareness in reference to self. The first is the consciousness of the narrative self and the second is the consciousness of the present moment, or rather the momentary states of self, known in Buddhism as mindfulness, or mental presence. In Farb's research cerebral activation was studied using two experimental conditions: one condition of a "temporally extended self," with focus on narrative self (NF, narrative focus); the other, a condition of "awareness in the present moment," with focus on experiential self (EF, experiential focus).

Two groups of subjects participated in this study: a group of subjects without previous experience of meditation (novices), and a group of subjects with eight weeks training in mindfulness meditation. In the novices, scientists observed reduced activation of the medial cortex structure, in particular in the prefrontal medial cortex, during the EF condition in comparison to the NF condition. The subjects with training in meditation showed an even more pronounced and extensive reduction in the prefrontal medial cortex during the EF condition when compared to the NF condition and to the novice subjects. They also showed an emergence and significant activity of a neuronal network located in the right hemisphere, involving the prefrontal lateral cortex, the insula, and inferior parietal lobule. Following training in mindfulness, the EF condition resulted in a shifting of activation from the amygdala toward the prefrontal lateral regions. This shift indicates a more objective and detached analysis of external sensorial and corporeal-emotional events, rather than a subjective and affective evaluation in reference to the self. Further analysis showed that cerebral areas associated with awareness of the present moment, such as the anterior insula, and areas associated with the narrative self, such as the prefrontal medial cortex, are functionally linked in the novices. This evidence indicates that mindfulness meditation can separate the two referenced forms of consciousness (associated with the narrative self and with fields of experience in the present moment). The separation allows one to develop the ability to give priority to a mental awareness of the body, thought, and feeling states, experienced as relatively detached from the self. When these states are viewed from a position of relative detachment, they are treated as passing mental states that can be simply registered or observed instead of being attached to a self.[17]

In "The Parable of the Arrow" the Buddha tells of a man who is hit by an arrow. The man's suffering, says Buddha, is caused by two arrows: the one that is physically shot into his leg and the other that is his mental reaction to the pain caused by the first. By removing the second arrow, true awareness can be obtained of the first. The empiric evidence presented throughout this section shows that the practice of meditation facilitates separation of the "two arrows," distilling, as it were, the analysis of one's own interior experience. This process is similar to that which happens in the course of psychoanalysis. The patient starts from a state in which his experience is characterized by the submerged and silent intense activity of his unconscious. The activity of his unconscious expresses itself mostly through his symptoms and, many times, the patient is unaware of the causes. In continuing the analytic process, the "I" gets to the point where its territory is widened to include those thoughts that were previously unthinkable.[18] The patient can therefore observe, in a more objective way, the second arrow and ache only from the first.

METAMORPHOSIS OF CONSCIOUSNESS THROUGH MEDITATION

During our conversations at Santacittarama, we tried to better understand the phenomenology of a "non-judging mental presence." This mental state is one characterized by openness to experiences in the here-and-now without craving, aversion, or attachment (as defined by the Buddha). One of the monks expressed the benefits of developing this mental presence:

> One ends up dwelling more and more in this simple awareness, with an inclusive perspective and a field of experience that is no longer differentiated between I and others, subject and object. The senses, of course, continue to function; one can think, conceptualize, but there is no longer this heavy sense of I, of being identified with one's thoughts and perceptions. Everything becomes more spacious, tranquil. The components of experience become lighter and unsubstantial: it's like acquiring a "sense" of space. Our senses and our attention, generally, focus on objects and cannot "see" the space between visible objects. It seems that we do not notice this space because we cannot focus on it . . . When we step back a little though, and we widen the field of vision, then we can sense the space, the no-thing in the middle. In meditation, we therefore become aware of the "space" in the mind as well, and as there is no limit in matter, there is no limit to mental activities. Mental activity is only a small part of a larger whole, and when one has the sense of space one is aware of the objects in it. So while the objects and activity continue to exist, they do not provoke reactions as strongly as they do outside this type of awareness. This is because space gives a sense of serenity, of being with the background. Instead of a very narrow consciousness, one acquires a wider perspective. Thus, on the level of the interior world, we can say that there are, metaphorically, silence and space in the background. Events and processes that come and go do not overcome us, and we have a better perspective on things. We are able to observe without being completely overcome and taken in by appearances.

This mental state is a borderline area between two worlds: between a conventional, entropic one (the source of suffering) and another free of any illusion. In the words of one of our monks:

> There are some moments during meditation in which the sensation of being distinct falls away, the mind is tranquil and silent and one is present and truly aware. There is no sensation of being distinct from something different from us. Then, in the normality of the day, the sensation of being distinct returns. This sensation is needed to be able to function in the "conventional" world . . . Since the activity of the mind in the body is something that is continually

> changing, there is not a strong sense of identification, of the kind "I am this." One becomes more centered on pure awareness as opposed to awareness focused on a material, or specific, object or condition. It can be described as being present on the borders of the world of phenomena, conditioned on the one hand, and unconditioned, infinite on the other. It is like finding oneself on the shared border of these two environments: there is the ability to act, to be responsible for oneself, to function perfectly in the world, but there is still this sense of infinity, of the unconditioned.

This particular state seems to be the ideal plateau from which to observe, free from the ordinary processes of categorization, the panorama of one's own internal experiences:

> Formal meditation practice tends to slow down mental processes, making them appear as if in slow motion. It tends to create spaces between mental phenomena, so that it is easier to develop a sense of mental presence, of awareness. . . . The important thing about being able to stay with things as they are is to investigate the experience in a direct way instead of being captured by the habits, opinions and preferences that characterize our usual reactivity. It is a little like knowing that one can be open to the flow of conscious experience without adding anything to it . . . in a very simple way."[19]

A MENTAL STATE OF PURE AWARENESS

The well-known neuroscientist Semir Zeki (2003)[20] recently formulated a theory in which he proposed a hierarchic organization of consciousness structured on three levels: "micro-conscious," "macro-conscious," and "pure conscious." Zeki refers to this last level, that of the Kantian pure or "transcendental" consciousness, in terms of the awareness of the person as a subject of their own perception, of being aware of awareness itself.

In a similar way, approaches to the study of consciousness based on the practice of meditation refer to a state of consciousness called "transcendental." Transcendental meditative practices include those centered on concentration and focalization of attention and often employ the repetition of a mantra. The state of concentration typical in transcendental meditation is, however, without the conative aspects that usually characterize the effort paid in concentrating the attention.

Maharishi Mahesh Yogi (1967),[21] who brought transcendental meditation to the West from the Indian Vedic tradition, describes the resulting state of pure awareness as follows: "When consciousness flows into the field of thought and activity, it identifies with many things and that is how we have experience. Instead, when consciousness turns inside towards itself, it generates an integrated state . . . This is pure awareness." The form of consciousness thus defined as "pure" is so in the sense that it is without any content of knowing. It is a state of awareness in which the individual is fully conscious, gathering within his awareness only the consciousness itself.[22] Those who practice transcendental meditation relate that the absence of any effort at concentration creates a state of "infiniteness" and a "loss of the sense of time, space and body." This experience of "pure consciousness" or "awareness without thought" is associated with a profound relaxing of the body, characterized by the slowing down of breathing and by important and diffused variations of neural functions.

Numerous studies on the subject suggest that consciousness of the self can be deeply altered in the practice of meditation and that, even in the absence of any consciousness of oneself as subject (as happens in the deepest meditative states), there remains an awareness "without object." Similar to what the Santacittarama monks described, a state of consciousness that is free of references to any form of self can exist, characterized by an intuitive, non-referential, consciousness. In this meditative experience, the aspects of consciousness described above, in reference to "I" and "Me," undergo some modifications: the "Me" is substituted by a temporary state of pure mental presence, while the "I" melts away and is replaced by an experience that the abbot of the Santacittarama monastery defines as a "field of experience without subject." Moreover, in Buddhist meditation, the reflective aspect of consciousness is associated with the detached observation of the contents of experience and mental processes, thus "transcending" the concepts of self-agency and self-identification. And while a state of mindfulness, or pure awareness, is well within the reach of every individual (and not only of expert meditators), it remains important to note in this context, as the monks themselves repeatedly pointed out, that the cognitive reference to a conventional self is not surrendered but maintained as a crucial faculty for the integration of ordinary conscious experience (see Edelman and Tononi, 2000)[23] and for social interaction.

The concept of mindfulness, derived from Buddhist texts and recently emphasized by clinical psychologists (see Cahn and Polich, 2006),[24] offers a unified paradigm which helps us comprehend the workings of endogenous attention, self-monitoring, and executive control functions—all of which are essential to self-awareness (Raffone and Srinivasan, 2009).[25] Siegel (2007–2009),[26] referring to mindfulness meditation or open mental presence, has recently enriched the semantic field of mindfulness studies by proposing a distinction among various forms of awareness. He states that a receptive or mindful consciousness implies "openness" to anything that presents itself to the mind in the present moment. He also claims that this state has been demonstrated to create an increased flexibility in regulating one's own internal processes, thus allowing a profound change in habitual ways of adapting and reacting. The author later describes what he defines as "a mindful observation of our own self," linking mindful consciousness with the meta-cognitive investigation of one's own mental processes. The integration of these states with receptivity is characterized by four aspects: curiosity, an open mind, acceptance, and love. Lastly, Siegel describes a reflective awareness, implying a more immediate ability of the mind to know itself, without effort or words, which leads in turn to an understanding of the nature of "awareness of the awareness itself."

CONCLUSION

A practice existed in the 1800s whereby women of nobility hung large, richly decorated mirrors in their bedrooms. The mirrors were called Psyche, as they were meant to reflect the image of the noble owners of the household, held to be as lovely as the Greek Goddess of the Soul. Psychein is the Greek verb for "to blow" or "to breathe." Paradoxically, one might then suggest that the word psychoanalysis has its very roots in the observation of the breath! Psychè–anemos: the systematic exploration of the quality of one's own image, reflected in the frame of the psychoanalytic mirror or conveyed into an élan vital of words and thoughts. It is from such an observation of the breath that our investigation of the Buddhist monks began: of breathing as both bodily and spiritual act, a metaphor of the process of construction and deconstruction, of creation and destruction. In Hindu philosophy, Atman, the "individual self" and Brahman, the "universal self" are two words also derived from verbs that mean to breathe in and to breathe out. The interplay of Atman and Brahman, then, may correspond to that which in Buddhism is called Samadhì, a state of profound concentration that transcends the dualism of subject and object.

Neuroscience, as we know, has evidenced the numerous inflexions of the nature of self alongside the multiple dimensions of consciousness. The monks we've interviewed have enhanced these scientific observations with first-person descriptions of their experiences, while psychoanalysts—with their increasing emphasis on the role of mirroring and empathy in the formation of healthy human relationships—add a third epistemological vantage point from which to observe human nature. It is our hope that research will continue in the direction of an increasingly unified vision which may more fully integrate the intuitions and findings of all three disciplines.

NOTES

*The authors would like to thank the monks of the Santacittarama Monastery for their frequent hospitality and gracious collaboration; Dario Doshin Girolami and Henk Barendregt for their friendship and guidance; and the many monks and expert meditators who generously gave of their time in assisting with our research.

1. From an interview with Ajahn Chandapalo (2010).

2. Nagel, T. 1974. "What is it like to be a bat?" *Philosophical Review* 83.4: 435–450.

3. Hofstadter, D. R., and Dennett, D. C. 1982. *The Mind's I: Fantasies and Reflections on Self and Soul*. New York: Bantam Books.

4. Molino, A. 1998. "Zen, Lacan, and the Alien Ego." In *The Couch and the Tree*, edited by A. Molino, 290–304. New York: North Point Press; De Martino, R. 1960. "The Human Situation and Zen Buddhism." In *Zen Buddhism and Psychoanalysis*, by E. Fromm, D.T. Suzuki and R. De Martino. New York: Harper & Row.

5. Blanco, I. M. 1975. *The Unconscious as Infinite Sets: An Essay in Bi-Logic*. London: Duckworth & Company Ltd.

6. Hofstadter, D. R. 1979. *Gödel, Escher, Bach: An Eternal Golden Braid*. New York: Basic Book.

7. *Khandhas* (*skandhas*, in Sanskrit) is a term that literally means "pile, heap"; they are the base of the personality on which is formed the idea of the existence of the "I."

8. James, W. 1892. *Psychology*. New York: Henry Holt and Company.

9. Ibid.

10. Ibid.

11. Gallagher, S. 2004. "Philosophical conceptions of the Self: Implications for cognitive science." *Trends in Cognitive Science*, 4: 14–21.

12. Damasio, A. 1999. *The Feeling of What Happens: Body and Emotion in the Making of Consciousness*. New York: Harcourt, Brace. Zelazo, P., Frye, D. 1998. "Cognitive complexity and control: II. The development of executive function in childhood." *Current Directions in Psychological Science*, 7: 121–128.

13. Howe, M. L., Courage, M. L., Edison, S. C. 2003. "When autobiographical memory begins." In *Theories of memory* (Vol. III), edited by M. Conway, S. Gathercole, S. Algarabel, A. Pitarque, T. Bajo. Hove: Psychology Press.

14. Gillihan, S. J., Farah, M. J. 2005. "Is Self special? A critical review of evidence from experimental psychology and cognitive neuroscience." *Psychological Bulletin*, 131: 76–97. Northoff, G., Heinzel, A., de Greck, M., Bermpohl, F., Dobrowolny, H., and Panksepp, J. 2006. "Self-referential processing in our brain—a meta-analysis of imaging studies on the Self." *NeuroImage*, 31: 440–457.

15. Thompson, E., Varela, F. 2001. "Radical embodiment: neural dynamics and consciousness." *Trends in Cognitive Sciences*, 5,10: 418–425.

16. Farb, N.A.S., Segal, Z.V., Mayberg, H., et al., 2007. "Attending to the present: meditation reveals distinct neural modes of Self-reference." *Social Cognitive and Affective Neuroscience*, 2: 313–322.

17. Michael Eigen would say: a self that "does not run after or get ahead of time but, instead, seems to simply move with it," "an unpressured sense of self that is not easily stampeded" (Eigen, M. 1993. "Breathing and Identity." In *The Electrified Tightrope*, edited by A. Phillips, 46. Northwale: Jason Aronson).

18. Citing Freud: "The intention of psychoanalysis is to strengthen the ego, to make it more independent of the super-ego, to widen its field of perception and enlarge its organization, so that it can appropriate fresh portions of the id. Where id is, there shall ego be" (Freud, S. 1933. *New Introductory Lectures on Psychoanalysis*, 11: 184. London: Hogarth Press).

19. This state of consciousness, evenly suspended, is surprisingly similar to that described by Freud (1912*): "It . . . consists of not concentrating the attention on something in particular, of maintaining the same type of calm, quiet attention, evenly-hovering attention towards everything that one hears." A more explicit contribution is offered by Nina Coltart (2000**), psychoanalyst and practicing Buddhist, when she spoke of the benefits that years of meditation brought her in her work as an analyst:

> I refer to something for which there is no one exact word, but it has to do with patience, with waiting, with "negative capability" which, inseparably linked with the continued exercise of bare attention, create the deepest atmosphere in which the analysis takes place . . . The more one learns to trust the intuition which arises from the less rational and cognitive parts of self . . . the more open one is also to a full and direct apprehension of the patient and of what is actually going on.

*(Freud, S. 1912. "Recommendations to physicians practicing psychoanalysis." In *The Standard Edition of the Complete Psychological Works of Sigmund Freud*, edited by J. Strachey, Vol. 12. London: Hogarth Press. 111–120.)

**(Coltart, N. 1992. *Slouching towards Bethlehem*. New York: The Guilford Press. 173–174.)

20. Zeki S. 2003. "The Disunity of Consciousness." *Trends in Cognitive Sciences*, 7, 214–218.

21. Mahesh Yogi, M. 1963. *The Science of Being and Art of Living*. New York: Penguin Books.

22. Arenander, A., Travis, F. T. 2004. "Brain patterns of Self-awareness." In *Self-Awareness Deficits*, edited by B. Beitman and J. Nair. New York: W.W. Norton.

23. Edelman, G. M., Tononi, G. 2000. *Universe of Consciousness: How Matter Becomes Imagination*. New York: Basic Books.

24. Cahn, B. R. J., Polich, J. 2006. "Meditation States and Traits: EEG, ERP, and Neuroimaging Studies." *Psychological Bulletin*, 132: 180–211.

25. Raffone, A., Srinivasan, N. 2009. "An adaptive workspace hypothesis about the neural correlates of consciousness: insights from neuroscience and meditation studies." *Progress in Brain Research*, 176: 161–180.

26. Siegel, D. J. 2007. "Mindfulness training and neural integration: differentiation of distinct streams of awareness and the cultivation of well-being," *Social Cognitive and Affective Neuroscience*, 2.4: 259–263; Siegel, D. J. 2009. "Mindful awareness, mindsight, and neural integration," *The Humanistic Psychologist*, 37.2: 137–158.

REFERENCES

Arenander, A., Travis, F. T. 2004. "Brain patterns of Self-awareness." In *Self-Awareness Deficits*, edited by B. Beitman and J. Nair. New York: W.W. Norton.

Blanco, I. M. 1975. *The Unconscious as Infinite Sets: An Essay in Bi-Logic*. London: Duckworth & Company Ltd.

Cahn, B. R. J., Polich, J. 2006. "Meditation states and traits: EEG, ERP, and neuroimaging studies." *Psychological Bulletin*, 132, 180–211.

Coltart, N. 1992. *Slouching towards Bethlehem*. New York: The Guilford Press. 173–174.

Damasio, A. 1999. *The Feeling of What Happens: Body and Emotion in the Making of Consciousness*. New York: Harcourt, Brace.

De Martino, R. 1960. "The Human Situation and Zen Buddhism." In *Zen Buddhism and Psychoanalysis*, by E. Fromm, D. T. Suzuki, and R. De Martino. New York: Harper & Row.

Edelman, G. M., Tononi, G. 2000. *Universe of Consciousness: How Matter Becomes Imagination*. New York: Basic Books.

Eigen, M. 1993. "Breathing and Identity." In *The Electrified Tightrope*, edited by A. Phillips, 46. Northwale: Jason Aronson.

Farb, N.A.S., Segal, Z.V., Mayberg, H., et al. 2007. "Attending to the present: meditation reveals distinct neural modes of Self-reference." *Social Cognitive and Affective Neuroscience*, 2: 313–322.

Freud, S. 1912. "Recommendations to physicians practicing psychoanalysis." In *The Standard Edition of the Complete Psychological Works of Sigmund Freud*, edited by J. Strachey, Vol. 12. London: Hogarth Press. 111–120.

———. 1933. *New Introductory Lectures on Psychoanalysis*, 11: 184. London: Hogarth Press.

Gallagher, S. 2004. "Philosophical conceptions of the Self: implications for cognitive science." *Trends in Cogntive Science*, 4: 14–21.

Gillihan, S. J., and Farah, M. J. 2005. "Is Self special? A critical review of evidence from experimental psychology and cognitive neuroscience." *Psychological Bulletin*, 131: 76–97.

Hofstadter D. R. 1979. *Gödel, Escher, Bach: an Eternal Golden Braid*. New York: Basic Book.

Hofstadter, D. R., Dennett, D. C. 1982. *The Mind's I: Fantasies and Reflections on Self and Soul*. New York: Bantam Books.

Howe, M. L., Courage, M. L., Edison, S. C. 2003. "When autobiographical memory begins." *In Theories of Memory* (Vol. III), edited by M. Conway, S. Gathercole, S. Algarabel, A. Pitarque, T. Bajo. Hove: Psychology Press.

James, W. 1892. *Psychology*. New York: Henry Holt and Company.

Mahesh Yogi, M. 1963. *The Science of Being and Art of Living*. New York: Penguin Books.

Molino, A. 1998. "Zen, Lacan, and the Alien Ego." In *The Couch and the Tree*, edited by A. Molino. New York: North Point Press. 290–304.

Nagel, T. 1974. "What is it like to be a bat?" *Philosophical Review* 83.4: 435–450.

Northoff, G., Heinzel, A., de Greck, M., Bermpohl, F., Dobrowolny, H., and Panksepp, J. 2006. "Self-referential processing in our brain—a meta-analysis of imaging studies on the Self." *NeuroImage*, 31: 440–57.

Raffone, A., Srinivasan, N. 2009. "An adaptive workspace hypothesis about the neural correlates of consciousness: insights from neuroscience and meditation studies." *Progress in Brain Research*. 176: 161–180.

Siegel, D. J. 2007. "Mindfulness training and neural integration: Differentiation of distinct streams of awareness and the cultivation of well-being." Social Cognitive and Affective Neuroscience, 2: 259–263.

———. 2009. "Mindful awareness, mindsight, and neural integration." *The Humanistic Psychologist*, 37.2: 137–158.

Thompson, E., Varela, F. 2001. "Radical embodiment: Neural dynamics and consciousness." *Trends in Cognitive Sciences*, 5.10: 418–425.

Zeki S. 2003. "The Disunity of Consciousness." *Trends in Cognitive Sciences*, 7: 214–218.

Zelazo, P., Frye, D. 1998. "Cognitive complexity and control: II. The development of executive function in childhood." *Current Directions in Psychological Science*, 7: 121–128.

Chapter Eight

Meditation Off the Cushion

Practice in Inconceivable Ordinary Life

Dorothy Yang

INCONCEIVABLE LIFE

Zen master Katagiri Roshi told a story that he called "Inconceivable Cosmic Life," a story that has always inspired me. It was about a hundred-year-old Chinese nettle tree in an area of Hiroshima that had been destroyed during the bombing and was presumed to be dead. It had no leaves or branches. One day, forty years after its death, several buds appeared to everyone's astonishment. School children built a fence around it with a sign that said, "The atom bomb turned even this once beautiful tree into an ugly thing. It has struggled to survive until today. The poor little tree has experienced strength and life. We must protect it." A very old tree surgeon known for saving 900-year-old trees and famous trees, heard about this tree and came to examine it. He was reputed to have the ability to tell if a tree was alive just by feeling it. He dug into the ground to see if he could find any living roots. They were all dead except for a single central root. He gave it a shot of nutrients, packed it with new earth and said that in one year, the tree would be covered with blossoms. And true to his prediction, the following year brought out numerous buds in the tree. The life and death of this atom bombed Chinese nettle tree was inconceivable. We all have this cosmic universal life: not only humans but all things in nature.

For Katagiri Roshi, life is inconceivable and vast, beyond our limited knowledge, our limited speculations and notions. We know so little about life or death and are full of judgments about ourselves, other people and life and death as well. If we could drop our judgments and develop a genuine curiosity about life and people, we could develop a capacity to see inconceivable life and experience increased connection to the universe. Inconceivable life is not limited to only beneficial things that happen; it can also manifest in destruction and human suffering. "In the truth of zazen, life and death are merging, moment after moment. And thus, because our lives are supported by all beings through the merging of life and death, we bring forth inconceivable life" (Katagiri, p. 33).

This chapter touches experiences with inconceivable life on and off the cushion in daily life, showing surprises that are possible when our conviction of separateness lessens. I will begin with sitting practice and move to the experience of swimming, a new world for me and expand to the larger environment, the practice of mindfulness and meditation any time, anywhere.

Buddhist students learn to give attention to the breath while sitting in formal meditation. Breathing unites body, mind, and heart in the present moment. We become mindful of whatever comes up in the practitioner's mind, the spontaneous arising in the moment. In sitting, there is an opening and deepening of non-goal oriented awareness which informs our being in the world. Sometimes we have an experience of life beyond our typical expectations. Off the cushion we often forget or lose contact with this open attitude. Yet the benefits of meditation in action can be profound.

PRACTICE IN ORDINARY LIFE

In zazen, we explore how to pay attention to body, mind and heart in ordinary daily activities as a form of practice. My practice of focusing on routine, familiar moments and encounters with others in everyday life and in psychotherapy is my way of integrating formal Buddhist teachings and practice into normal worldly activities. I am aware of a tendency to split the practice on the cushion and the rest of one's life. It is relatively easy to notice the breath when doing nothing else but breathing. It is more challenging to bring this level of consciousness to one's encounter with a New York City taxi driver when rushing to get to an appointment while simultaneously worrying about unfinished taxes. As Buddhism is a primary focus in my life and I integrate it in psychoanalysis and psychotherapy with patients, I find that it is all the more important that I study my mind in the "outside" world. It is this awareness that "inconceivable life" exists in each and every moment that I seek to live out: inconceivable life is life that is more than meets the eye.

What is it that distracts us off the cushion? Is it the wish to stave off death and impermanence? Is it our struggle to endure more aliveness? Or are we at odds with the renunciation required for the degree of mindfulness we seek to practice in daily life? Can we tolerate giving up attachment to addictive habits for a greater and more genuine source of freedom but one that requires more work?

It seems that most people, including seasoned meditators, distinguish between on-cushion and off-cushion experience, so I find myself wondering: Is the mind equally challenged on and off the cushion and where does that leave the practitioner? Wherever we are, we can practice meditation. The great Zen master Dogen said that to study the Buddha Way is to study the self, to study the self is to forget the self. And to forget the self is to be realized by the ten thousand things.

LEARNING TO SWIM

Growing up, I had been taught by my parents to fear water and thus never learned to swim. I avoided it and had only timid contact with it until years later when I had serious medical problems and surgery. Then water became the best environment for my body to heal. For years, I maintained excuses to avoid learning to swim. What I did not realize was that my mind was fraught with many dangers related to water.

First, there was loss of family members connected to water. Back in China before World War II, my father's youngest and favorite brother died from drinking unsanitary tap water. Coming from a rural town where country people drink water out of a well, my uncle did not know that city tap water was contaminated. He was only sixteen years old when he died after two years of illness.

During World War II when the Japanese were bombing Shanghai, my mother's family escaped to a boat with her box of jewelry as paper money had lost all value. Amid the bombs flying overhead, with all the frantic, terrified people pushing and shoving and rocking the overloaded boat, my mother's younger brother got knocked into the dark water. He had been the one in charge of holding the box of jewelry that would pay for passage and escape. It was winter and freezing. With his heavy coat on, he was unable to stay afloat for long. He held on to the family box of valuables needed for food, shelter, and necessities. My grandmother begged him to let go of the box so that he would not drown. His life was more precious than the money. Finally barely able to breathe, my uncle let go of the family treasure.

When my younger sister was eight years old and we attended a dinner party with our parents, one of the guests called herself a "fortune teller." She focused on my sister as being at risk with water and warned that she should be careful, even if the water was a puddle. From that time, my sister was not allowed to lock the bathroom door when she took a bath and had to sing so we knew she was all right. Once she stopped and forgot to continue to sing and the family rushed through the door. When she went on a school field trip, my mother would be sure to have someone keep a special eye on her.

To further discourage us from dangerous sports like going to the beach, my mother would read tragic accounts from the newspapers. "Oh, listen to this! A mother's only son who came back from the United States with his PhD drowned while swimming at the beach. The poor mother's hair turned white overnight in inconsolable grief." My parents instilled fears in us to protect us.

The last but most traumatic fear of water has to do with growing up in Taiwan during the crises with China with only the Straits of Taiwan between the two. My father had been a fighter pilot who defended his country when the Japanese attacked in World War II and later fought against the communists. In 1949, the Nationalists were defeated by the communists and fled to the islands of Taiwan. Taiwan is 111 miles from China but also established a military first line of defense on two smaller islands, Jinmen and Mazu, which were much closer to China. Jinmen is only two miles from China and Mazu ten miles. Both places were used by Taiwan as military bases. No civilians lived there. These islands were considered as possible launching pads to regain control of China.

The United States policy toward East Asia in the early Cold War added to tensions in the Taiwan Straits because it first supported unification of Taiwan with China. With the outbreak of the Korean War, the United States sent its Seventh Fleet to monitor the Taiwan Straits in order to prevent the Korean war from spreading southward, signed a treaty to support Taiwan. The area remained volatile.

My family went to the United States for three years, 1955–1958, when my father was posted in Washington, DC. The communists bombed Jinmen in 1958, the year my family returned to Taiwan. We were returning to a potential killing ground. China and Taiwan reached an agreement to bomb each other on alternate days and this continued for twenty years until the United States normalized its relationship with China. Taiwan's major protection from annihilation was this strip of water, the Taiwan Straits. Those of us in military families on Taiwan were aware of how precarious our position was. My father was assigned the job to oversee the group of young pilots who flew over the straits everyday to guard against major military assaults. Many of these pilots lost their lives. Phone calls in the early morning hours meant some pilot's plane had been shot down and off my father would go. What saved us on Taiwan was this crucial body of water that separated us from our enemies and from destruction.

With these stories in mind, I did not think I could ever learn to swim. Five years ago, doctors recommended I walk in a warm pool. From walking I went on to swimming. I had to find a way to exercise and strengthen my body without impact. I needed to walk in water since I could not walk on land without severe pain and a cane. I had to face my fears for the sake of my body and mind.

What I learned in Buddhist meditation as the study of the self carried over to my experience in water. Since I had many fears and preconceptions about swimming, I had to face old habitual patterns. Judgment, self criticisms, self doubt, and struggles to master something new quickly impeded my learning. The goal to improve manifested as aggression toward my self. Feelings surfaced that impeded the experience of "just being" in the water. The fear of the water made me feel separate from it.

There are also many fears that arise in sitting meditation. Fear of the unconscious, fear of the unknown, fear of what may come up, fear of not doing it right and then having to start all over again.

In learning to swim, terror unconsciously affected me. I wanted quick mastery of swimming as if I were a robot able to skip over the process of getting to know and accept all experiences of body and the water in varied interactions: clumsy, uncoordinated movements as well as smooth gliding. A difficulty was that I only wanted the "correct" moves and wanted to cut out the "incorrect" experiences. Immersed in water, I did not know or practice how to just let myself be. I could not bring what I had learned about watching my breath or being mindful of my body and environment in the water. I forgot about compassion and loving kindness toward myself and habitual discomfort arose, including being plagued by fear of not being good enough, constant self-correction (a traditional Chinese value), and demand for instant mastery.

In zazen practice, all the thoughts, feelings, and bodily sensations that arise are expressions of one's self. The focus is not to aggressively and ambitiously pursue, attain, and achieve improvement. Rejecting "imperfections" or "mistakes" in one's practice along the way would create a sense of pitting one side of the self against the other. Uncomfortable experiences like swallowing water or gasping for air are also part of swimming. As long as I treated them as something I had to avoid or to get rid of, I could not relax and accept all experiences without discrimination. I would have to learn to be receptive, let go and open myself to spontaneous movements, thoughts and feelings in interaction with water as "practice realization" or "spontaneous arising in the moment."

In swimming, as in formal meditation, there is "posture." The head is face down in the water with the top of the head like a beam heading forward. One of the first things I noticed in swimming was how difficult it was to coordinate the turning of my head and body in order to easily inhale and exhale air. Breathing in the water did not come easily and naturally. I moved my arms quickly to pull the water behind me only to notice that I had forgotten to breathe and felt my lungs ready to burst from holding my breath. It did not help much when my teacher said, "You can't drown in four feet of water and you can stand up when you feel that way."

One day, as I struggled hard to build momentum so that my feet would stay up, self criticisms, maras (neurotic demons) chased me while I fought to escape them. Finally my lungs could hold no more air and my arms and legs collapsed in exhaustion. I gave up and surrendered the struggle to become an expert swimmer. I feared I would start swallowing water or start to sink. Instead, my arms and legs moved easily as I glided through the water more slowly. Suddenly, I noticed only the sparkling bright sunlight dancing in the water and the rippled patterns that formed. Small dark tiles amid the light blue ones, guided me forward. The sense of a separate, isolated "self" disappeared and I was sunlight, water, and myriad colors. I felt free. Sensory stimuli freed me from the attachment to my "self" and my appearance. Interpenetration of environment and interdependence of me and the universe took over—oceanic feeling, loss of fear of being one with the water. Swimming became delightful, relaxed, blissful. Empty rather than solid and real. In surrendering the "I" who had to perform a certain way and master my environment, I came to trust the universe around me and felt completely supported.

LEO AND ME

As noted above, I began wading and swimming for medical reasons. In doing so, I had to stop avoiding what I most feared. I hoped doing so would help me physically. I did not expect the many other benefits that spontaneously arose. One was my encounter with Leo, a man in his late sixties.

The first time I arrived, Leo was the only other person in the pool. I was much shorter than he. Lifeguards offered to raise the floor which was attached to ropes on all four sides, so I would not have to climb down the steps. Being short, I needed the floor raised so that the water could be brought down or I could not walk without it being over my head, especially at the beginning when I could not stand up straight well. Leo's face bunched into a scowl and his bushy eyebrows pinched together. Balding with jowls, his body was stocky and he appeared to be around 5'10" tall. He and I were the only ones who used the warm pool early in the morning and he had been coming years before me. He was used to having the pool to himself. He walked in the pool or floated slowly facedown with his snorkeling mask. The change in height did not make a difference to his activity but he took offense. The change to his environment felt like a personal affront.

Seeing his displeasure, I offered to go at a time when he was not there and asked if I could call or email him to work it out. He responded with an emphatic shake of his head no. "That's too intrusive," he said and walked away, dismissing my attempts to negotiate with him. I needed the warm pool as much as he did and he refused to share it. Days later I heard that Leo repeatedly complained to the pool manager. I felt shocked. We were both members and I had the same right to use the pool as he did.

One morning he and a female friend stood on either side of the pool speaking loudly about me as if I were not there, making unpleasant remarks, referring to me as "she." "I wondered if she showered before coming to the pool. She's new and doesn't know that we've been coming here for years." I appeared to be one of a very few Asians who used this gym which encourages cultural diversity. I counted my breaths as I walked back and forth in the warm pool between the two of them. I did not say anything back to them. I felt I had no voice.

An old fear arose. It brought me back to the painful time when I was seven years old in an all white school, the three years when my father was assigned to Washington, DC. My parents had not explained we were moving to another country and that I would need to learn a new language. I was placed in the back of the classroom and given paper and crayons to draw with. No attention was paid to me and the teacher did not include me when she taught. I had been the best student in my school in Taiwan. What happened? It was a total mystery to me. No adults, including the principal and teachers, approached me. The children must have thought I was someone to stay away from. Without knowing or understanding what was going on, I kept silent like the good Chinese girl I was brought up to be. Months went by and I did not complain to my parents. It was not until I got a "D" in reading that my parents reacted. "Chinese people don't get 'Ds' in reading," they told me. I told them I could not read the alphabet because there were no pictographs (as there are in Chinese) to help me. I was clueless. My father said, "You'll have to learn the alphabet tonight." Learning the letters all at once was torture, but learn I did.

In the pool, I faced a similar state of panic with another intolerant male figure, Leo. I became so afraid of him and his expressions of dislike that I finally went to the director of aquatics to try to find a solution to the problem. In spite of all his complaints to the management, Leo found he could not get rid of me. He and I used the pool in silence and avoided any eye contact.

My physical recovery took a long time but eventually I learned to walk again and no longer needed the water lowered. Leo and I continued to share the pool in silence. I wanted to reach out to him but dared not. I realized by then that I was not his enemy but that he projected negative qualities onto me. I was not afraid of him anymore. Sometimes I would just include him in my thoughts. "Everyone wants to be happy, no one wants to suffer, and we all want to experience peace of mind."

Three years passed. Here we were: both of us suffering from pain and both of us wanting to be free from pain. We shared the same needs to cope with pain and cope with our sufferings. One day, our glances met by chance. Neither of us turned away. I said hello and he responded. We crossed the pool and started to talk. Without actually apologizing, Leo told me that he had gone through a very difficult time the past two years. He suffered from intense chronic back pain following a bad surgery many years ago. I also learned that his wife was suffering from cancer. We stood there talking for about an hour like long lost friends. It turned out that was a time I was working on writing a professional article on how Chinese culture impacts clinical treatment. He listened with interest and shared that he was a retired newspaper editor who now wrote interactive children's books online. We broke the ice and parted as friends.

I was amazed at the transformation of aggression–aversion to genuine friendliness. We were no longer one against the other. This transformation was inconceivable to me. After three years of avoidance and silence, Leo and I had begun to communicate. From then on, every time we met in the pool, we shared news about our current physical condition, found out that we shared similar interests in spiritual paths and meditation. In addition we offered each other advice on good healers. I went to his physical therapist and benefited a great deal from treatment with him. He too meditated. Leo and I e-mailed each other things that might be of interest and the progress of the projects we were working on. We became good friends who supported and encouraged one another. So there was a live root in our seemingly "dead" relationship. The change that occurred seemed inconceivable after our years of silence.

It was not just *my* transformation: something had indeed happened to both of us. A shared transformational field. In Zen there is a saying: not one, not two. Not one means not just one thing or any one foreclosed system of thought and feeling and not two means not separate. Either side alone can be hindering. If we separate from things, they may feel unreal and threatening. If everything is one, people can get sticky with oneness. We need to go beyond one or two. Don't cling to either. In Buddhism, "not" can mean vast and interconnected. To say "no form," "no feelings," "no perceptions," means not caught or limited by form, feeling, perception. If not caught, contrived, contracted, possibilities arises of feeling-form-perception opening vast access to inconceivable life.

A PSYCHOANALYTIC CASE

Dan, age sixty-eight, was a semi-retired surgeon who came to therapy upon his daughter's advice. Tall, longish grey hair and long beard, he was dressed in a faded short sleeved Hawaiian shirt that revealed tattoos on both sides of his arms. His eyes behind round blue-rimmed glasses were wary as he entered the room cautiously. This was his first therapy consultation. His daughter had given him my contact information a year before and alerted me that her father did not believe in psychotherapy, God, or anything except AA. He had a drinking problem and AA helped him. He felt he knew what happiness was since he never experienced it. He looked for faults in himself, judged himself constantly. Our work was like digging at granite rock.

When I asked him why he sought help now, Dan answered that both his daughters had moved out of his apartment to be with their boyfriends. He and his daughters were very close, their attachment intensified by loss of their mother thirty years earlier. Now Dan was left alone with his third wife of ten years, without his daughters to divert him from problems in his marriage, which fast deteriorated. Communication and connection were minimal.

The only woman he ever loved, his first wife Maria, was also a doctor. She had been out shopping for Christmas with their two small daughters when she suddenly dropped to the floor and lost consciousness. The store manager asked the five year old daughter for her father's telephone number. Dan was called and rushed to his wife but failed to resuscitate her. He and his daughters rode with her in the ambulance but she died on the way to the hospital.

From that time on, a pall set in every Christmas. He and his children went through irreconcilable mourning and grief, but each kept their feelings to themselves. He regretted not seeking bereavement therapy for his family. Too traumatized by loss, he could not figure out what to do. No one offered help and he did not know how to ask for it. He was unhappy with his current wife of ten years, dreaded going home at night, and when he was home, he hid behind his books. He felt he read so much to shut out and escape from his wife. He felt the two of them had nothing in common and was more lonely when she was there. Now that his daughters were gone, he wanted to end the marriage but feared being alone might lead him back to drinking.

Dan had been lonely since he was a child. After his wife died, he had to do everything himself. He did not seek any resources in his environment and could not confide in anyone or ask for help. He struggled to bring his children up, and married a divorced woman with a daughter a year after his wife's death. He hoped his new wife would be a mother to his girls. However, the second wife did not provide love for him or his daughters and twelve years later, he divorced her. Over the years, his rage grew and the pain of his pent up emotions led him to numb himself with alcohol. Left alone with his third wife and their lack of relationship, he came to therapy to talk about leaving her.

In the past, he resorted to drink when he was alone. He drank especially heavily after Maria died and did not want to return to that place. He grew up with working-class parents who trained him to do as he was told. His mother was a bitter, caustic, emotionally distant woman who rarely responded to Dan's simple requests. He had asked for loafers but got instead got ugly brown lace-up shoes. He already felt excluded by the other boys since he was small and scrawny. At home, he repeatedly asked his mother to fry his eggs longer so that he would not have to eat runny egg whites, but his mother did not respond. His father had been an engineer but became wheelchair bound when Dan was ten. His father expressed only disappointment over what his son did, never praise, encouragement, or support. He insisted Dan go to medical school, preferably Harvard and refused to hear that Dan wanted to work with his hands and fix motorcycles.

Small and thin, his body absorbed the toxic nourishment of his upbringing. He spent a great deal of time alone from an early age. After many years of loneliness and feeling invisible, he decided to go to Italy for medical school. The years he spent there were his happiest. He could do what he wanted. He showed me a photograph of himself from that time. A long-haired "James Dean," with dark sunglasses on a motorcycle. Dark sunglasses, perhaps, to hide his feelings. Later in Italy, he met his future wife, made friends, came out of his shell and relished his first experience of spontaneous, loving contact.

When we began treatment, we discussed ways for him to engage in new activities. He tried taking an art class, a tai chi workshop, yoga, going to art exhibits, and renewing old friendships. One day, Dan told me he felt his life was going pretty well and he wondered about cutting back from once a week to once every other week. I was very surprised. I thought about it and decided to give him my truthful response. I told him we had not spent enough exploring his inner life and wasn't he curious too? Wasn't one of the major issues in his life to connect with himself and others? He said, "Curious? What does that mean?"

He coped with his external situations better, yet I could not suppress a sense that so much needed to be done, why break off now? I suggested he come twice a week. He said that felt "too intimate." By then I knew he could handle my sense of humor. "Too intimate? What are you waiting for? One of us to die first?" He confessed being afraid of what he might find if he went deeper.

That week, Dan had a very vivid dream, the first he remembered ever having. He and his family were watching TV in the parents' bedroom when a very large poisonous snake slithered up the stairs toward them. It was orange and black. It was supposed to be one of the most rare and venomous snakes on earth. I asked him for associations but he could not come up with anything.

After some weeks, Dan had to reschedule an appointment, explaining that he had to have surgery. He said he had no stomach wall, from all the years of alcohol, and that there was some leakage of blood. The doctors wanted to try a new method which would decrease the amount of blood he lost. "I'm anemic. That's why I get tired a lot." When I asked him how come he never mentioned his medical condition to me, he answered, "I don't know why. It wasn't that I was trying to hide anything from you. I guess I didn't think it was related to therapy."

I asked for more information about his surgeries and he said, "I've been cut open from sternum to abdomen ten times. I have a lot of scars on my body from surgeries for gastric bleeding. One time, I found myself on the floor lying in a pool of blood. I was entertaining a woman friend in between divorces and thank God she was there. I couldn't move and had to ask her to get me to the emergency room as soon as she could. Fortunately she was able to get me there in time or I would have died from loss of blood." I asked, "Still you didn't stop drinking after that?" Dan said no but felt he would never let anyone open him up again. Perhaps the prospect of getting worse and dying enabled him to make use of AA. He was so barricaded and unaware that his loneliness had been created from his wall of fear, hurt and loss.

Through our work and staying with it, he became more aware of his limited emotional range. In time, I introduced him to meditation and he found a meditation center that had a recovery program. These days, he is like another person and has come to realize that this moment is all we have. Inconceivable life here and now, both ordinary and amazing.

Through therapy and mindfulness, he re-contacted his early urge to work with his hands, which proved to be a most rewarding experience. His daughter gave him soapstone and carving equipment. At one point, he tried to carve a whole body image of himself, letting the process take over. Afterwards, he realized he had carved a sarcophagus with him imprisoned in it. Another time when he ran out of words, I asked him about his many tattoos. He had a story behind each one. He did not get the whole tattoo done all at once but added images that were meaningful, like milestones. I wondered if he could do a life-size drawing and show where the tattoos were. He brought in a doll he'd sewn which showed all his tattoos.

Dan had thought happiness came in the form of joie de vivre, something dramatic that he would recognize as joy in life. Over time, this belief began to shift. I asked how he was feeling in the moment while talking to me. I asked if it was conceivable or inconceivable to him. He never thought he could talk to anyone who would listen and who he felt he could trust enough to open up to. He began to recognize this moment, in the present, was all he really had. One breath at a time, one moment at a time. He began to criticize less and study his own mind more. His relationship with his daughters got better as he respected their boundaries. Communication changed from giving advice and telling others what to do to just listening. Appreciation grew.

Just as things were going so much better, calamity struck. His thirty-five year old daughter who was pregnant was diagnosed with cancer in her lymph nodes. Dan was shocked beyond belief. How could this happen again! First his wife, and thirty years later, his daughter. It was inconceivable. What was the point of living?

He could not face the possibility of his daughter's death. I felt sad with him and did not know what to say. No words could save his daughter and I did not want to raise false hope. I could see him slipping into the past. Not knowing what to do, I offered him a cup of hot water. To my surprise he accepted it. I asked him to bring it to his abdomen, to his hara, with both hands and to close his eyes and focus only on the heat in his abdomen. After five minutes, I asked him how he felt, he answered, "calmer." He was able to bring himself back to the present by focusing on his body and connecting with himself.

Days later, Dan realized that what was happening now is not exactly what had happened when his wife died. He was thirty years older, his daughters grown, and he had many friends in his support group. He skyped his daughter and saw she was alive now, still alive. He had buried her already, foreseeing the terrible loss of thirty years ago. He told me that this time, no matter what the outcome, he wanted to be fully aware and awake for his daughter and deal with each moment, each breath as they came up. He realized he will treasure every moment and be alive so that he can connect more with her. In this way, he was able to find in himself aliveness, like the Japanese tree surgeon found life in the bombed Chinese nettle tree.

REFERENCES

Katagiri, D. 1998. *You Have To Say Something*. Boston, MA: Shambala Publications.

Chapter Nine

The Relief of Being

Pilar Jennings

Many years ago, when in the throes of attempting to deepen my spiritual practice, I attended a lecture on the relationship between the psyche and Buddhist meditation. In the crowded auditorium, a young man stood up and asked with a gushing and flowery description of his meditation experience, why sitting on a cushion, shutting his eyes, and watching his breath—felt so good. The audience laughed in knowing appreciation. There were many others who had clearly experienced similar good feelings merely by being still, keeping the mind attentive, and observing the breath.

After a pause, the lecturer suggested that this very good feeling arises when we give up the burden of sustaining our notions of identity or self. These porous constructs, he suggested, require our every waking moment of energy and attention. They spur us on to do things we don't enjoy, to sacrifice what we find meaningful, and to easily feel that life is by its very nature an endless act of drudgery. When we give up rigid notions of who we are—even for a few minutes at a time—there is a pervasive and rather sweet feeling of relief.

In response to his sage words, a discernible wave of "ahs" was heard throughout the audience as we considered this pithy analysis of the ancient tradition of just being. The lecturer was Joseph Goldstein, one of the founding members of the New York Insight Meditation Society. As a long-term meditation practitioner, author of several excellent texts on Buddhism, and with a presence that exuded a life of spiritual exploration, he seemed a reliable source. We had been giving up the burden of self in our meditation practice, and it was good to know.

As the year progressed, this compelling phrase—giving up the burden of self—reappeared in my thoughts. There may have been obvious triggers for its reappearance—moments of acute stress, attachment to a pending relationship or job, etcetera—but mostly I remember that it appeared simply as a comforting reminder. In these moments I was reminded of the feeling of spaciousness, the sense of sinking down into some vast and flexible part of myself, and tabling the many chronic worries that can consume a lifetime. Fear of unexpected sickness, financial disaster, and relational upheaval, moved into a well-contained storage unit in my mind. Instead, I contacted something I had felt before, long ago perhaps, and for a few glorious moments or if I was lucky a whole thirty minute uninterrupted stretch, I felt the relief of being.

In his analysis of ego development as the foundation for object relations (a rather unfortunate term for human relations), British psychoanalyst Harry Guntrip offers a theory that evokes this earliest experience of living without burden. Building on D. W. Winnicott's theory of the good enough mother—a mother who is necessarily imperfect yet protects the infant in critical ways—Guntrip dives into the infant's reality as it interacts with such a mother. From Guntrip's perspective, the good enough mother allows the infant the gift of just being. Such a mother imparts the first experience of being cared for in such a way that the infant can bathe in a deeply experiential sense of being at rest, or what Guntrip calls "inbeingness" (1969, p. 249). Feeding takes place in response to the baby's hunger signals, sleep ensues after unforced and unhurried feeding, and slowly the baby takes in the merged sense of being, and being at one with the mother (Guntrip, 1969, p. 266).

This capacity to simply be without undue stress or concern for one's environment is, according to Guntrip, the root of object relations. From his perspective, learning to be is born directly out of relationship with the mother who is able skillfully to sensitize herself to the baby's reality. The mother ideally develops what D. W. Winnicott called, "primary maternal preoccupation," a finely tuned empathic state designed to protect the baby from an otherwise impinging environment. It is for this reason that Guntrip refers to this capacity for a sensitized intunement with others, along with an emotionally susceptible state, as the female element (p. 251). He is quick to clarify that the female element is not unique to the female gender, and in fact must be fully integrated into both genders. But as the infant is first literally housed by the mother's body and then, with good fortune, psychically held by the mother in an unobtrusive and deeply empathic manner, it is through the female that this capacity for being is imparted.

When I first read Guntrip's evocative description of the female element as a doctoral student of psychology, my mind flashed on the stillness I had experienced in meditation practice. Even as a young child when I was first exposed to Buddhism, I felt enveloped and soothed by quiet sitting, as if it were an adult-sanctioned play space of the mind. In the midst of my parent's divorce and the many turbulent years that followed, I looked forward to meditation as a way to re-enter the experience of worryless existence. As a reference point, I remembered lying on my parent's bed in the afternoons, clad in my favorite Levis watching *Lost In Space*, with the warm sunlight dancing on the pretty yellow comforter. I had known this feeling of conscious rest.

Years later, after beginning my studies in psychology and reading Guntrip, I recalled sitting in meditation after exceptionally trying times in adulthood, the times that challenge our sense of reality and potential for making meaning. The first weeks after 9/11, for instance, loomed large in my mind. At the time, I had been mourning the loss of close friends whose grizzly deaths felt like the stuff of science fiction. The whole catastrophe felt so fundamentally "other," as if we'd collectively been catapulted into some alternate universe where formidable structures disintegrate and people are sucked into the ether of timelessness, like the weirdly compelling scenes from Logan's Run. Adding to the Dantesque trials of this time was an unexpected lay-off from work the week before 9/11. Thus, like so many, my mind was awash in chronic worry. Every facet of life felt infused with instability requiring a vigilant attention that was physically and psychically exhausting.

It was at the peak of these worries that I decided to revisit my local meditation center. The steady flow of unsettling thoughts and concerns had become increasingly unmanageable. Yet, throughout the years of studying the Dharma (Buddhist teachings) and practicing meditation, some part of me understood that even during such dreadful and bizarre circumstances, I was responsible for how I chose to work with and relate to the pain and suffering I felt. What had happened was beyond my control. How I responded, however, was up to me. It was also becoming clear that the practical efforts I made to address these various losses—the resumes submitted, the strenuous workouts, and fruity affirmations—had done little to allay the feeling of distress that had attached itself to my very core.

I began regularly attending a Buddhist center I had sporadically visited in years prior. In the beginning, I worried that there wasn't time to be sitting on cushions, envisioning placid lakes in my mind when life was so tenuous. I worried that the Dharma talks were too simplistic and lacking the intellectual rigor necessary to help me snap out of my woeful mental state. Surely there was something more substantial I could be doing to rectify the unfortunate turn my life had taken.

And yet, remarkably, even as life seemed to be disintegrating into a morass of unfathomable loss and confusion, for an hour at a time I found myself harkening back to some fundamental experience of rest that seemed to reside within me. With eyes shut, surrounded by others sitting quietly, I was able to relinquish each worry for a limited period of time. I reminded myself repeatedly that each worry in all its harrowing glory would be there waiting for me at the end of the meditation, that nothing catastrophic would happen as the direct result of calming my mind for one hour. I tried to convince myself that in such circumstances, I might need to wrestle, yet again, with my sense of what constituted productivity.

With the help of a soothing instructor whose soft voice guided us into a place of rest, I began to reclaim the right to simply be. The grip of fear that had held me in its vise for weeks, turnings into months, slowly softened and a recognizable feeling of safety returned. I watched my breath as it touched the tip of my nose, I relaxed my shoulders, my neck, and I kept my mind focused on an object of attention, a loving Buddha, a calm body of water, something warm and still. So too, I took note that while nothing about my life had changed in the course of the meditation, I felt better, as if my life were less inherently problematic than I had previously imagined. Just being seemed to purify my perception of reality.

After our meditations, the instructor would occasionally congratulate us for having made our way to a Dharma center. It was suggested that perhaps some of us were Buddhists in previous lives, or better yet, Bodhisattvas or enlightened beings who were there to affirm these ancient wisdom teachings and live them out in our troubled world for the sake of all beings. I will admit to moments of a delicious grandiosity when I thought, oh yes, I have heard these teachings before. Look how easily I can just be! Look at me—I'm a Bodhisattva! But as I began reading Guntrip and Winnicott, I imagined that perhaps I was reconnecting with something I had known before in this life, as a much smaller person and with far less hair.

From the expressions of my fellow meditators, I suspect I was not the only one prone to feelings of great spiritual achievement, and perhaps a simple happiness at having experienced a sense of being at peace. There was often a quietly celebratory quality at the end of a group meditation as we returned from our collective trips back to early infancy before our worlds began to impinge upon our capacity for unfettered joy. When speaking with new practitioners, I was struck by the profound feelings of relief that were often experienced. A sense of having a sanctioned release from chronic doing, even if that doing were confined to mental processes—worry, planning, fretting, etcetera—seemed to permeate the initial exposure to meditation. And indeed, it could feel so good.

Guntrip suggests that the female element in us all, male and female alike, is experienced as being-ness. It is the beginning of ego-identity, of having a sense of sacred and unique subjectivity that stems from a quietness at the core of our personality. If adequately instilled, it is sustained as "the secret foundation of stillness, security, and peace" (p. 269). It is through this primary experience of being that all 'being in relationship with' other transpires. The feeling of resting easily in the presence of another, of having the capacity to intuit the 'beingness' of others and respond with sensitivity, evolves directly out of this capacity to be. By extension, Winnicott suggested that the capacity to be alone without anxiety, stems from this very experience of resting in the presence of another that gets woven deep into the fabric of our psyche (1958, p. 30). For both Winnicott and Guntrip, there is a dynamic "we" at the core of our ego. Without it, we cannot tolerate aloneness or stillness.

It is interesting to note that in Buddhist teachings, the ego is considered to be an inherently problematic phenomenon. It is described as that part of the mind that is experienced as discrete, or a fixed sense of "I," like a high security monolith that must be protected at all times. It is said to wreak havoc in our lives, to usher in a faulty and delusional sense of separateness from others that causes pervasive feelings of loneliness and grandiosity. The ego, from a Buddhist perspective, is the part of the mind that corrupts our capacity to just be. With its unquestioned presence and impact, we feel too easily dissatisfied with who we are, how others treat us, and with what others have that we don't. There is nothing relational about the ego in Buddhist teachings.

It is for this reason, that most Dharma talks demonize both the ego and Western psychotherapy as a method for bolstering this problematic and inherently delusional mental construct. It is not uncommon for Buddhist teachers unfamiliar with contemporary Western psychological theory, including the work of Winnicott and Guntrip, to emphatically suggest that we are wasting our time working through childhood hurts and losses, and talking to therapists about the many ways in which we have felt wronged by others. This is the stuff of ego—the benighted effort to reinforce our flawed sense of individuality, of being a separate person who is so easily harmed or slighted by others. Do the work of getting to know the truth of the mind, says the Dharma, and we find that there is no lasting and fixed "I" to be defended. We are always changing, always co-determined by others, and therefore intimately in connection with all beings.

For the last sixty years, much of Western psychology has been saying something quite similar: that we are inherently relational. And furthermore, that if our individual development from the very beginning of life does not honor this reality, we will suffer terribly. In Winnicott and Guntrip's object relations theory, we find a precise and poignant description of what happens to us if the primary experience of being, as we are held in being with another, has been thwarted. Says Guntrip, there are mechanisms employed to whip up a feeling of existence that are akin to a Buddhist notion of ego-defense. Selfhood can only properly develop within the context of caring and highly attuned relationship, and if we have lost access to our inherent capacity to be with ourselves and others, we will find alternative, albeit faulty methods to affirm our subjectivity.

It is these very methods, along with the suffering they so easily generate, that are consciously explored and potentially released in the meditation process. While Western psychotherapy has traditionally focused on the interpersonal dynamics that cause and fuel these problematic methods for fostering a sturdy subjectivity, Buddhist meditation addresses the psycho-spiritual results of these methods. Thus, these two contrasting traditions have both paid close attention to our female element, our capacity to just be, yet they emphasize different stages of its development and potential impact.

The nascent student of meditation is encouraged to carefully watch what happens to his or her mind when there are no obvious distractions. When we're sitting in meditation, do our thoughts flood us with dramatic narratives and charged affect that we long to release? Do we fidget and fantasize about the cheeseburger or sushi platter we'll be inhaling as soon as we're released from the incarceration of our meditation class? Do painful or tantalizing memories transfix us with their wrenching or thrilling details? Is it too much for us to be still and do nothing?

The Buddhist method for addressing these struggles of being involve the conscious release of the impinging internal and external environment. The very thoughts, feelings, or repetitive planning that manifest as tension in the body, a furrowed brow or clenched solar plexus, are acknowledged when they appear but not engaged. In the Vipassana tradition this is referred to as noting, where each mental process is merely observed without judgment. Students learn to watch the contents of their minds with friendly curiosity, neither engaging nor ignoring what arises. This spare and powerful technique can facilitate a conscious absorption into the sensations we experience in response to the myriad thoughts and ensuing feelings that so often define our sense of being. There is a sense of sinking below the radar of storylines and memory, into a primordial and generative space, into beingness itself.

When this ability for stillness and absorption has been cultivated, a natural curiosity about the nature of the mind typically develops, often leading practitioners to explore and question human consciousness, of beingness as they had formerly understood it. Meditators tend to get curious about their minds and the ways in which the mind is used to create our sense of what is real and reliable. With continued practice, one may begin to experience a mind at rest, in which beingness is simply felt rather than fought for. The hard work of existence begins to slip away and the more tender, vulnerable experience of surrendering into a vaguely familiar sense of spaciousness, returns.

This is the very beginning of giving up the burden. In this way, meditation is offered as an inroad back to a time when just being was the primary feature of existence, and doing flowed spontaneously from the delight of existing without crippling fear, anxiety, or mental gymnastics. Indeed, a lovely sense of being in relationship with oneself and by extension, with the larger world of other beings, typically evolves. The mind feels porous, and by extension the world of which we are a tiny but precious part. We notice our fellow meditators, their tender humanness and dear wish for happiness.

So too, we begin to notice that our minds seem to share something foundational, a simple and lovely state of unhurried being that transcends the trappings of conventional identity. This is what the young man in the lecture hall described—a reclaiming of the female element—all under the guise of watching the breath.

But this is only half the story. A follow-up question from a slightly more experienced meditator might have addressed why meditation can feel so bad. The pervasive discomfort, agitation, and distress that can arise from simply sitting on a cushion, watching the breath and keeping the mind attentive, is well known to anyone who has attempted to sustain a meditation practice. It can feel utterly unbearable to sit without moving, to forsake the planning and musing on yesterday's fiasco du jour. It can feel as though we are destined to disintegrate into a pile of useless dust while everyone else gets ahead in life.

And yet, for most, there is some amorphous incentive to keep trying, even if the primary motivation is the desire to aggressively control the recalcitrant mind. Or perhaps, there may be an intuitive sense that the very discomfort that can arise from meditation is likely a pervasive mental state in one's lived experience. The sense of dissatisfaction, of being at odds with our own mind, is reminiscent of our default waking state. If we get curious, the discomfort won't necessarily go away, but we'll begin to see that it's not only while meditating that we feel so acutely dissatisfied with ourselves and our lives.

On a Buddhist retreat some years ago, I found myself repeating the phrase—Buddhist purgatory—over and over again in my thoughts. A feeling of having been incarcerated in my own mind with its unrelenting assessment of others, disappointment, and bubbling anger consumed large segments of our ongoing meditation sessions. To what good end is this, I asked myself repeatedly as I fantasized about calling a friend to come rescue me from the stultifying doldrums of my internal chatter. I worried about the research I had tabled for the duration of the retreat, the many students who were waiting to meet with me, and my intolerable NYC rent. I didn't have six days to sit around watching the air hit my nostrils! Life was racing by and I was indulging once again my unrelenting interest in the spiritual realm. Meanwhile the physical realm was likely crumbling to pieces in my absence. It is reasonable to suggest that my female element was well-camouflaged for vast portions of the retreat.

Guntrip theorized that when the female element is integrated into the psyche, a natural counterpart evolves. This is the male element, the part of us that spontaneously takes action, and moves into doing rather than merely being (p. 263). It is as unforced as a baby reaching for its mother's face, touching her nose, her mouth. It is exploration, learning, and discovery that emerge from authentic being. It is the natural curiosity that pulls toddlers from their mothers out into a colorful world, and young adults into romantic love and creative expression. Without it, according to Guntrip, our beingness fails to thrive. These two central elements—being and doing, male and female—compose a whole person. Without one, the other cannot survive (p. 271).

Invariably, when one part of the whole is missing, it is the female element. Indeed, this part of the person that allows for our very experience and sense of being (and, as a result, for our capacity for relationship), can become powerfully dissociated. What gets generated, then, instead of a deeply rooted sense of "me-ness," is a terrible feeling of being nobody in particular, of not counting or having meaning (p. 250). Guntrip describes this as the likely outcome of a baby or child parented by a primary caretaker who expects to be accommodated by the child. This, via enforced feedings, or bathing and other rituals that reflect a mis-attunement with the child's natural timetable and capacity for stimulus. Such a child may come to feel that his true self is lodged in a more peripheral part of his psyche, like a membrane that merely obscures a deeper and unknown center. Babies do not cultivate the capacity to surrender to an unfettered experience of being, and being at rest, when in a prematurely stressful and impinging environment.

It is when this essential experience of being, of having a sense of sacred "me" is missing, that doing moves in with the overwhelming job of constructing a substitute sense of being. The nature of this doing in such instances will typically take on a compulsive quality that leaves the person deeply fatigued. Guntrip called this mechanism of doing without a core sense of being, the pseudo male element. For without the initial experience of spontaneous being, we become easily addicted to work, to thinking, to stimulus, as a means of dismantling the disturbing sense of vacancy at the center of our personhood.

It is this very sense of insubstantiality managed by fierce attachment to doing and thinking, that is uncovered in meditation. And it is for this reason, among others, that meditation can feel miserable and defeating. I would conjecture that it is the rare Western practitioner of meditation who does not bring to their practice the effort to use the pseudo male element as a means of fortifying a deeper sense of being. If it could fairly be conjectured that some Buddhist students may never have adequately cultivated their female element during infancy, and that most, if not all, Western Buddhists have been pickled in a culture that denigrates all things female, especially as it manifests in the vulnerability of beingness, I suspect that meditation quickly evolves into yet another skill-set, something to either do poorly or well. We wonder incessantly whether we've got the right technique, if we are we achieving the right kind of clarity for the right kind of spiritual development we've thought so much about.

Yet, most Western students also bring to their efforts at meditation a genuine wish to heal, to feel and be at rest. None of us arrive at our meditation centers off the wings of victory, but I would suggest that all of us intuit a remarkable potential for something ameliorative, something that will genuinely and steadfastly improve the nature of our lives. And it is at the intersection of this tension between our need to do as a means of feeling real, to master our chosen technique of Buddhist meditation, and the effort to release our doing through meditation and thus to risk more aliveness, that the horrific pain known to every practitioner of meditation arises.

Guntrip is right in suggesting that doing, when there is too tenuous a sense of being, will generate overwhelming anxiety and destructive tension. The same is true when we attempt to stop this compulsive doing before a sense of being has authentically emerged.

In the midst of a guided meditation, the practitioner would aim at releasing their grip on thoughts, fantasy, or memory. The point is not to deny that thoughts arise, nor to work toward a mind that no longer generates distracting thoughts, feelings, or concerns. To do so would be to morph into an altogether foreign species. The primary and initial aim of meditation is to discover that our thoughts, worries, or powerful waves of feeling, do not have to be engaged or wrestled with. Rather than repressing the outpouring of mental activity, meditation serves as a means to actively observe without becoming identified with our mental activity. It's a model for relating that is kind and curious, but not controlling or obtrusive. It's a good way to be with oneself and others.

In Buddhism, this ability to pay close attention to thoughts and feelings without repressing or taking action based on thoughts/feelings is referred to as bare attention. The point is to develop a more harmonious relationship with the mind, so that the many powerful thoughts we think and feelings we harbor are honored for being merely transient states of mind. They are not indicative of a fixed identity, nor symbols of unchanging selfhood. They are simply impermanent internal states that we can either observe and learn from, or use to cultivate a false sense of concrete "me-ness." When this understanding is fully ingested, the potential to experience being at rest emerges with remarkably ameliorative impact.

But when our capacity for being has been dissociated or never adequately developed, whole identities can be cultivated around our ability to remain in action. For some, this action is primarily mental in nature and takes the form of incessant ruminating and planning. This tendency to do rather than be does not, alas, necessarily result in productivity. Often it simply generates guilt, and leaves people feeling that it is somehow detrimental to exist without a constant sense of doing even if confined to repetitive mental activity. Thus, an ongoing meditation practice can trigger tremendous feelings of discomfort. If a practitioner has been relying heavily upon their pseudo male element for a sense of self, relinquishing this active doing can underscore dramatic feelings of having nothing but empty, meaningless space at the very core.

Attempting to merely observe one's thoughts without actively participating in an internal drama, can feel counterintuitive. If identity has been intimately tied to a capacity for doing, thinking, or being in motion, stillness can be experienced as annihilating. Who are we if not thinkers of thoughts, workers, seekers of stimuli, information, and relationship? For those for whom a secure and primary sense of being has been thwarted, there is no sense of reliable meaning underneath the continuous doing (p. 257). As a result, meditation with its emphasis on experience beyond the realm of thought and doing, can run dramatically against the frenzied action that protects people from a devastating sense of meaninglessness.

In his extensive writing on object-relations, Guntrip explores the poignant drama that unfolds when an infant's ego moves into regression from self and others. He describes the unmanageable anxiety that ensues when an infant is unable to make meaningful connection with their primary caretaker. This anxiety begins to infiltrate the infant's internal world which results in a retreat into an illusory, womb-like state (p. 237). Guntrip referred to this process as resulting in a regressed ego. For the adult coping with such a regression, the female element remains elusive, setting the stage for an over-reliance on the pseudo male element as a means of generating a substitute experience of ego. This regression has far-reaching impact in the relational sphere, leaving people feeling cut off from themselves and from the many people who inhabit their world. A sense of fundamental aloneness ensues, and an impenetrable feeling of gaping space exists between the self and others (p. 225).

Guntrip was quick to clarify, however, that regression can also serve a healing purpose. He described a healthy regression as the process of taking space and time to allow oneself the possibility of reconnecting with the deeply obscured female element. His description of such space and time sounds remarkably like meditation, a conscious clearing away of internal and external doing. Meditation is an intentional pulling inward, a decision to observe the experience of being so that the specific things that impinge upon our ability to simply be, become clear and stark.

Experienced meditation instructors will invariably inform their students that they are merely reminding them of the inherent capacity to experience a sense of freedom in being. The ability to be at rest, to sense the specialness of our being by nature of stillness and peace, is not an anomalous gift for the lucky few. It is the essence of human life, the nature of our minds, and the foundation for fulfilling relationship with ourselves and others.

Unfortunately, when the female element is obscured, it can feel as foreign as an arcane and unknown language. But as Guntrip suggests, there are effective and life-changing means to reclaim the lost female element. A healthy regression which can be accessed via meditation, is one mode of reclaiming the right to be.

In the midst of a Buddhist retreat I attended while reading Guntrip, I struggled with the regression that is a central part of the meditation process. I worried incessantly about the various projects and people I felt responsible for. I imagined running out of time—that the summer would pass by without having fulfilled my many pending commitments. In short, I fought against the regression, the temporary cocooning of meditation practice that is the first step toward the simplicity of being. Throughout the retreat, the particular obstructions to this pulling inward appeared continuously. In particular, I was bombarded with bouts of unresolved anger. In between inhalations and exhalations, the "oms" and the "ahs," I repeatedly fantasized about confronting the people I felt anger toward, telling them with no uncertainty how little I thought of them, how misguided they were, how benighted. Intermittently I would return to the inhalation and exhalation, listening to the sound of the birds, the rustling of the trees, only to find myself mentally kicking a former romantic partner in the groin before the morning meditation ended.

After three days of detailed fantasies about excoriating various people in my life, including the meditation instructor for his unprocessed psychological wounds that were (from my perspective) routinely enacted in his Dharma talks, and my roommate for her weird adherence to the recommended silence, and the chefs for cooking such attractive food laced with my full spectrum of allergens that cause undue suffering, I was faced with an obvious impingement. I could not rest, and certainly could not experience my female element when infused with unresolved feelings that had taken on the additional hindrance of sweeping narrative drama.

On the last day of the retreat, I made my way down to the 6:00 a.m. meditation session, still engaged in a stream of expletives I longed to unload on the people who had triggered my anger. I sat through the next hour indulging in various acts of fantasized physical and verbal assault, only to notice once again the melodic chirping of birds just outside the meditation hall.

I opened my eyes, and turned to watch the small gray birds flying from tree to tree. The early morning light was soft, and the birds seemed noticeably unhurried in their activity. As I observed them congregating on branches, eating seeds, chirping away, I felt a softening that I sometimes feel in those last few moments before falling asleep. I think of this time as a key moment of surrender, when the relinquishing of thoughts, and worries, allow for a temporary respite from the mind gone awry. It is this concentrated surrender that allows us to rejuvenate, to reconnect with some semblance of peaceful existence sans frenzied efforts at control.

For Guntrip, this could also be called a healthy regression. These are the moments when our doing is merely tabled in the service of our capacity to exist without terror, fury, and the unrelenting drumbeat of doubt. These are moments critical to our well-being, and for most, they require a conscious pulling in of our attention. A willingness to stop engaging our constant flow of thoughts and feelings, and move closer to the core of existence, is the first step.

In the morning of my spontaneous bird-watching, I began by simply observing the happy flight of the small birds. I watched them hop from branch to branch, eating berries. The soft early morning light had turned the leaves a beautiful sage green and the berries a warm maroon. After a few minutes passed, I realized that I had inadvertently released my grip on the great Strindbergian drama brewing internally. In the midst of this more undefended state, I was able to note the constant presence of angry feeling for much of the retreat. For those few key moments, I had put the locus of my being on a softer, more malleable place in my psyche where the need for dramatic narrative was greatly alleviated. Instead, like a good enough mother, I noted that underneath the anger was a well of hurt, and underneath the hurt a rather tender heart I was reluctant to acknowledge. For this tender heart lacked a fiery protective armor, and was thus more vulnerable than I ever consciously cared to be.

***

In the throes of just being, we notice more, and observe the thoughts we tend to replay with compulsive ferocity. Our beingness can serve as a buffer zone allowing us to see that there are feelings, thoughts, and dramas that may be serving as so much armor to protect us from a more fundamental vulnerability. This tender heart I recognized underneath the unrelenting anger was the center of my female element, my self at rest. Of course, when we're at rest, we are vulnerable. Any hurt feeling or wounding that breaks into consciousness after hiding beneath our chosen narratives, may leave us feeling pierced. This is the risk of sustaining the female element: to let ourselves crack open, to feel whatever pain we have worked hard to defend ourselves against. The risk of keeping it psychically entombed, however, is far greater.

Meditation practice is an ancient and multi-layered process. It has myriad variations in technique as divergent as global weather patterns, but the intention is the same across traditions. The process of slowing down, bringing our attention to the mind with greater and more skillful concentration is a commonly used method to re-enter a sphere of existence that is highly attuned to one's own being, and that of others. The capacity for a deeply sensitized intuition for our self-experience that Guntrip describes is a central result of long-term meditation practice. It is a reclaiming of the nature of our existence, which through layers of uncertainty, disappointment, and fear can become all too easily obscured.

With each breath and still moment, meditation offers the opportunity to move temporarily away from the internal and external chaos that can result from a life where the male element has become a dominant feature. At first there is a conscious regressing, a concentrated effort to relinquish the steady flow of unresolved feelings or concerns we harbor. With practice, there is an increasing willingness to trust that time spent sitting on cushions can be time well spent. It tends to be a slow process, just as the infant learns over time that they can rest easily in the presence of others. Guntrip describes a foundation that is established for the infant, where the good enough mother repeatedly affirms that she is present to care for the infant's many needs.

But it might be helpful to remember that even the most skillfully cared for infant will experience moments of stress, physical discomfort and fear. No sentient being can be successfully spared those fraught moments when our very aliveness feels like too much to bear. Nonetheless, if the foundation for a sense of being at rest, of simply and safely being, is carefully created and bolstered, the capacity to endure any difficulty can be safely relied upon.

Just so, a foundation is built for each practitioner of meditation, predicated on a disciplined repetition of conscious breathing, sitting, and observing the mind. Having a spiritual practice does not prevent life circumstances from causing pain and duress. Terrible things happen to us all the time. But when the female element has been accessed and this soft and vulnerable part of the self is repeatedly integrated into the lived experienced, there is relatively little that can trigger the unmanageable angst and suffering that results from a life severed from the deeply rooted comfort provided by our female element. Even when our lovers die, or our children fall ill, or terrorists wreak havoc, the ability to rest in that deeply embedded sense of "we" that is the fabric for our female element, remains.

Toward the end of Guntrip's written work on object relations is a poignant reminder that the most fundamental part of human nature is the experience of togetherness. We begin our lives cocooned within our mothers, and are eventually expelled into a world where our psychic survival remains closely tied to our relationship with others. But unless a feeling of oneness with the mother continues, and is routinely reinforced, our ego—that part of us that is inherently relational—will lack the fortification necessary for sustainable relationship with others. Guntrip suggests that we never forget this initial physical and psychic connection with the mother—it remains a private realm of peace, safety, and stillness (p. 269). Ultimately Guntrip tells us that this private relational foundation must be sustained in order to maintain a fulfilling sense of relationship with the self and others. For some, this preservation happens through a regular revisiting of stillness, a conscious choosing to release our adult lives where relationship to self and other may seem almost irrelevant to our male elemental lives.

Over time, meditation can reawaken the awareness that the capacity to simply be is something we carry within us waiting to be reactivated. Despite the many psychological and cultural incentives to remain ensnared in identity predicated on doing, the lived experience can take on the meditative quality of observing ourselves in our being. The psychic exhaustion of continuous mental and physical doing, is at the very least contained in regular intervals so that the tenderness of the female element can begin to emerge. Being alive can evolve into something decidedly more restful in which the relief of being carries us through.

REFERENCES

Goldstein, J. 2002. *One Dharma.* San Francisco: HarperCollins.

Guntrip, H. 1969. *Schizoid Phenomenon, Object Relations and the Self.* New York: International Universities Press.

Winnicott, D. W. 1971. *Playing and Reality.* London: Brunner Routledge.

———. 1958. "The Capacity to Be Alone." In *The Maturational Processes and the Facilitating Environment.* London: Karnac Books.

IV

Parallel Convergences

Chapter Ten

Amae and Western Buddhism

Roberto Carnevali

Some years ago, at the time of my third (and fortunately final) analysis, I found myself drawn to books with captivating—or at least unusual—titles, in the hope of finding something to inject new life into my way of thinking and feeling, which by then had become rather confused. Of these books, I was particularly drawn to *The Anatomy of Dependence* by Takeo Doi. I was not familiar with this author at the time, but was intrigued by the thought that there existed a Japanese psychoanalyst addressing the theme of dependence within his own culture and using a term like "anatomy" to describe it. The book resonated deeply with me; indeed, I found myself believing that I had truly accessed a quality of Japanese culture and "understood" that which was apparently considered to be beyond comprehension outside of Japan. I felt that *amae*, the core concept of Doi's book, was something that I had always known, and that—although I had not grown up in Japan and did not belong to that culture—I had experienced something similar in my own life, which had always been with me, was still with me and would be with me in the future. It all remained within me. Little or nothing of the experience surfaced during my therapy, at least not explicitly; I was left only with a sense of something important which I felt on a preconscious level, and which had something to do with my maternal world.

In the spring of 2008—many years after I'd ended my third analysis—I took part in a conference in Milan focusing on the relationship between psychoanalysis and Buddhism; and it was here that I met Anthony Molino. Many aspects of his talk impressed me, among them his manner of presentation and way of relating to his audience, with which I felt a deep affinity. By continuously acknowledging his own subjectivity, at times through autobiographical references, Molino emphasized the highly personal nature of his ideas, with the associated feelings and emotions acting not as accessories to, but integral parts of the discourse. (By reading these few opening lines it should be apparent that I rely on a similar manner of presentation.)

Amid the autobiographical references in his talk, Molino referred on more than one occasion to the importance of his encounter with Richard De Martino, one of his university professors from his years in America. I knew De Martino for his chapter in the book *Zen Buddhism and Psychoanalysis*, a book co-authored by Erich Fromm and D. T. Suzuki. I was well acquainted with the book, being a great admirer of Fromm's work. When Molino subsequently gave me a copy of *The Couch and the Tree*, published in Italian as *Psicoanalisi e buddismo*, I noticed that one of the chapters that had been omitted from the Italian version was by Takeo Doi addressing the subject of *amae*.

Please pardon this long autobiographical introduction, but it is necessary in order to understand how I found myself forging connections between authors and ideas developed at different times and in different places; and to understand furthermore how a series of unique circumstances linked them in my mind, and allowed me to give more complete shape to my own thoughts and emotions.

In a piece published in *Setting* (Carnevali, R. 2008), I addressed the same issue, which I would like to consider in greater detail here.

AMAE: A DEFINITION BY APPROXIMATION

It is difficult to define the concept of *amae* in any language other than Japanese, as no other culture—not even other oriental cultures—experiences it directly in quite the same way. As such, any attempt to define it must be through the use of similes and by employing the closest available terms in one's own language. "Dependence" is the first of such terms that I would like to consider. However if, on the one hand, this term is universally associated with the maternal realm, where all individuals begin their lives, on the other, it is also a term with predominantly negative connotations in Western culture: dependence on tobacco, drugs, or gambling, and in recent years, on video games and the Internet. These constitute some of the foremost afflictions of our time and are the source of great problems of a sociological and psychological nature, considered to be genuine pathologies. Indeed, in Lombardy, the reality closest to me, the service that was formerly known as SerT (Servizio Tossicodipendenza) ["The Drug Dependence Service"] has now become SerD (Servizio Dipendenza) ["The Dependence or Addiction Service"], and it now tackles (or should tackle) precisely all the varieties of pathological dependencies within our society.

The term "pathological" acquires particular significance when considered alongside the title of Doi's book. Generally speaking, anatomy is the scientific discipline which considers the structure of the human body. Within this field, there is a sub-discipline that has in turn become a discipline in its own right called anatomical pathology, which specifically considers the structure of the diseased body. The main job of an anatomical pathologist is to perform autopsies—that is, to study and dissect corpses in order to determine the anatomical cause of a person's death. A metaphorical application of this concept to the one that is our main topic of discussion reveals the great disparity between "pathological" interpretations of *amae* and dependency in general, which have arisen from the Western approach to the issue, and Takeo Doi's ideas. Indeed, these interpretations convey neither the complexity of the concept of *amae*, nor that of the Japanese notion of "dependency" in its wider sense.

To give an example of a "negative" interpretation of *amae*, I will quote two brief passages from an article published in the Electronic Journal of Sociology (2000), entitled *Is Amae the Key to Understanding Japanese Culture* written by Herman W Smith and Takako Nomi of UM–St. Louis:

> A Japanese mother is expected to carry or hug her child as connotated by the dependence inherent in *amae*.
>
> . . .
>
> The Japanese mother who supervises or monitors her child is rewarded with uniquely identity—confirming responses like clinging and serving behaviors from the child not predicted for mothers and children in the United States.

It is clear here that the authors believe that the Japanese mother has a negative responsibility, insofar as she is understood to raise children with "clinging and serving behaviors." This same mother, in a different passage, is likewise said to indulge "overprotective and overindulgent attitudes"—a complete misconstrual of the meaning of *amae*, which is in fact antithetical to hyperprotectivity and is founded on trusting others to accept us.

In light of all that has been said thus far, we may claim to have taken an essential step toward reaching our "approximation" of the concept in question: *amae* has something to do with dependency—but, unlike in the Western world, in Japanese society this term has a positive, or at very least neutral connotation, with no implication that it is something that needs to be "cured." This gives rise to a preliminary problem regarding pathology and psychological treatment. If, for the most part, social considerations can be more or less removed from the assessment of that which is normal or pathological at a bodily level, this is no longer true when dealing with the psyche. When defining so-called mental illness, the social structures within which the "illness" is being defined cannot be ignored.[1]

Amae may thus be seen as something that invites our (Western) society to question the principles on which the concepts of mental "sanity" and "illness" are grounded. What I mean by this is that in order to understand *amae*, we must be willing to broaden our notion of what is sane and what is insane and refrain from taking for granted certain categorical distinctions that are present in our thinking and representations.

Let us consider the example of an everyday custom in our society which caused Takeo Doi some difficulty, as he simply did not understand it.

> The "please help yourself" that Americans use so often had a rather unpleasant ring to my ears before I became used to English conversation. The meaning, of course, is simply "please take what you want without hesitation," but literally translated it has somehow a flavor of "nobody else will help you" and I could not see how it came to be an expression of good will. The Japanese sensibility would demand that, in entertaining, a host should show sensitivity in detecting what was required and should himself "help" his guests. To leave a guest unfamiliar with the house to "help himself" would seem excessively lacking in consideration.
>
> This increased still further my feeling that Americans were a people who did not show the same consideration and sensitivity toward others as the Japanese. As a result, my early days in America, which would have been lonely at any rate, so far from home, were made lonelier still. (Doi T. 1973, p. 13)

This difference in perspective between the Japanese and American mentality brings us one crucial step closer to grasping the concept of *amae*. In American culture, where the idea of "doing something yourself" is promoted, it follows that there's something not quite right in fostering forms of dependence. Therefore, being urged to "help yourself"[2] only goes to underline that, even if circumstances might arise in which it would be nice to have someone take care of us, our ability to get by on our own, without having to "depend on anybody," will allow us to face the world with an extra "something" whereby we will always be able to fend for ourselves.

For the Japanese (and it is a position I share), developing the ability to "get by alone" means forgoing *amae*, and thus losing something fundamental, for which the ability to finish any given task on one's own is no recompense.[3]

Now, with psychoanalysis and psychotherapy in mind, a question arises: When we look after someone, do we consider "dependence" to be a symptom? Or even a syndrome? If someone expects help from others, or trusts others by submitting to their assistance without verifying their reliability, should he or she be treated for this? Is someone who expects to be treated fairly and affectionately a dreamer who needs to be set straight, perhaps through relentless interpretations? Of course, my ironic tone reveals my own opinion; but I am convinced that in the treatment of patients, many analysts—at times not explicitly but in their daily work—tend to be guided by the belief that one of their objectives, perhaps their primary one, is to make their patients independent. And if the patients have ever had any sense or experience of *amae*, it will need to be eradicated like the root of a deadly disease.

And so we have reached an understanding of what *amae* is by approximation, without giving it a precise definition. It is something that may be expressed as a type of dependence, which springs from our relationship with our parents, especially with our mother; a dependence which fosters in us certain expectations about the surrounding world, leading us to trust openly and not be afraid of being dependent, to be indulgent with ourselves and others, and to believe that our own needs will be met wherever we go because there will always be someone who understands us.

AMAE AND THE MOTHER

Now we can look at the relationship between *amae* and the maternal world—a relationship to which I've hinted and will now dedicate the attention it deserves. Obviously, everyone's first experience of dependence involves the mother. Those psychoanalysts who operate in a relational or inter-subjective perspective often refer to Winnicott's idea of the inseparability of the "mother–child" dyad when evaluating the way in which the structure of a subject's personality develops. This does not mean, however, that relational psychoanalysts are unequivocal about what the "pathological" developments linked to this inseparability might entail if it were to continue into adult life. Most of them focus on detachment, separation and the severing of the umbilical cord, but the more perceptive ones suggest the possibility that a trace of the maternal tie accompanies the subject into adult life and colors his or her encounters with the world.

I believe that if there is something of *amae* visible in Western culture, it manifests itself in relation to the aforementioned concept. And here Erich Fromm's idea returns. It is not, in my opinion, a matter of chance that Fromm is considered to be one of the founders of interpersonal psychoanalysis and was also one of the few psychoanalysts to deal with Eastern thinking, particularly Zen Buddhism. Later on we will address the relationship that I believe exists between my own ideas and Buddhism; for now I will limit myself to suggesting an analogy between Doi's understanding of *amae* and Erich Fromm's notion of the necrophilia–biophilia bipolarity centered on the maternal figure.

Erich Fromm, who, as mentioned, was one of the early proponents of relational psychoanalysis, concerned himself with the idea of human destructiveness[4]—both in the renowned *Anatomy of Human Destructiveness* and in a slightly earlier work, *The Heart of Man*,[5] published in Italy with the unfortunate title *Psicoanalisi dell'amore* [Psychoanalysis of Love]. One of

Fromm's central theses, which I wholly embrace, is that there are two distinct forms of aggression. The one form that is natural and found in all animals is the expression of "motion-toward" things to appropriate them in a reasonable fight for survival. The other, which is virtually absent in animals, can be correctly defined as "destructiveness"; and since it is unrelated to the fight for survival, it is understood as the overcoming and elimination of the other simply for the pleasure of destroying. Fromm finds an explanation for this second form of aggression by looking to the subject's relationship with the maternal figure. He speaks of a tendency toward biophilia or necrophilia, depending on whether there is a tendency on the mother's side to favor a confident and open attitude toward life, or, conversely, a mistrustful withdrawal from life itself.

The necrophilic tendency is to see danger in every element of the outside world and potential enemies everywhere, prompting overprotectiveness and overcautiousness. Destructiveness would be the natural consequence. A child brought up to feel a sense of mistrust toward the world and taught to identify danger and enemies everywhere experiences his surroundings as hostile; his first instinct, therefore, in defending himself is to attack. That which Melanie Klein calls the "schizoparanoid position" and sees as naturally and unfailingly present in every subject, is attributed by Fromm to the necrophilic tendency of the mother. Indeed, it is reasonable to presume that necrophilic and biophilic mothers do not exist as separate figures, but rather that a bipolarity on the necrophilia–biophilia axis effectively characterizes the maternal figure and each subject in relation to her. The destructiveness of every individual can thus be traced back to the influence of the necrophilic polarity in the relational climate of his or her early childhood.[6]

What I intend to argue here is that the predominantly biophilic mother establishes a relationship with her child that is characterized by *amae*. Though the link between destructiveness and necrophilia is relatively direct, it may be not quite so simple to identify the effects of a biophilic relational mode.

Indeed, it would be too simplistic to locate something we may generically define as creativity or even constructiveness at the opposite pole from "destructiveness." Both of these concepts are, in fact, connected to the idea of "giving life" to something, of "producing," which is not intrinsic to the concept of biophilia, as "philia" implies a relationship of harmony with the object, which does not necessarily lead one to renew or transform it, but simply to "welcome" or accept it.

If we return to Fromm's conception of aggression, we may also accept the legitimacy of natural aggression, of "motion-toward" things to take possession of them in the fight for survival, if these things do not come to us "naturally." If something offers itself to us, it obviously does not need to be "attacked"; thus, if we know how to seize the opportunities with which life presents us, then we can limit our aggressiveness—even the non-destructive kind—to those situations that truly require it; at the same time, we can also develop the ability to recognize those situations in which the world reaches out to us. It is at this point that *amae* enters the picture. Indeed, the biophilic mother is the one who responds to her child's needs, not just satisfying them when she is able to, but also by helping the child understand which situations and people merit his trust, thereby helping him achieve an attitude of trustfulness toward the outside world. This implies that the child builds up expectations that his needs and wants be met—expectations which, through dependence on the mother, can be extrapolated to certain elements present in the world around him. This is *amae*.

SOCIAL AND PEDAGOGIC ASPECTS OF THE NEGATIVE VIEW OF *AMAE* IN THE WEST

Our limited sense of *amae* in the West, where no one has (to my knowledge) previously attempted to detect elements of it in our daily life, is likely due to the political and pedagogic principles on which our culture is based. These are principles that, even in more enlightened times (certainly not the current ones), we have been unable to separate from certain foreseeable assumptions, rather like indisputable axioms that we perpetuate and rarely question. And the bitterness that appears in much of Fromm's written work is evidence of the difficulty he had finding the conditions within his own culture for a way of life centered on valorizing man's resources.

Here are two examples of these "indisputable axioms": competitiveness as the propulsive force behind the economy, as well as most social relationships;[7] and the "punish and reward" mechanism regulating these relationships, in a conception of legality that bases respect for others on the fear of punishment. If one considers these axioms as a point of departure, then trust becomes a handicap, dependence even more so. The biophilic mother would by this logic be a deluded dreamer, promoting values that produce children who are destined to be failures with no future.

Some years ago, while in office as Mayor of New York, Rudolph Giuliani coined the still-popular phrase "zero tolerance" to express the policy of intervening radically against any deviant behavior, with the intention of eradicating it entirely—a stance he put into action wholeheartedly. Aside from my doubts about the effectiveness of this method, I find the vision of the world that this idea presents to be incredibly problematic and harmful. It presumes that tolerance is a luxury only available in situations where nothing particularly significant occurs, and that, conversely, situations requiring a solution can only be resolved by heightening repression and punishment. "Zero tolerance" is described as a sort of reversal of tolerant thought, because anyone who transgresses has in so doing surpassed the uppermost limit of acceptability; though in actual fact, the concept entails a lack of tolerance at the origin that is in place prior to the infraction. He who approves of Giuliani's method is methodically intolerant, hypocritically propagating a false tolerance and waiting only to justify his intervention with an "iron fist." He believes this is the only effective solution and applies it—with the utmost sense of being justified—in the most extreme cases, which are the only ones he regards as truly important.

Similarly, we can observe that the only remedy suggested by rightwing governments, especially—and, to some degree, leftwing governments, too—for anything that represents deviation from the norm is to increase repression. This attitude persists, despite the fact that even in the much-lauded United States, the experience of Prohibition had a devastatingly negative outcome (even in practical terms), criminalizing situations that could have been dealt with much more effectively had they been handled differently—as, in some cases, they were. I am referring, for example, to prevention, education, and a pedagogical approach focusing on "real," unwavering tolerance, whatever the circumstances, to be implemented methodically and not as a fallback for situations that are not excessively problematic.

The lowering of the legal age for prosecution; the general "tightening up" of sentences implemented whenever a particularly serious crime enrages public opinion,[8] often a policy of the government in power, be it right or leftwing; neighborhood watch patrols; punishment for personal use of drugs and the banning of alcohol for minors; not to mention the driving license points system—in my opinion, one of the most ridiculous sanctions ever invented—which is still in force even though current statistics have shown it to be completely ineffectual. . . . All of these things are the expression of a society that believes the only possible remedy for any deviation from the norm is an exemplary punishment; a society that has abandoned its principal task of promoting justice as a value, rather than merely a dispenser of punishment.

All this also applies to the so-called phenomenon of "bullying," which is still prevalently tackled through repression and punishment, rather than by educating the families of children who become "bullies," and suggesting a different pedagogical approach. In recent years, too, the practice of grading children's behavior has been reintroduced in Italian schools—with a grade of C—being enough for the student to fail the entire year and have to repeat the grade: this, despite no indication of the effectiveness of this method.

AMAE IN A RELATIONSHIP, ANALYTICAL OR NOT

To believe that no tolerance whatsoever should be applied in cases of severe aggression is to believe that man is not capable of constructive behavior, and that tolerance can only be used when nothing important is at stake. It also implies that when human nature finds its full expression, there can only be destructiveness (a "natural" death instinct, along the lines of Freud's theory of instincts), and that destructiveness should be punished and repressed to prevent it from surfacing. The assumption is that only the fear of being punished can prevent individuals from carrying out certain destructive actions. However, this notion is contradicted above all by facts; for not only is it false that the most repressive regimes have the lowest crime rates, but in point of fact, the complete opposite is true.

Instead, it is the biophilic mother who, in recognizing the constructive capacities of the subject she cares for, promotes his development by helping him make positive contact with the world. And the foundation of this positive contact is a relationship of trust between the mother and the child, and between the mother and the world—with the latter generating the child's trust in the world. This is what I conceive *amae* to be: an aura which accompanies the child of a biophilic mother, permitting him to relate to the world by believing in his own resources and in the possibility of meeting people with whom and places where these resources can be activated.

Amae and the biophilic mother do not create "spoilt" individuals or "parasites," as Western common sense commonly missupposes. On the contrary, they create individuals who function in the world with a certain ease because they are ready to take the hand of those—few or many—who are willing to offer it; and they recognize these people instinctively whenever they encounter them. Strictly speaking they are not "independent" people so much as they are less worried about looking after themselves or being a burden on anyone, accepting help whenever it is offered. They do not worry about having to return the favor as quickly as possible because they do not consider the bond to be a burden, but rather an essential component of life. They are dependent and are conscious of it, choosing the people on whom they depend—and are ready to help when these people ask for assistance, without being eager to do so to settle a score and "free" themselves of their debt.

Moreover, to debunk another common cliché present in society and a certain branch of modern psychology, their primary goal in relating to others is not to avoid being "manipulated" by them. Indeed, they do not see the world as full of potential manipulators, and are therefore able to make contact with others without immediately being on the defensive. This, in turn, often prompts greater trustfulness on the part of the interlocutor, which does away with the need to put up defensive barriers.

Analysis is a setting that can accommodate *amae*; and *amae* can become a useful tool for analytic work. Unlike many people, particularly within the psychoanalytic community today, I believe that one of the main functions of analysis is to act as a corrective emotional experience (Alexander, F. 1948); and I place great deal of importance on the way the therapist presents himself to the patient, not only in creating an empathic "relational climate" (Carnevali, R. 2003), but also to set an example of a relational "style" that can result in just such a corrective emotional experience. As an analyst I put *amae* at the forefront of my work. Many colleagues tell me that I am naïve in always believing everything my patients say to me, and that I need to learn to be more mistrustful, because they are cunning and often manipulative. I have no doubt I am naïve, but I am not interested in doing anything to change this about myself. I am not interested in finding out if my patients are telling me the truth or are trying to manipulate me; I simply want to let them know that I trust them, and that we are capable of building a relationship based on trust in which the individuals involved have no need to deceive one another and can thereby avoid deceiving themselves. In an analytic relationship, *amae* can act as a method of exchange between therapist and patient that is not found in the exchange between the child patient and his mother's necrophilic polarity, thus opening the door to a more trustful way of relating to the world. This is the fundamental concept I try to put into practice in my work as a therapist and analyst.

AMAE AND BUDDHISM

How can I begin to help someone relate to the world and let down at least some of his defenses if I am the first one to behave defensively toward him, in an effort to avoid his potential attempts at manipulation? What is more, use of the term "manipulation" when referring to a patient in this context seems wholly inappropriate to me, as is labeling him "cunning" (a term many therapists use), as the sole advantage he would ultimately gain from these defensive maneuvers would be secondary to his pathology. Such behavior would leave the patient deep in his suffering, due to his inability to embark on new treatment paths. He will only dare embark upon these paths if he succeeds in finding a "biophilic" therapist who, defenseless, opens the door to him, and is prepared to share in the mutual risk of trust.

The link between *amae* and biophilic mother is thus summarized in the idea of the subject seeking a place for himself in the world, to live in a relationship of mutual exchange with the environment in which he is immersed and from which he consequently requires a relationship of trust.

With regard to one of my essays mentioned above (Carnevali, R. 2008), someone once pointed out to me that the link between *amae* and Buddhism—

which I touched upon briefly in that paper—is anything but evident, and that not everything that is derived from Eastern culture can be related directly to Buddhism.

In order to argue against this point, and in support of the idea that the concept of *amae* can indeed be traced back to Buddhism, I wish to quote from a conversation between Dalai Lama and the late psychoanalyst Joyce McDougall, included in *The Couch and the Tree* (Molino [ed.], 1998). At a certain point in the text the narrator, Francisco Varela, quotes His Holiness as follows, which surprises those listening to the conversation (p. 269):

> We could make a distinction between the grosser level of mind and subtle mind. In terms of the gross mind, there could be a connection from the parents to the child if, for example, one or both of the parents has such very strong anger or attachment that physiological changes take place in their bodies as a result of those mental tendencies. In this case the mind influences the body. Thereafter they produce a child whose body is influenced by the parents' bodies. The child's body, produced by the parents' bodies, could then influence the child's state of mind so that it similarly experiences very strong anger or attachment. In this case you'd see a gross level of mind, be it anger or attachment, going from one generation to another. That's a possibility. It's not just a pure mind-to-mind relationship, but a mind-to-body and body-to-mind sequence.

Later in the conversation, when talking about the ego in relation to experience, the Dalai Lama returns to the concepts of "gross consciousness" and "subtle consciousness" (p. 275):

> The 'I' can be designated on the basis of gross consciousness or subtle consciousness. One way of looking at this statement that the mere-I is the repository of mental imprints, is to look at it from a conventional point of view. When a person has done an action, that leaves certain imprints, he now has a certain propensity due to that experience. That's all there is to it. You don't need to posit a substantial basis that exists as the repository for that propensity.

Leaving aside a potential dispute over Freud being a follower of Lamarck when it comes to the theory of evolution, I will limit myself to emphasizing that the views expressed here by the Dalai Lama are very far removed from the idea, which goes against any sort of relational perspective, that "being oneself" means "freeing oneself from all influence to rediscover the true nature of the self." Indeed, the Dalai Lama is proposing an idea of the self as something that is continuously becoming, thanks to a relationship of constant exchange with the surrounding world. Moreover, this view has at least one fundamental point in common with the most orthodox Freudian psychoanalytic theory.

It appears evident that the background of the Dalai Lama's speech relates to a view that strongly runs counter to the idea of "detachment" from worldly things, in the sense of indifference or avoidance of relationships (which many people often associate immediately with Buddhist thinking). The expression "seize the moment" can be seen as urging us toward true contact, fusion with the world, an all-absorbing "immersion" with everything around us, capturing all the nuances. Awareness of the moment is awareness "in relating"; it is the possibility of understanding oneself and the "other." And a biophilic outlook and the presence of *amae* as described herein can only favor this process, thus deeply connecting it with Buddhist thought—at least in the sense we have provided thus far, based, as we have seen, on the words of its main exponent.

I would like to conclude this chapter with a reflection on psychoanalytic technique (or, to be more precise, the theory of psychoanalytic technique). The use of *amae* in analytic work may perhaps seem obscure or overly complex, and many people may well believe that my arguments touch on issues of potential interest from an epistemological perspective, but of little or no applicability—having, therefore, virtually no effect on analytic practice. On the basis of my daily work, however, I can assert that the opposite is true, as in my previous statement that "in an analytical relationship, *amae* can act as an element of exchange between therapist and patient," "opening the door to a more trustful way of relating to the world," which, as I mention, "is the fundamental concept I try to put into practice in my work as a therapist and analyst." With these statements, I am expressing something that for me is a state of being, a lifestyle, a virtually constant immersion in a relational dimension that accompanies me not only in my work, but in my private life—a humus in which I try to grow those seeds that the outside world constantly "plants within me." *Amae* is constantly within me; thus it need not be evoked. It is continuously alive, as well, in my analytic practice, except when subjected to defensive processes of repression (in counter-transference), which I try to anticipate and thereby prevent. This does not mean that the concept of *amae* as an analytic tool is one that is easily passed on; indeed, perhaps the most meaningful aspect of this chapter is its attempt to give a "loose" portrayal of the concept, which will hopefully prompt others to approach a "biophilic" way of working analytically, founded on amae.

***

The English translation of this chapter has offered me a further opportunity to reflect on *amae*, leading me to offer one final consideration.

When I came up with the original Italian title for my chapter, *Amae e il buddismo in occidente* [*Amae* and Buddhism in the West], I conceived the terms *Amae* and Buddhism to be connected by the conjunction "and," with both elements seen in relation to the Western world. When I learned of

Anthony Molino's table of contents for this book, I found that the title had been changed to "*Amae* and Western Buddhism"—a change in meaning that directly connected Buddhism with the Western world, leaving *amae* to measure up to the Western reinterpretation of Buddhism. I immediately realized that the new title was much more fitting. The translation, which partly betrayed my conscious intention in formulating the original one, picked up on unconscious aspects that I had not considered, and the new title appeared more complete in its meaning. As I am not a scholar of Buddhism and have no direct knowledge of Eastern Buddhism, it is clear that what I talk about in my work is the relationship between *amae*—which, deep down, is a concept I adhere to despite never having been to Japan—and Western Buddhism, something I can experience directly and with which I am at least slightly familiar, as part of the world I live in.

I bring this up because I feel it serves as evidence of *amae* within me. The great film director Ingmar Bergman used to say, "I shoot a film and only later do I understand from the critics what I meant." I do not think this was a joke; on the contrary, I believe he wished to convey how deeply enriching it can be when somebody else is able to "read" certain aspects of our personality that we have not detected, or catch a meaning of which we are unaware when we express ourselves.

Perhaps the most profound meaning of *amae* is precisely this: the possibility of allowing ourselves to be penetrated by the thoughts of someone else, who is able to understand us beyond our own intentions. If, by virtue of amae, we can be so humble as to accept these thoughts, which are "alien" but not "alienating," we will be able to expand our awareness of ourselves, carrying others within us and allowing ourselves to be carried in others.

NOTES

1. Without calling on Foucault and his *History of Madness*, we may think of Soviet dissidents interned in psychiatric hospitals or the protagonist of Clint Eastwood's film *Changeling*, who is locked away in a psychiatric clinic in 1930s America because she maintains that the child that has been found by the police is not her disappeared child.

2. *Arrangiati*, probably the most suitable Italian equivalent of the expression, often possesses negative connotations as well.

3. Drawing on my own experience, I will provide an example of my personal affinity with the Japanese outlook and the concept of *amae*. When I go shopping with my wife (who, in this sense at least, is obviously very "Western"), I notice that she succeeds in buying beautiful, good quality items at low prices, sifting through dozens of clothes in stores where hundreds of people serve themselves and come into contact with salespersons only to pay for their purchases or to ask the odd fleeting question. In these moments, I realize that I require a different type of shopping experience altogether, where a salesperson welcomes me and attends to me as soon as I enter the store, guiding me through my purchases and leading me, step by step, to payment at the till and then the exit. Moreover, being colorblind, I also depend on others for choosing colors, and therefore ask for advice both from whoever is accompanying me (usually my wife) and the salesperson, to be certain that I am not making a mistake. I have never

perceived all this as a personal limitation that I should overcome, nor have I ever taken any steps to espouse the "help yourself" shopping mentality.

4. Fromm E. 1973. *The Anatomy of Human Destructiveness*. New York: Holt, Rinehart and Winston.

5. Fromm, E. 1964. *The Heart of Man, Its Genius for Good and Evil*, New York: Harper and Row.

6. To complement Fromm's thinking while maintaining the necrophilia–biophilia bipolarity as our key of interpretation, we can also envisage the paternal figure playing a fundamental role in the establishment of this climate. A rereading of the Oedipus myth in a relational key is central to my argument. A necrophilic attitude toward the world invests, first and foremost, the figure of the unborn child: what we might consider a natural attitude of "rejection" toward an element of discontinuity (the birth of a child disrupting the continuity of a couple's life) may assume a spectrum of varying positions on the necrophilia–biophilia axis. Before considering Oedipus's destructive impulse toward his father Laius, we should therefore look at the prophecy that sees Oedipus as the usurper and induces Laius to send his son to death. Before there being a baby destined to kill his father and sleep with his mother, there are two parents who envision their son's fate and construct a situation to prevent it from occurring: precisely the situation which eventually leads to that destiny's fulfillment! In other words, we could say that it is the parental couple in which the necrophilic attitude prevails. The couple, in fact, perceives elements of the outside world as threats that must be thwarted before materialize and they destroy us. It is this perception that makes the first and most important "mark" on the unborn child. Thus Oedipus, who does not already bear the fate of being Oedipus, is turned murderous and incestuous by the defenses that his parents act out for him.

7. To not overcomplicate this chapter, I will only develop this point in a brief endnote. For centuries now, a considerable part of the Western world has espoused a capitalist economy, but it took the fall of the Berlin wall to mark the true end of communism; and over the last twenty years we have begun to assume that the *homo novus* theorized by Marx is a utopian figure. Indeed, in the West, man is now conceived as solely devoted to the pursuit of his own interests, excluding the possibility that he may have a natural propensity to socialize and commune with others. According to this view, man's sole means for self-realization would be to "attack" the world and make it his own, in a sort of struggle for survival. Here again we can observe that the necrophilic attitude prevails as, in order to not succumb in a world populated by wolves, man must activate all possible defenses and overpower others to avoid being overpowered. Silvio Berlusconi is a striking example of this mentality, and the support that he received for nearly twenty years demonstrates that an outlook abolishing the natural human inclination to interact with both others and the world is a widely shared one. A crude but significant example of this is Berlusconi's statement that any entrepreneur or professional who votes leftwing is a *coglione* ("an asshole"), as he deems it unthinkable that a citizen's vote could depend on his or her sense of justice or need for social equity, rather than individual interests.

8. I also want to spend a few words on increasing prison sentences for pedophiles, which is justified by the public outcry over the crime's particular repugnance. This public indignation is understandable, and the disgust even more so, but what does this have to do with increasing prison sentences? What would be the logic behind doing this? Does anyone really think that before grooming and abusing a child, pedophiles ask themselves how many years they would face; and if the sentence is only three or four years then they go ahead, whereas they would refrain were it fifteen or twenty, as the risk is too great? We need not be skilled psychologists to understand that the order of thoughts in the mind of a pedophile is quite different, and that the risk of punishment has no impact whatsoever on his actions. At the end of 2007, the Italian Society of Clinical Psychology and Psychotherapy organized a conference in Milan entitled "Pedophiles today: Shall we attempt to cure them?" which raised issues that are, in my opinion, of great interest. Despite the conference being very well attended, however, the ideas circulated only within this narrow circle of professionals who have virtually no impact on public opinion and policy.

REFERENCES

Alexander, F. 1948. *Fundamentals of Psychoanalysis*. Oxford: W. W. Norton.

Carnevali, R. 2003. *L'immaginario e il diavolo*. Milano: FrancoAngeli.

———. 2008. "C'è qualcosa di nuovo . . . anzi d'antico." *Setting*, 26.

Doi, T. 1973. *The Anatomy of Dependence*. Tokyo: Kodansha International.

Fromm, E. 1964. *The Heart of Man, Its Genius for Good and Evil*. New York: Harper & Row.

———. *The Anatomy of Human Destructiveness*. New York: Holt, Rinehart and Winston.

Fromm, E., Suzuki, D. T., and De Martino, R. 1960. *Zen Buddhism and Psychoanalysis*. London: Allen & Unwin.

Molino, A. 1998. *The Couch and the Tree*. New York: North Point Press.

Smith, H. W., and Nomi, T. 2000. "Is Amae the key to understanding Japanese Culture?" *Electronic Journal of Sociology*.

Chapter Eleven

Two Unexpected Guests

Graziano Graziani

How should we consider the pairing of psychoanalysis and Buddhism? Does it refer us to the comparison between a scientific discipline and a religion, or to something else?

In most of the literature, authorial perspective determines how the polarized "Other" is viewed and/or interpreted. When psychoanalysts write on Buddhism, a scientific attribution prevails; conversely, practicing Buddhists are likely to give a spiritual reading of psychoanalysis. Often, it seems that even the writings of psychoanalysts who themselves are Buddhists are host to an internal, dichotomous dialogue in which views of an allegedly scientific nature and spiritual visions examine each other. Indeed, in actual fact, these two polarities do not fully correspond to their explicit assumptions.

Despite its scientific claims, classical psychoanalysis favors principles that would in fact be more suited to a pseudoscience or a religion than a scientific discipline. One of the basic propositions of psychoanalysis is that its theoretical premises are considered truths that do not need to be proven. All that is required for a theory to be considered valid is that it explains the facts for which it was formulated. In other words, a theory (which could even—let's say—be the theory of fairies) formulated to explain an event is considered valid precisely because it explains said event. As is the case with religions, such theories are evidently not falsifiable.

A comparison between psychoanalysis and Buddhism could therefore also be construed as a comparison between religions, with one—psychoanalysis—claiming scientific status. Although many psychoanalysts today still share the attitudes described above, since the 1960s others have taken action to guarantee the survival of psychoanalysis as a scientific rather than a religious discipline. To spell out the risks of this religious drift, Cremerius (1995) highlights the similarities between Freud and the founding figures of a church. Indeed, Freud (1923) regarded psychoanalysis as truth ("We possess the truth"), defined his doctrine as sacred rules ("No one who cannot accept them all should count himself as a psychoanalyst") and created an International Psychoanalytic Association (the IPA) which, much like the Church, was to act as the repository of "true psychoanalysis." However, clearly aware of the discipline's ecclesiastical shift, the most recent leaders of the IPA have attempted to distance psychoanalysis from classification among the pseudosciences. And this is how we should read the warnings of two of the most recent IPA presidents, with Wallerstein (1988) defining the classical theories as "articles of faith" and Kernberg (1996) comparing analytic training institutes to religious seminaries. Nevertheless, despite being a religion in some respects, classical psychoanalysis has the great merit of having proposed a set of procedures which are useful on the therapeutic plane, so that, in actual fact, "a technique developed to make it rain (knowledge of the unconscious) has proven extremely useful as therapy" (Fossi, 2005, translated from the Italian). For several contemporary analysts, the empirical dimension of the analytic process and its anchorage to cognitive sciences are the elements that can confer scientific status to psychoanalysis, and which future inquiry should address.

On the religious front, natural selection (in this case, cultural rather than biological) has seen to it that of the thousands of faiths that man has espoused throughout history, four major religions, of which Buddhism is one, are primary across the globe. More so than with other religions, though, some of the observations that can be made concerning Buddhism act as a sort of photographic negative of what has been said about psychoanalysis. As with all religions, there are areas of Buddhism in which dogmatic, obscurantist mysticism prevails, or has prevailed: from the medieval Tibetan theocracy that endured up until the last Dalai Lama, to the murder of the democratically elected president of Ceylon at the hands of Buddhist monks in 1959. Buddhism is, however, rather different if compared to the theological religions. For all its references to a spiritual and divine sphere, it addresses no deity. Furthermore, it does not reject logical thinking, which purportedly led Jung to define it "the religion of pure reason" (McGuire, 1984). Its precepts are, in fact, much closer to what we could define as psychology rather than religion. The attitude taught by the Buddha is to explore perceptual reality, in order to dispel the mist of erroneous convictions overshadowing our vision of ourselves and the world. Therefore, in the same way that classical psychoanalysis produced excellent technique, Buddhism defined good practice for unveiling reality. Among these, vipassana or "clear-seeing" meditation is a fine way to explore individual consciousness and reach greater awareness of what is happening at the moment in which it happens. For over twenty years now, the procedures of vipassana meditation (Mindfulness) have been adopted by Western medicine. Indeed, when subjected to meta-analysis (Grossman et al.,

2003), treatment protocols for Mindfulness-based therapies have been proven undoubtedly effective.

At this stage, future comparison between Buddhism and psychoanalysis should not be articulated as a comparison between a religion and a pseudoscience (which, in itself, is a religion), but rather as a dialogue between praxes. The grounds of this comparison should therefore be the simple facts and experiences that psychoanalytic and meditative practice either do or do not have in common. Furthermore, if a psychoanalyst is to have a say in the comparison, he or she should be acquainted with the other praxis, that is, have had first-hand experience of meditation. Otherwise, the risk is that a psychoanalyst who has built his identity on the speculative dimension (of metapsychology) might be prone to falling back on theoretical and abstract formulations.

***

It may come as a surprise that among the limited numbers of analysts who have practiced meditation and explored the parallelisms between psychoanalysis and their meditative experiences, two Italians analysts, Roberto Assagioli and Emilio Servadio, are rarely mentioned. They are our two "unexpected guests," as important as they are overlooked, whose little-known but important contributions I propose to revisit.

The first of the two guests, Roberto Assagioli, is not usually associated with psychoanalysis, although he was the first to make the discipline known in Italy. (He is undoubtedly more well-known as the creator of Psychosynthesis, a personal and original form of psychotherapy.) Assagioli graduated in medicine in 1910 with a thesis entitled "Psychoanalysis," at the time a real novelty in Italian psychiatric milieu. He then studied at the Burghölzli Clinic in Zurich under Eugen Bleuler, the psychiatrist who coined the term "schizophrenia," and was first among his colleagues to welcome Freud's ideas. At Burghölzli, Assagioli met C. G. Jung (Bleuler's assistant at the time) and the two became friends; indeed, their friendship was deep and lasting, and Jung introduced Assagioli to Freud as the doctor who could introduce psychoanalysis in Italy. Assagioli became a member of the Freud Society in Zurich, along with Bleuler, Jung, Binswanger, and other Swiss psychiatrists, and went on to be the only Italian member of the newly-formed International Psychoanalytical Association, two years before being joined by Edoardo Weiss, an analyst from Trieste (at the time part of Austria). In the 1920s, Weiss went on to become the true father of Italian psychoanalysis and, after immigrating to the United States in 1939 due to the racial laws introduced in Italy, was among the founders of ego psychology. Assagioli was the only Italian to have the privilege of publishing in the early psychoanalytic journals founded by Freud, the "Jahrbruch für Psychoanalytische und Psychopathologische Forschungen" and the "Zentralblatt für Psychoanalise." (His contribution to the latter, an article on sublimation, featured certain aspects of what later became known as Psychosynthesis.) Though the first essay on psychoanalysis to be published in Italy was by Barontini (director of the Imola psychiatric hospital) in 1908, Assagioli followed this shortly after with an article in 1910 for the renowned literary journal *La Voce*. In 1912, Assagioli even succeeded in having the March–April issue of *La Voce* devoted to psychoanalysis. He then founded *Psyche*, a journal of his own, and published (with the author's consent) the first essay by Freud ever to appear in Italian, which he translated himself. Assagioli maintained correspondence with Freud, which lasted even after he decided to leave the psychoanalytic movement.

Assagioli's interest in psychoanalysis was precocious, but his interest in Eastern thought was even more so, dating back to his childhood and the teachings of his mother, a member of the Theosophical Society. In 1907, when Assagioli was only nineteen years of age and frequented the literary avant-garde that gathered at the Florentine café Le Giubbe Rosse, he published an article in *Il Leonardo* (a journal founded by his friend Papini) entitled "For a new Aryan Humanism," in which he wrote: "In a few years' time, the progress of internal psychology in Europe will require us to adopt many Oriental technical terms to denote the states of consciousness, for which the European languages do not have equivalents. We will thus speak of Pratyahra, Dharama, Dhyanam and Samadhi" (translated from the Italian). Assagioli's interest in oriental philosophies and the spiritual dimension grew after his exit from the psychoanalytic movement in 1914, which coincided with Jung's. In 1930, he penned the Italian introduction to Alice Bailey's commentary of the Yoga Sutras of Patanjali, while continuing to develop his own method of treatment, which he called Psychosynthesis. Assagioli felt the term was apt as it related, in cultural terms, to the synthesis between East and West and, in psychological terms, to the Synthetic Centre that organizes personality. While psychoanalysis is predominantly concerned with the lower floors and the foundations of the human building (as Freud wrote to Binswanger to differentiate the discipline from the latter's Daseinanalyse), Psychosynthesis (like Daseinanalyse, but with greater emphasis) aims to study the higher stories of human existence, "to open up the terrace where you can sun-bathe or look at the stars" (Assagioli, 1965). According to Assagioli, there are various ways for man to reach these higher stories, one of which is the meditative path. Meditation is thus one of the tools of Psychosynthesis, alongside other practices such as listening to music, drawing, keeping a personal psychological diary, visualizations, etcetera.

Assagioli appears to have drawn inspiration from Buddhist psychology when he argues, in an unpublished set of notes ("Exercise in Disidentification and Self-identification," 1931), that man should first gain awareness of the multiplicity of the various aspects of the self, then disidentify himself from them in order to regain personal unity, his own transcendental summit—or what Assagioli calls the Ego or the Center of Self-consciousness. While the various aspects of the self may be in conflict with one another, the Center of Self-consciousness is compatible with all of these aspects, comprehending them in a way that is objective and superior. If man strays from his Centre, he will eventually begin to identify with thoughts and emotions that do not correspond to his true essence, and which will end up devouring him. In Assagioli's book *The Act of Will* (1973) (one of the few cited in psychoanalytic literature—rather unsurprisingly by a Buddhist analyst, Nina Coltart, in 1996), he suggests practicing all morning following the outline: "I have a body, but I am not my body. I have an emotional life, but I am not my emotions. I have an intellect, but I am not my intellect. I am I, a Centre of pure consciousness." Assagioli devotes an appendix of *The Act of Will* to meditation, as he had done in his previous book, *Psychosynthesis: A Manual of Principles and Techniques* (1965). Entitled "Meditative Techniques and Psychotherapy," this latter appendix—which makes extensive reference to Schultz's autogenic training and Desoille's idea of the directed daydream—was not written by Assagioli, but by Wolfgang Kretschmer, the most well-known European psychiatrist at the time. I believe that Assagioli chose Kretschmer to write the appendix to his book for two reasons. The first was that doing so would associate meditation with an authoritative figure and show that the practice could be welcomed by some of the greatest minds in European psychiatry. The second reason—revealed by the content of the appendix—was to fulfill Assagioli's intention to define a meditative practice that drew from Eastern tradition, but was also able to differ from it and follow the canons of Western psychology. Indeed, the practice described by Assagioli in appendix to his second book, *The Act of Will* (1973), contains many elements that are personal or of psychodynamic derivation.

The meditative process that Assagioli describes is divided into three consecutive phases. The first phase, called Reflective Meditation, revolves around contemplation, concentration from the periphery to the Center, persistence and tenacity. This is phase in which the individual disidentifies from thoughts and emotion, and concentrates entirely on a single subject, immersing himself in it. Assagioli suggests that meditation should focus on subjects ranging from spiritual qualities such as courage, faith, serenity, etcetera, to specific symbolic images and certain phrases suggested by the author, which he calls "seed-thoughts."

The second step is Receptive Meditation. While during the first phase, Reflective Meditation, the mind's "inner eye" is directed horizontally and observes aspects of the individual's personality, during Receptive Meditation it is turned upwards to discover what is hidden beyond ordinary consciousness. For this to occur, the stage of inner silence must be reached through the visualization of symbolic images. Once this stage of silence is attained, the individual will receive messages of awareness expressed through visions or illuminations. Reception is always followed by the registration of what has been perceived, which may also be noted down.

The final stage, known as Creative Meditation, is one in which the individual vivifies the content that has been transmitted by the meditative experience, in a creative and personal way. Although Assagioli's technique differs from traditional meditation, I believe he deserves much recognition for having attempted to systematize the meditative process and, above all, for having introduced it in psychotherapy as early as the 1920s.

***

Matters are somewhat different when it comes to our second unexpected guest, Emilio Servadio. In practicing meditation, Servadio did not stray from what he had learned in the East and, unlike Assagioli, he remained orthodox in his analytic practice. Despite being a very important figure in Italian psychoanalysis, and well-known at an international level, Servadio's observations on the relationship between psychoanalysis and meditation are virtually unknown. There are probably three reasons why Servadio is never mentioned in literature regarding the dialogue between psychoanalysis and Buddhism.

The first is that Servadio did not write an exhaustive study on the subject. His thoughts on the matter were, instead, published in about ten short articles from the years 1938 to 1986 (commendably collected by psychologist Biancamaria Puma,[1] a student of Servadio's, and is available at www.emilioservadio.it). The second reason stems from the fact that Servadio generally wrote for the wider public, rather than specifically addressing psychoanalysts. Lastly, when Servadio's thought is linked to Eastern philosophy, it is often in relation to Hinduism and Yoga, rather than Buddhism. Indeed, Servadio was fascinated by Indian philosophy from a very young age and adhered in particular to the monistic Vedanta of Shankara, founder of Advaita Vedanta. However, Shankara adopted many Buddhist views, and his rejection of the dualistic view of Upanishad philosophy was a result of the Buddha's teachings. For this reason, in fact, Shankara also became known in India as a prachanna bauddha, or a Buddhist in disguise. Servadio also practiced Yoga, following the Yoga Sutras according to the teachings of Patanjali, and often compared Yoga and psychoanalysis in his writings. In its meditative nature, however, Yoga Sutra is very similar to Buddhist practice; and some of the comparisons that Servadio draws also make explicit reference to Buddhist meditation, as well as Yoga.

If these are the likely circumstances that led to the exclusion of Servadio's name from the list of analysts worth mentioning in the psychoanalytic dialogue with Buddhism, there are also several reasons why Servadio should instead be counted among them. The first is of a historical nature, as he was among the first to take an interest in the matter, as early as 1938. Second, Servadio was more than simply an enthusiast of the subject as he practiced meditation and did so throughout his entire life. Though, as a man of his time, he cannot but be considered a classical psychoanalyst, the cross-references of Servadio's long personal practice place his comparison between analysis and meditation on the experiential, rather than metapsychological, plane. What is most original about Servadio's work is precisely this comparison of practices—and from this point of view, his observations have never been more timely and worth exploring. Before looking at Servadio's work, a brief reconstruction of the biographical events that influenced his thinking is required.

Servadio's interest in Oriental philosophy began well before he became a psychoanalyst. He turned his attention to the East as early as 1920, when writing for *Ur*, the journal directed by Julius Evola, who later became a point of reference for fascist mysticism. Collaborating on the Italian encyclopedia, Servadio met Edoardo Weiss, at the time the only Italian psychoanalyst, and Weiss became his analyst; with the help of a few others, the two worked together to found the Italian Psychoanalytic Society in 1932. That same year, Servadio struck up a deep and lasting friendship with Anna Freud. Servadio also met Freud and presented papers at the International Psychoanalytic Congresses of Wiesbaden (1932), Lucerne (1934), and Paris (1938). Servadio spent the following eight years in India, after being the first Jewish members of the Italian Psychoanalytical Society to emigrate due to racial laws introduced in Italy by the fascist regime in 1938. Ernest Jones suggested the move, as psychoanalysis was only just starting up in India, and a tiny Indian Psychoanalytic Society had begun to operate in Calcutta. Jones sent him to Mumbai (then Bombay), where no psychoanalyst was operating at the time. Shortly after his arrival, he was appointed teaching analyst by the Indian Psychoanalytic Society. He also became a professor at Madras College and was, in turn, a student of famous yogis such as Shri Kuvala Vananda. He began to practice meditation, which, he says, was his way of "going home." On returning to Italy, at the end of World War II, Servadio re-formed the Italian Psychoanalytical Society with some colleagues, founded the Rome Institute of Psychoanalysis, and went on to be President and then Honorary President of the Italian Psychoanalytic Society until his death in 1995.

Despite belonging to the psychoanalytic establishment and underwriting its theories, in his writings, Servadio does not hesitate to dismiss much of the metapsychological speculation around conceptualizing a model of comparison with meditation. "It would not flatter psychoanalysts"—he writes (1986)—to continue to refer to meditative practices with such definitions as: "regression to the oceanic stage" (Freud, 1929); "infantile erotic pleasures" (Lewin, 1950); "the child's dependence on parental figure" (perhaps a reference to Ferenczi, 1913); and "primary narcissism" (Federn, 1929). Servadio's decision to break with past theories, and Freud himself, can only be explained by his insistence on remaining firmly rooted in praxis, which allowed him to avoid being seduced by the "witch metapsychology."

The parallelism that Servadio draws between psychoanalysis and Buddhism (1961, 1986) develops from a basic view of mental functioning that is common to both: namely, that the mind proceeds in an automatic, uncontrolled fashion. Thoughts follow thoughts, reasoning follows reasoning, and the subject is captured by the "fascination" of thinking and the anxiety that its interruption would provoke. Buddhist tradition teaches us that what is obscured in the continuous flow of thought is our ability to see that "thoughts are just thoughts." Servadio (1961, 1986) goes so far as to maintain that when an individual produces thoughts, he is not actually thinking but, rather, "being thought" by a particular instance of thought—of which he has no awareness (vasana).

Indeed, one of the objectives shared by analytic practice and meditation is full awareness of the mind's continuous wanderings. Thich Nhat Hanh (1987) writes that, for the meditator, "the essential thing is not to let any feeling or thought arise without recognizing it in mindfulness, like a palace guard who is aware of every face that passes through the front corridor." For its part, psychoanalysis relies on the therapeutic method devised by Freud, which, according to Servadio, contains several elements that have equivalents in meditation.

The first of these elements is the analytic setting, many characteristics of which also feature in meditative practice, albeit with different names. Servadio (1961) compiles a list of these characteristics, which include: constancy, patience, use of bodily postures, non-habitual experiences, renunciation of immediate gratification, neutrality and acceptance. Second, Servadio (1986) sees an undeniable similarity between the "suspension of critical faculties" invoked by Freud and the precepts given to those who meditate. Those who begin an analysis are asked to communicate all the thoughts that pass through their minds, disregarding any logic, finalism, self-judgment and moral conventions. This is the fundamental "golden rule"—otherwise known as "free association"—that makes the analytic process possible. As well as being the main source of information for the analyst, free association is also a unique form of "self-knowledge," comparable, according to Servadio (1986), to the attitude and experience of the meditator. Indeed, the naked attention to the flow of thought required for meditation is open, impartial, non-judgmental, interested and impersonal in nature. The only difference with Freud's "golden rule" would therefore be in the verbalization of the ideational content and, of course, in the presence of a listener.

We know that subjects who meditate learn that it is not a mistake for them to be captured by thoughts distracting them from meditative focusing, as this is how the mind normally functions. Subjects are, nevertheless, advised to relinquish a given thought when their naked attention contemplates it, and return to focusing in a gentle and non-judgmental way (generally, through breathing). In fact, Buddhism teaches that to attain a clear vision of the self and balanced ego flexibility, subjects must overcome attachment, in this case, to their ideational content. In relation to attachment, Servadio (1961, 1985) interestingly transposes meditative practice onto psychoanalysis. Premising that narcissistic defenses are the main obstacle to the development of transference, Servadio (1961, 1985) wonders what these defenses might be. He goes on to argue that they are, in fact, a form of attachment to one's self "crystallized" by feelings of arrogance, pride and unshakeable convictions; a form of attachment that carries suffering. Incidentally, in recent years, Mark Epstein (1995), a practicing analyst, has pointed out how narcissistic attachments constitute a major obstacle to good meditative practice. If the subject is able to overcome the attachment to his thoughts (even narcissistic ones) through analysis or meditation, this would allow him to acquire a "metacognitive awareness" in which thoughts are experienced as thoughts (mental events), rather than as aspects of the self. Servadio (1961) relates Freud's (1923) idea of "internal foreign territory" (i.e., something that belongs to us but is perceived as external to us, such as: "I was taken by anger") to the metacognitive awareness of the individual who meditates or is in analysis. Developing a clear vision of the "internal foreign territory" would thus coincide with the onset of a process of disidentification. Like Assagioli before him, Servadio also sees disidentification as the cornerstone of awareness practices. Through meditative practice, he says, "little by little, the ego moves away and frees itself from what had become egosyntonic, using it more or less at will, in the same way that we would make use of a vehicle knowing full well that we are not the vehicle and that we can get by without it" (Servadio, 1961, translated from the Italian). The subject can therefore begin to relate to his thoughts, rather than "becoming" them, as if they were simple events occurring in his field of consciousness. On this level, the apparent aim of both analysis and meditation would be not so much to alter the subject's mental content, but rather the way in which he or she relates to this content.

The great value that Buddhism assigns to the "present moment" is, in many respects, identical to the importance that Freud attributes to the *hic et nunc* of the session; indeed, both practices share the common goal of "detaching us from the past and the false realities holding it down" (Servadio, 1961, translated from the Italian). Servadio (1986) identifies another analogy in the similar state of consciousness that both psychoanalyst and meditator are asked to attain. According to Servadio, the "evenly hovering attention" that Freud (1912) recommends to the analyst ("He should simply listen, and not bother about whether he is keeping anything in mind") is largely interchangeable with the attentive state that the meditator is taught. Such a condition, “familiar to anyone who meditates,” would allow the analyst to listen in an impartial way, in a state of “silence” that “filters” the words from the “noises.” The analyst would direct his listening, which is “hovering” and free from attachments, to the words of the patient, as well as his own thoughts; and through this listening, argues Servadio (1986), a form of communication touching the deeper levels of self could be established. Moments of empathy and counter-transference would develop within the frame of consciousness that meditation has always sought to expand. It is a case of “feeling before understanding” (Servadio, 1986)—a characteristic of the best Buddhist teachings: “Words are only fingers pointing at the moon. They are not the thing itself. The actual experience lies beyond the words” (Gunaratana, 1991). Indeed, Gunaratana teaches that, as meditation progresses, there is a sudden, fleeting moment when the subject begins to become aware of an object but has not yet conceptualized it, in which he or she has pure awareness of that object. These moments in which we experience an object before objectifying it, perceiving a thing as a non-thing, would coincide with the levels of profound awareness that analysts recognize as empathy and counter-transference, and which meditation teaches us to cultivate. It would therefore be desirable, even for his own work, for an analyst to have had direct experience of meditation. In this sense, Servadio (1961) is citing and supporting the views of Geraldine Coster (1934) when she writes that: “the analyst of the future should be one who knows experimentally something of the process of meditation.” Servadio (1961) maintains that a first step could also be for analytic technique to show a deeper consideration for body state, relaxation and breathing rhythm. Both analytic training and technique could therefore potentially benefit from greater knowledge and integration of meditative practices. Despite his views, however, when he became the director of the Institute of Training (where I myself trained), Servadio did not put forward any proposals in this direction, probably deeming it premature, politically speaking, to introduce any links to meditative practice in psychoanalytic training.

Nothing seems more persuasive than the quotation from the Svetasvatara Upanishad that Servadio (1961) cites as the ultimate goal of meditation: “Just as a mirror shines brightly after it has been cleaned, so the yogi who has realized the true nature of his soul becomes integrated as one in his body, attains sense of fulfillment and remains free from sorrow.” However, as fascinating and useful as meditation may be, he feels he must warn against the disavowal of our Western therapeutic practice “in favor of a darshana that does not belong to us.” In this sense, Servadio is in agreement with Jung (1943), who “very wisely” points out the risks of salvific illusion and an absolute adherence to Eastern philosophy, when, in actual fact, “Truth appears differently in different lands and ages, according to the living materials out of which its symbols are hewn.” Like certain psychoanalysts today (Pensa, 1994; Epstein, 1995), Servadio unfalteringly underlines that meditative practices should not have a therapeutic purpose, even if they may ultimately prove beneficial. "In India," Servadio tells us (1961, translated from the Italian), "I learned from Shri Kuvala Vananda himself that the majority of Westerners who wish to devote themselves to meditation are neurotic in the clinical sense of the word—neurotics, he said, who should seek the help of a psychoanalyst rather than squatting down every day trying to meditate." In all likelihood, Servadio would agree with the views recently expressed by Corrado Pensa (1994, translated from the Italian): "On the path of meditation, the risk of self-deception is very high . . . A good psychotherapy can make the practice of awareness more well-grounded, lively and insightful. In turn, meditation can deepen and dramatically accelerate the psychotherapeutic process."

For the most part—as I mentioned above—the observations in Servadio's writings prevalently concern experience and practice. He makes a bold metapsychological interpretation on one single occasion, considering Kundalini—the goddess or sleeping serpent symbolizing the Yogic idea of corporeal energy—a sublimation of proto-instincts (libido and destrudo); but this was 1938, before his departure for India and his personal practice.

Concluding these brief remarks on Emilio Servadio's thoughts and his role as precursor in the comparison of psychoanalysis and meditation, we may summaries his thinking with these few words: "Without knowing it, psychoanalysis has always been rather Eastern in its technical aspects and Western in its theoretical aspects" (Servadio, 1986, translated from the Italian). In truth, while there is no doubt that Freud's ideas are rooted in the tradition of Western philosophy, only some of his technical devices are Oriental, albeit not consciously so. Indeed, many of the therapeutic factors that characterize the analytic method cannot be found in Eastern tradition, such as the significance of interactions, analysis of transference, interpretations, the role of dreams, etcetera. Nevertheless, the elements in common highlighted by Servadio's careful examination can provide the basis for a comparison between the two practices and an enrichment of psychoanalysis itself.

NOTES

1. Whose work made the writing of this short chapter possible.

REFERENCES

Assagioli R. 1965. *Psychosynthesis*. New York: Penguin Books.
———. 1973. *The Act of Will*. New York: Penguin Books.
Coltart N. 1996. *The Baby and the Bathwater*. London: Karnac Books.

Coster G. 1934. *Yoga and Western Psychology*. London: Oxford University Press.
Cremerius J. 1995. *Die Zukunft der Psycoanalyse*. Frankfurt: Suhrkamt.
Epstein M. 1995. *Thoughts without a Thinker*. New York: Basic Books.
Federn P. 1929. *Ego Psychology and Psychosis* (Weiss E., Ed.). New York: Basic Books.
Ferenczi S. 1913. *Stages in the Development of the Sense of Reality*. *Selected Papers*, vol. 1. New York: Basic Books.
Fossi G. 2005. *La Psicoterapia Dinamico-Evoluzionistica*. Milano: Franco Angeli.
Freud S. 1912. *Recommendations to Physicians Practicing Psychoanalysis*, vol. 12. London: Standard Edition.
———. 1923. *Two Encyclopedia Articles: Psychoanalysis and the Libido Theory*, vol. 18. London: Standard Edition.
———. 1929. *Civilization and its Discontents*, vol. 21. London: Standard Edition.
Grossman P. and Niemann L. 2003. "Mindfulness-based Stress Reduction and Health Benefits. A Meta-Analysis." *Journal of Psychosomatic Research*, 57: 35–43.
Gunaratana H. 1991. *Mindfulness in Plain English*. Boston: Wisdom Publications.
Jung C. G. 1943. *The Psychology of Eastern Meditation*, vol. 11. *Collected Works*. Princeton University Press.
Kernberg O. 1996. "Thirty Methods to Destroy the Creativity of Psychoanalytic Candidates." *International Journal of Psychoanalysis*, 77.5: 1031–1040.
Lewin B. 1950. *The Psychoanalysis of Elation*. New York: Norton.
McGuire W. 1984. *Dream Analysis: Notes of the Seminar Given in 1928–1930 by C. G. Jung*. Princeton: Princeton University Press.
Pensa C. 1994. *La tranquilla passione*. Roma: Ubaldini.
Servadio E. 1938. *Considerations psychanalitiques sur le yoga*. XV International Conference on Psychoanalysis, Paris. cited in: Servadio E (1947). Psicoanalisi e Yoga (II parte). Luce e Ombra. www.emilioservadio.it.
———. 1947. *Psicoanalisi e Yoga (II parte)*. Luce e Ombra. www.emilioservadio.it.
———. 1961. *Psicoanalisi e Yoga*. Ulisse. www.emilioservadio.it.
———. 1985. *Scoprire l'inconscio praticando lo yoga*. Il Messaggero Veneto. www.emilioservadio.it.
———. 1986. *Psicoanalisi e pensiero orientale. Relazione alla IX Giornata dello Yoga*. Roma. www.emilioservadio.it.
Thich Nhat Hann. 1987. *The Miracle of Mindfulness*. Beacon Press. Boston.
Wallerstein R. S. 1988. "One Psychoanalysis or Many?" *International Journal of Psychoanalysis*, 69: 5–21.

Chapter Twelve

Mandalas of the Mind

Katriona Munthe and Anthony Molino

> I tried in my comment (to *The Secret of the Golden Flower*) to create a bridge of intimate spiritual understanding between the East and the West.
>
> —C. G. Jung

The practice of meditatively passing through a "mandala palace" or, as the people of Oddiyana used to call it, walking the stepped path to enlightenment in the "Land of Initiation Circles," is a Buddhist practice that enables unification of the outer world, the body and one's inner state of mind. The Buddhist is able in this tantric practice to experience, moment after moment, the process of human development, replete with fantasy and symbolism. He is able to move through the codes and languages of a mythological expression of the passions, the emotions, ideas, and sensations—the mind objects—along an inner spiritual journey toward emptiness by visualizing the deities and using subtle energies to cleanse the outer (cosmological) and the inner (personal) wheels of time.

Indeed the Mandala, in its fundamental secrecy, is actually a mirror of the cosmos, not just of the outer cosmos but also of the inner micro-cosmos. In Jung's words, "In complete harmony with the oriental concept, the symbol of the Mandala is not only a form of expression, it also exercises a retroactive effect on its author." Indeed, there hides in this symbol a magical effect that derives originally from the protective magic circle, the *sulcus primigenius,* that is traced around the center, the *templum* or the *temenos* (sacred precinct) of our most intimate personality. This is in order to avoid "dispersion" and to keep at bay the distractions of the external world. And it is precisely this "magical activity" that turns, in the end, into the discovery of a *transcendent function*. That is to say: into the unifying energy that allows the images of harmony, balance and integration slowly to emerge, pushing their way through conflicting emotions and clashing oppositions to allow for awareness of the nature of light and the inner kinship of all beings. To become aware, in other words, of the Buddhahood that is present but latent, and therefore not basically different, from the very state which we strive to overcome. Or, as Jung writes:

> It is a question of recuperating—with the help and mediation of an external tool—one's capacity to pay attention to, or one's immersion in, an inner sacred enclosure which is both the origin and the goal of the soul. Here we find contained that unification of consciousness and life that once we knew and then we lost, and which therefore we must find again. [1]

This chapter, "Mandalas of the Mind," is not the exploration of a *structure*, the way in which the mind has been conceived in visual-spatial imagery through centuries of Buddhist practice. It is not even an attempt to describe a *process* interior to the deepest brain, the combining of incoming information, including language and relationships, ultimately to find some mytho-cultural system of understanding. No, the hope here is humbly to retrace the footsteps of an *experience* whose historical significance has still not been properly evaluated. I refer to that of Jung's own journey through what he called "Active Imagination," and its relevance today as a Western approach to Buddhist meditation practice.

We are now more aware of what ancient Buddhist Psychology can truly offer modern psychology: a genuine opportunity for dialogue. As an integrated and complete system of thought, it offers us a complementary vision of our fundamental human questioning about the nature of mind, the limits of our potential for human evolution, the possibilities of developing mental health and the methods and practices for psychological and physical transformation. More specifically, the study of the mind through meditation practice can bring us to a profound transformation of ourselves. And where as our clinical practice is concerned, we can experience the energy of being present, in the here and now, independently yet also in the same place as our patient: for together and yet in autonomy we are carefully watching without participating in the theaters of the mind—including our own!

Now, through the systematic and inspiring research of Junghian historian Sonu Shamdasani, we are discovering more of Jung's previously unpublished works and, as a result, become newly open to hear to what his friend Walter Evans-Wentz (well-known translator of *The Tibetan Book of the Dead*) said of him on 25 October 1936: "Dr Jung's contribution has a unique value; it shows the advanced scientific attitude of Europe's foremost psychologist and suggests how in future ages the sages of the Occident and those of the Orient will grasp each other's hand in mutual understanding and respect."[2] It seems feasible therefore, almost eighty years later, to approach

Jung's thinking again, rich in our own experience of the ever-expanding dialogue among Western psychology, neurobiology, and Buddhism and, most particularly, in light of the ever growing practice of Mindfulness meditation among psychoanalysts.

What is this affinity of which Jung speaks in his commentary to *The Secret of the Golden Flower*, where he also presents anonymously his own mandalas from the *Liber Novus*? What was this sudden breakthrough and the feeling that he could establish at last "ties with someone, with something" as he recalled to Aniela Jaffe?[3] As Sonu Shamdasani reveals, Jung's active imaginations, as recorded in his *Black Books*, tailed off in the 1920s; but in 1928 he suddenly found himself drawing and painting a most exquisite work which he called *The Yellow Castle*. It seemed to him to have a Chinese atmosphere. The central image is something that he himself likened to "the Imperial City in Peking" and to "the Heavenly Jerusalem of the Book of Revelation"—but above all to "the city of Brahma on Mount Meru" (Liber Novus).[4] Oddly enough, this particular Mandala emerged from his mind simultaneously if not synchronistically with a text that arrived to him from the other side of the world in ancient China, from Richard Wilhelm, *The Secret of the Golden Flower; A Chinese Book of Life*.

Jung was being asked to write a psychological commentary, an introduction, to a world that as a European he had not until then believed possible to approach—save for doing so with profound wariness and a sense of estrangement. And we know how throughout his work he warns only too often that we not allow ourselves to be dragged into superficial synchretisms in our studies of comparative cultures. He hated the confusion of rituals and values, what he called *cultural tourism*. But as he writes:

> I had been investigating the processes of the collective unconscious since the year 1913 and had obtained results that seemed to me questionable in more than one respect. They not only lay far beyond everything known to "academic" psychology but they also overstepped the bounds of any medical, purely personal, psychology. They confronted me with an extreme phenomenology to which hitherto known categories and methods could no longer be applied. My results, based on fifteen years of effort, seemed inconclusive because no possibility of comparison offered itself. I knew of no realm of human experience with which I might have backed up my findings with some degree of assurance. The text that Wilhelm sent me helped me out of this difficulty. It contained exactly those items I had long sought in vain among the Gnostics. Thus the text afforded me a welcome opportunity to publish, at least in provisional form, some of the essential results of my investigations.[5]

THE COLLECTIVE UNCONSCIOUS

Jung was looking at "results" that were "as yet completely unknown and only in the process of transformation": "The collective unconscious—so far as we can say anything about it at all—appears to consist of mythological motifs or primordial images, for which reason the myths of all nations are its real exponents. In fact, the whole of mythology could be taken as a sort of projection of the collective unconscious . . . We can therefore study the collective unconscious in two ways, either in mythology or in the analysis of the individual."[6]

Already in 1898 Jung had been immensely influenced by the work of Eduard von Hartmann (1842–1906). Jung had found in the Basel Library a copy of his *Philosophy of the Unconscious* where the emergence of the unconscious was not accidental but represented an inherent teleological striving toward a higher state of consciousness. He even envisioned the redemption of the world as a return to an original state before its commencement. For Hartmann the ultimate goal of the individual should be "the complete devotion of the personality to the world-process for the sake of its goal, the general world redemption."[7] It is not difficult to hear the echo of a Buddhist's striving toward compassion for all sentient beings or the Bodhisattva's vow to forgo personal liberation until all sentient beings reach enlightenment. Similarly, we can here perceive intimations of the "Clear Light," that "original state prior to the world's commencement" expressed, for example, in Dzogchen and Nyingma Buddhism (the essential nature of the mind that is indefinable yet characterized as being of the nature of emptiness and luminosity).

Regarding Buddhist doctrine and its influence on him as well as on his own clinical practice, Jung would later write, in 1955:[8] "I but follow the trace of a design that exists since about 2,000 years through the spiritual history of humanity." He continues:

> The doctor must wage a war without mercy against suffering. It is therefore not surprising that he considers these philosophical and religious attitudes insomuch as they can be of service to him, as so many health systems or healing systems. And that he precisely recognizes the Buddha whose teachings had as a central theme the healing of suffering through the supreme development of Consciousness as the most trusted ally in the treatment of patients.[9]

Later, in his Commentary to the *Bardo Thodol*—"A faithful companion, to which I owe not only many suggestions and discoveries but also some absolutely essential ideas"—he discovered "the book had been created through connecting with the archetypal contents of the unconscious."[10]

Jung seemed, then, to be following in the wake of an oriental renaissance that had ushered in the possibility of a truly universal humanism, as Raymond Schwab used to say.[11] This was nourished by his readings, his huge collection of Indian materials and all thirty volumes of the *Sacred Books of the East*[12] that sat on his library shelf. But with the arrival of Wilhelm's challenge, his deepening understanding of Eastern thought came to inform his perspectives and his understanding of the phylogenetic collective unconscious of mankind.

Shamdasani says that for Jung the East could literally be found within![13] Yet this inner territory was so confusing and difficult to navigate that only by reading the *Secret of the Golden Flower*, and in the actual experience of *the mandala as a circumambulation of the center*, could Jung live the event that was truly to bring him out of his isolation. The commentary that he was to write would reveal for the first time his understanding of the significance of the mandala and allow a new style of writing, one that disguised his most personal experiences (now published in the *Liber Novus*) but which he then used as his guiding truth through the allegorical labyrinths of the Chinese text. He felt that the mandalas he himself was drawing were surging up in direct confirmation of the common archetypal deposit that one might call the *imaginarium* of humanity. Jung's experience was that of living a real expression of the inner powers of the mind manifesting themselves as symbols: symbols working, producing effects and rendering visible the structure of the process to which our need for inner transformation is subjugated.

THE MANDALA

Jung was looking for some way to convey the insights from his own visionary (and sometimes terrifying) experiences, from his own fantasies and precognitions of collective events and finally to understand that "incapacity"[14] —that emptiness—which could revitalize the power that animated the correspondences between private fantasies and public events. He had tried to dramatize his thinking in pictorial form and already in the *Black Books* had dated his entries and added his reflections on his state of mind and personal difficulties. He records his self experimentations as he attempts to recover his experience of the Soul and, finally, of the Divine in 1913 and 1914. Just a few years later, so much blood shed into the abyss of World War I anguished him "because people did not know that their brother was themselves."[15] It was necessary to overcome the hero in ourselves—the ego—a Buddhist might reply.

He had a dream of slaying Siegfried, the god within himself, and thus of slaying his own power, his own ruthlessness and pride. He began deliberately to re-evoke the dream image in his waking state and he practiced entering into the figure, dramatizing his mind's experience of being Siegfried. This is not unlike the widespread Buddhist method of contemplating that which constitutes our ego imprisonment in order to achieve freedom. To develop compassion, for instance, we are invited to fully enter our own greed and selfishness, our own ego centeredness, so that we may ultimately enter a state beyond it.

Jung was ever more disturbed and ever more committed to reaching beyond what he called his own schizophrenia.[16] He felt he might kill himself if he could not penetrate the significance of murdering the hero whose horn had sounded, when all had been drenched in a terrible rainfall. He found himself caught in the dynamic pattern (common, of course, to all depth psychology) that separates the conscious from the unconscious, and was basically struggling between the developing extremities of the dichotomy. What became juxtaposed, as a result, were the conscious psychological aspect of life with which the "I" identifies, and the repressed material of the unconscious: namely, that which heretofore had remain unseen, even ignored or denied, and gone on living as something "Other."

Jung had also observed, in the course of his clinical work, the centrifugal movement of the libido in those subjects directed toward the outer world—the extroverts—and he had contrasted this with the centripetal movement of those whose interests were directed principally toward the world within (the introverts). Somehow his understanding of the collective psychological dynamic of mankind was splitting into irreconcilable antitheses. The contraposition that he came to discover, however, in *The Secret of the Golden Flower*, was between two conscious principles, the Yin and the Yang, the dark and the light, the masculine and the feminine. The Eastern point of view embraces their complementarity, their continuous alterance, their circular interbeing. Willhelm gave him the possibility of reading into Chinese wisdom to see how, when the Yang had reached the pinnacle of its strength, deep within its structure, the seed of its opposite, the dark power of the Yin, would begin to expand in the turning of time. Jung understood this as the ancient Greek concept of *eniantrodomia*. He saw now how the day gives way to the night and the seasons find the rhythm of their cycles. Here, finally, was Jung's relief!

He discovered that beyond the clashing opposites there was ultimate freedom (*nirdvandva*). Moreover, he found in "the journey of the East that since immemorial times has been taken . . . by those incapable of completely separating the opposites of human nature," a way of himself not losing "all conscious reciprocal inter-connection between his extremes, a way of not losing that vitally necessary unity of the person."[17] The circular process could now become his new dynamic way forward and beyond the conflict. In his *Liber Novus* he thus comments on one of his own early mandalas: "This stone, set so beautifully, is certainly the Lapis Philosophorum. It is harder than the diamond. But it expands into space through four distinct qualities, namely breadth, height, depth and time."[18] Already here we perceive the inflections of alchemy, the study that later would so intensely preoccupy Jung and deepen his spiritual and psychological understanding. It was, indeed, in hermetic philosophy that he would find three basic laws that would serve to frame the symbolism of the individuation process:

1. The universe forms a whole whose unity is essential, as expressed by the symbol of the snake devouring its tail;
2. There is analogy and reciprocity between what is above and what is below, as indicated by the Emerald Tablet text of Hermes Trismegistus;
3. The visible represents the exteriorization of the invisible, and the spiritual is hidden behind the material and is a transformation of it.

Jung was discovering his "Way," the Tao, the unifying circular path, leading him to abandon the linear method of swinging like a pendulum in an ever expanding arc between division and dichotomy. This would also prove to be the "Way" that would slowly reveal how he could share his experiences and develop his own Western way of practicing with patients.

Let us turn now to cast back a glance at a Buddhist understanding of the Mandala. Buddhist cosmology is based on two main conceptual systems of the structure of the Universe. One is derived from the early Abhidharmakosha (fourth century AD), and the other from the Kalachakra Tantra that was introduced into Tibet only in 1024 AD. In the first case our world system is seen to have begun with an *inward* movement of four strong directional winds produced by collective Karma; these then converged into the void of space. According to the myth, the clouds and lightning and torrents of rain then churned within space producing a yellow foam that solidified into earth and sank below the surface of the water. At last, from the very center of this cosmic ocean, Mt Meru emerged out of the waters. Seven concentric rings of golden mountains formed around Mt Meru and, surrounding them all, another vast circular saltwater ocean was bounded on its outer circumference by a fence of iron mountains. Here in this ocean there arose the four directional continents. So it is that from space to the winds (clouds) to fire (lightning), water, and, finally, in the solidification of earth are manifested the five elements that permeate the whole cosmos. These even penetrate into the mandala of individual form and into the secret body mandala, where the movement of the winds passes through the subtle channels, or chakras, of the body itself. At the center stands the axis of the universe, Mt. Meru, which ultimately comes to be revealed as the spine and the central spiritual channel of the human body.

The other conceptual system structure, that of the tradition of the Kalachakra Tantra, assumes that many cosmoses arise, pass away and arise again in endless periods of time. Not all the atoms of the five elements disappear at the end of an epoch; they simply fall ever further apart and outwards, and become separated from each other by space atoms. As a result of the past stockpiled collective Karma from earlier ages of the world, the atoms again form new combinations. The air atoms come together and bring about storm winds which in turn ignite the fire atoms and cause lightning. Next follow the formations of water atoms which bring rain, and rainbows appear as manifestations of the first earth atoms that become thicker and result in solid earth. Space atoms fill in the void between the other atoms. The cosmos is concentric and is structured like a pyramid. Mt. Meru is not square (as it is in the Abhidharmakosha System) but round, and tapers toward the base where four colossal disks surround the center, along with six concentric land masses, six mountain walls, six oceans, and the twelve wind tracks on which the planets glide in concentric circles. The actual ritual geometric diagram is the symbol of the cosmic elements. In this mandala, the deities are assembled and situated in a clearly ordered pattern. In the end, the expanded three-dimensional symmetrical structure turns and falls back into the stillness of the center.

According to an important Tibetan source[19] four types of mandala can be distinguished: those made from powdered colors, those painted on textiles, those formed in the mind through meditation and finally the body itself, seen as the inner mandala to be offered to one's spiritual teacher and to the Buddha, to the Dharma and the Sangha. Now, is it possible to explain the mandala ritual? The Buddhist underlines the relativity of our knowledge, and the different levels and relative truths of our different stages of understanding. In this spirit, and in Jung's words: "The goal of contemplating the process depicted in the mandala is that the yogin shall become inwardly aware of the deity: that is to say, through contemplation he recognizes himself as the deity and thus returns from the illusion of an individual existence to the universal totality of the divine state."[20]

ACTIVE IMAGINATION

Jung had discovered with his patients that the important problems of life are all insoluble—necessarily so, given that they express the inevitable polarity inherent in all self-regulating systems. Therefore it is no longer a question of finding resolution but rather an ability to go beyond, to step outside the confines of the problem itself, to discover the interconnectedness within a totality, to go further than the schemata of our envisioning and thinking processes. Our mind tends to restrict itself to the field of prejudice and bind our sense of space inside the insuperable. To exemplify this, in a very simple way, we are reminded of an exercise often offered by Mindfulness instructors today, which is based on the challenge to interconnect nine points with four continuous strokes of the pen (never lifting the pen off the paper), so creating a geometric pattern that never overlays a line already drawn. One is faced with the conviction that there exists an invisible barrier that imprisons the drawing within a rectangle (expressed by the points) but rarely discovering instead, that in order to achieve the new shape one must only "step outside" this imaginary (and invisible) boundary, elongating only one line beyond the points.

This change of perspective frees the mind and breaks through the old, illusory habit of control. In Jungian terms, this suddenly animates the space between contrasting inner and outer forces. A sudden new understanding produces new movement, and there is a new flow and circulation of energy. *Something* pushes one out of the conflict and into new "sacred space." This process was evidenced in Jung's work with his patients who spontaneously, in states of psychological dissociation, seemed to present mandala images arising out of visions and dreams. Jung felt they were there to be painted or sculpted, to be danced in contemplation of the mind. They formed the basis of a ritual to be performed and, like the meditator who approaches the divine center from without, proceeded in concentric sequences of movement around the center of the mandala surface that would ultimately become the seat of their own *Mandala Deity*.

Where the images presented themselves as thoughts, they seemed to take on an abstract shape and crystallize in light, the origin of form itself. Jung spoke of the intensity of this incredible wakeful awareness—a source of vital energy—as True Being. This is the primordial, eternal spirit that he had encountered in *The Secret of the Golden Flower*. This is the creative point from which all emerges and, as in the Kalachakra Mandala, is the very source that enters into sacred union with life—space. Wheeling energy turns the circle, the Tao governs, and this rounding action then becomes non-action since everything that is peripheral must finally submit to the center. Jung then noted how each one of us, with our own personality, tends to condense aspects of this energy in spontaneous and significant figures, numinous symbols that seem to emerge ever more powerfully into the foreground, expressing, influencing and fascinating the psyche. As Shamdasani states: "Jung was composing a thoroughly scholarly psychology that at the same time placed the greatest emphasis on the spontaneous emergence of figures from within the individual without prior learning."[21]

Around this time, Jung's interests and influences were again becoming more academic. He was establishing the Eranos Conferences in Ascona (1933) where he began to focus on the history of religion and culture, especially on the connections between East and West. Understandably, the comparative study of the individuation process that was occupying Jung required the collaboration of experts in the field of comparative religion. So it was that important figures including Heinrich Zimmer, D. T. Suzuki, Giuseppe Tucci,

Karl Kerenyi and Mircea Eliade all came together to exchange and enrich each other's researches.

In this context, and directly concerning the individuation process, the Buddhist perspective in Deity Yoga may have inspired Jung to remember that the actual practice of self-generation depends on the relationship between the inner offering (the meditator who, after purification, presents himself as an offering) and the mandala (the outer circumference) that results from the identity of the emanated deities with the female and male Buddhas who reside in the Center. The meditator becomes the deity and then brings his breath under control so as to calm his mind and focus it on a single point. He observes either the form of the mantra letters in the heart-center or, by simply sounding the mantra, he may refine his meditation on emptiness in various stages and eventually realize that even the deity's body and mind are without inherent existence. The meditator has allowed light to radiate from the syllable in his heart, setting in motion the whole visualization: and "because of this the fire flares."[22] In Jung's own words:

> I personally know individuals who have experienced this phenomenon. For as much as I have discovered, the acute state of consciousness was as intense as it was abstract—a detached form of awareness. . . . The fact that common bodily sensations disappear during this experience indicates that their specific energy is redirected to reinforce an intense clarity of Consciousness. The phenomenon is usually spontaneous, it comes and goes autonomously. Its effect is surprising in so much as it produces a distancing from what we consider to be our inner personality, from emotional and intellectual involvement. It produces a unity of Being that is felt generally as ultimate freedom![23]

One of Jung's fellow Eranos researchers, the Tibetologist Giuseppe Tucci suggests that this experience of self-generation within the body of the central deity comes about in a body of light. Deities are visible because of the emitted or intrinsic light that radiates from them. They can be luminescent, opalescent or scintillating, or composed of fluid light. Tucci writes: "Everywhere a common fundamental trait is evident: photism, the great importance attached to light, whether as a generative principle, as a symbol of supreme reality or as a visible perceptible manifestation of that reality. Light, from which all comes and which is present in ourselves."[24] Jung's own experience in the construction of his yellow castle was of a golden light, which he recognized as the Tao. Here he found the origin of the Golden Flower itself; *the altar where Consciousness (Being) and Life (Space) are germinating together, inseparably merged in the One Single Sparkling Flame.* Surely these words must have been written by a man who had had the experience himself, even though he attributes to his patients the journey through such visualizations to reach what we might well call now our Buddha-nature.

Jung also found that some of his patients were able to surrender to this experience more easily than others: "I have been profoundly impressed to realize that which turns up as something completely new [in analysis] only very rarely or never in fact, corresponds to our conscious expectations . . . and yet this new image remains a peculiarly suitable expression of the integrity of that personality, in fact one could not imagine a more perfect representation."[25] Here, however, a question arises: what had these patients actually done to activate and express these images, to paint their mandalas or to bring about in themselves the power of this guiding principle?

"Inasmuch as I could see they had done nothing at all [*wu wei*] they had simply allowed it to happen." Jung's experience was unlike that of the Buddhist meditator: "Never had this been generated intentionally or consciously, rather the experience seemed to have been generated by and through the flowing of Time."[26] For someone to change, they actually cannot go on being the same, using the same tools, striving in the same way they have up until then, they must allow *change to happen* to them, they must be able to let go and get out of the way for real transformation to take place! Here Jung's own needs emerge, alongside his role as teacher and deep-seated longing to develop a method of his own. He was looking to elaborate a practice that could now become an intentional and conscious stimulation of "wu wei"—the attitude that could allow and accept that even these irrational and incomprehensible images take their respectable place in our lives, in our hearts, in our minds, there to work their transformations.

He is fully aware that the Oriental has the authority of his ancient culture and its many techniques to gain access to this higher consciousness. He bewails the Westerner's battle, on the contrary, against all his cultural, intellectual, and religious points of reference, and the fact that he will have to leave behind the security and convictions of his tradition. He will have to commit his very integrity, for only by virtue of this integrity will progress be won and the snares of inauthenticity avoided.

Jung sets about discovering *an art that almost no one knows*, that of learning to train the psyche to *let things happen*, the problem being that the rational mind constantly intervenes, trying to help, to deny or to correct and in any case seems unable to leave the psychic process undisturbed. So it is now a question of constructing a discipline. His method, Active Imagination, begins by observing with detachment or objectivity the developing inner image. He says that the process is not only due to an intense unconscious dynamic but also to that human tendency to distinguish with the conscious "I"—the eye that sees—that which appears before us. This conscious attitude then welcomes the vague and fragmentary connections and associations between the swirling parts of the emerging picture, welling up, as it were, from the underworld of the unconscious.

It is by welcoming and embracing the split-off or separated partial psychic systems that it becomes possible for the human being to encounter his own divinities and devils. It is a question of distinguishing and personifying the unconscious figures, of learning to recognize their psychic power, of entering into a relationship that can revere such images. Then and only then, when the emptiness of the phenomenon as such is experienced—when truly the individual feels a sense of insufficiency, loneliness and longing—is the transcendent function triggered and activated. This is the powerful desire of the soul to connect again with wholeness and totality, to merge again in the cosmological order of all things, into ultimate union with all human beings.

Practically speaking, we might think there is nothing simpler, at the start of such a process, than to observe the forming of the developing image. But often enough the image refuses to form itself, deemed by the ego to be too stupid or too banal. Judgment creeps in, justifying the pointlessness of the exercise, invoking boredom or distractions and a difficulty in concentrating. Reason raises all kinds of objections, the mind itself—as we know so well from our meditation exercises—is intent on constantly moving erratically in every other direction away from the one upon which we are trying to focus. And yet, as Jung points out, this image may well be the one that will lead us into ever more profound understandings, becoming powerfully present, god-like, and luminous: offering itself that we may merge temporarily with its radiance and therein allow ourselves to be touched, even transformed. Understandably enough, Jung admonishes that we take the image seriously and treat it with respect.

A first phase therefore requires that we arrest the "mad mind" (the monkey mind) as the Zen Buddhists call it. Once the ego is quieted, our inner space gives way to gradually ever more intense concentration on a specific stimulus, and the "I" trains itself to become indifferent to its thoughts. The second internal phase demands that images that are forming be welcomed, accepted, embraced and never ignored or allowed carelessly to dissolve. A third phase must be expressive and representative: some form must accommodate the mental images and allow them to be seen, whether through writing, painting, music or dance. This moment needs to involve the body and, as suggested, find material form. Herein, we could simply state, lies truly the mandala ritual of Active Imagination.

But here too the emotions are involved, and strong affects come into play, as the body participates and shares in the experience. Only too easily we lose connection with the visualization: for as its power becomes too strong, it risks overwhelming us. To this end, Jung states that the psycho-physiological altered state known in meditation must here be practiced. *Meditatio*, as it used to be called, is the conversation that can be initiated with a god, and has always been the word used when an intimate communication with the invisible or ineffable is invoked. And it is in the recognition of our uncertainty, of our condition of precariousness, our transience and our impermanence, that eventually we shall be brought to our knees before the unknown. We shall discover an attitude of submission toward that which transcends us.

The last phase requires that the person truly believe in what he is seeing and react as though he were in the reality of the visualization. Now we leave the audience, to walk onto the stage of the theatre of the mind where we become the actor, part of our own inner play. This practice of Active Imagination brings a capacity to live, even for brief moments, as acting subjects of our inner imaginative world, capable of "psicopoiesis," that longed-for symbolical reconfiguration of our lives. Yes, it's true, we still try to apply our critical faculties and continue to attempt interpretations; but it is a question of holding back the reins of our impatient intellectual need to understand, that impetuous principle of comprehension, which only too quickly tries to make sense of the emerging material without allowing it to evolve adequately. We need rather to confront and balance our attitude and face a peer player of sorts, another position of the mind that is equally strong: on the one hand the irrepressible ego-need enacted and personified, and on the other a still voiceless truth that spontaneously, on the inner psychic stage, is expressing itself uninfluenced by the individual's will, much as the outside objective world remains equally untouched by that which we desire or by that from which we escape. Ultimately we will be embraced by the significance of this dialogue and, in the Mandala, come to transform the autonomous complex into a relationship, wherein to activate "wu wei," a form of voluntary sacrifice, an active passivity, an intentional inertia of our consciousness that here abandons itself to the totality of Being.

Active Imagination for Jung is the "Way" (Tao) of awareness that reunites that which was divided, that activates the transcendent function and unifies opposites in a higher state of Consciousness.

> Only now do I come to what the Mandala really is: "Formation, transformation, the eternal mind's recreation, and that is the self, the wholeness of the personality which, when everything is well, is harmonious, but which can bear no self-deception. My mandala images were cryptograms of the state of myself, which were delivered to me each day."[27]

NOTES

1. Jung, C. G., Wilhelm, R. ed. 1981. *Il segreto del fiore d'oro*, 43–63. Turin: Boringhieri; Authors' translation.
2. Evans-Wentz to Edward Bing. 25 October 1936. Rascher Archives, Zurich Central Library.
3. Jung C. G., Jaffè A. ed. 1977. *Jung C. G. Memories, Dreams, Reflections*, 197. New York: Vintage.

4. Peck, J. ed. 1992. *The Visio Dorothei: Desert Context, Imperial Setting, Later Alignments: Studies in the Dreams and Visons of Saint Pachomius and Dorotheus, Son of Quintus.* Diploma Thesis, Zurich: CG Jung Institute.
5. Jung's Commentary to the secret of golden flower. Read, H., Fordham, M., Adler, G., McGuire, Wm. ed. 1953–1979. *The Collected Works of C. G. Jung*, 13: 3–4. Princeton: Princeton University Press.
6. The Structure of the Psyche. Read, H., Fordham, M., Adler, G., McGuire, Wm. ed. 1953–1979. *The Collected Works of C. G. Jung*, 8: 325. Princeton: Princeton University Press.
7. Berlin 1872, translated by W. Coupland, London: R. Paul, Trench, and Traubner, 1931.
8. Neumann, K. 1955. "The teachings of Gautama Buddha." In *La saggezza orientale. Raccolta di scritti di C. G. Jung*, edited by L. Arigemma. Turin: Bollati Boringhieri.
9. Ibid.
10. Read, H., Fordham, M., Adler, G., McGuire, Wm. ed. 1953–1979. *The Collected Works of C. G. Jung,* 18, 833. Princeton: Princeton University Press.
11. The Oriental Renaissance: Europe's Rediscovery of India and the East, 1680–1880, translated by G. Patterson-Black and V. Renning, New York: Columbia University Press 1984.
12. Muller, M. ed. 1879–1910. *The Sacred Books of the East.* 50 vols. Oxford: Oxford University Press.
13. "Il Futuro dell'Immaginazione; Il Libro Rosso di CG Jung," Lectio magistralis by Sonu Shamdasani, April 2012, National Library, Rome.
14. Jung, C. G., Shamdasani, S. ed. 2009. *The Red Book: Liber Novus*, 238ff. New York: W.W. Norton.
15. 18 December 1913, Murder of the Hero; Jung C. G., and Shamdasani, S. ed. 2009. *The Red Book: Liber Novus*, 241ff. New York: W.W. Norton.
16. McGuire W., Hull, R. F. C. ed. 1977. *Combat interview (1952), C. G. Jung Speaking: Interviews and Encounters,* 233–34. Princeton: Princeton University Press. Bollingen Series.
17. Jung, C. G., Wilhelm, R. ed. 1981. *Il segreto del fiore d'oro*, 36. Turin: Boringhieri; Authors' translation.
18. Jung, C. G., Shamdasani, S. ed. 2009. *The Red Book: Liber Novus*, 121. New York: W.W. Norton.
19. Lessing, F., Wayman, A. ed. 1978. *Mkhas-grub-rje's Fundamentals of the Buddhist Tantras.* Paris: The Hague.
20. Read, H., Fordham, M., Adler, G., McGuire, Wm. ed. 1953–1979. *The Collected Works of C. G. Jung*, 9.1. Princeton: Princeton University Press.
21. Shamdasani, S. 2003. *Jung and the Making of Modern Psychology: The Dream of a Science.* Cambridge: Cambridge University Press.
22. Brauen, M. 1997. *The Mandala, Sacred Circle in Tibetan Buddhism*. London: Serindia Publications.
23. Jung, C. G., Wilhelm, R. ed. 1981. *Il segreto del fiore d'oro*, p. 51. Turin: Boringhieri. Authors' translation.
24. Tucci, G. 1949. *Teoria e Pratica del Mandala*. Rome: Ubalini Editore.
25. Jung, C. G., Wilhelm, R. ed. 1981. *Il segreto del fiore d'oro*, 39. Turin: Boringhieri; Authors' translation.
26. Ibid., 39.
27. Jung C. G., Jaffè A. ed. 1977. *Jung C.G. Memories, Dreams, Reflections*, 196. New York: Vintage.

REFERENCES

Arigemma, L. ed. 2009. *La saggezza orientale. Raccolta di scritti di C. G. Jung*. Turin: Bollati Boringhieri.

Beer, R. 1999. *The Encyclopedia of Tibetan Symbols and Motifs*. London: Serindia Publications.

Brauen, M. 1997. *The Mandala, Sacred Circle in Tibetan Buddhism*. London: Serindia Publications.

Gyatso, T., the fourteenth Dalai Lama. 2004. *Dzogchen: The Heart Essence of the Great Perfection*. New York: Snow Lion Publications.

Innocenzi, R. 1990. *L'Immaginazione Attiva in CG Jung*. Rome: Melusina Editrice.

Jung, C. G., Jaffè A. ed. 1977. *Jung C. G. Memories, Dreams, Reflections*. New York: Vintage.

Jung, C. G., Wilhelm R. ed. 1981. *Il segreto del fiore d'oro*. Turin: Boringhieri.

Jung, C. G., Shamdasani, S. ed. 2009. *The Red Book: Liber Novus*. New York: W.W. Norton.

Kabat-Zinn, J. 2009. *Full Catastrophe Living: Using the Wisdom of Your Body and Mind to Face Stress, Pain, and Illness*. New York: Bantam Dell.

Lessing, F., Wayman, A. ed. 1978. *Mkhas-grub-rje's Fundamentals of the Buddhist Tantras*. Paris: The Hague.

Muller, M. ed. 1879–1910. *The Sacred Books of the East*. 50 vols. Oxford: Oxford University Press.

Peck, John. ed. 1992. *The Visio Dorothei: Desert Context, Imperial Setting, Later Alignments: Studies in the Dreams and Visions of Saint Pachomius and Dorotheus, Son of Quintus*. Diploma Thesis, Zurich: CG Jung Institute.

Read, H., Fordham, M., Adler, G., McGuire, Wm. ed. 1953–1979. *The Collected Works of C. G. Jung*. Princeton: Princeton University Press.

Sambhava, P. 1994. *The Tibetan Book of the Dead*. London: Aquarian.

Segal, Z. V., Williams, J. M. G., Teasdale, J. D. 2012. *Mindfulness-Based Cognitive Therapy for Depression*. New York: Guilford Press.

Shamdasani, S. 2003. *Jung and the Making of Modern Psychology: The Dream of a Science*. Cambridge: Cambridge University Press.

Tucci, G. 1949. *Teoria e Pratica del Mandala*. Rome: Ubalini Editore.

———. 1976. *Le Religioni del Tibet*. Rome: Edizioni Mediterranee.

Postscript

Reflections on Buddhism and Psychoanalysis

Adam Phillips[1]

If we ask where can we find ourselves, where are the various versions of the self we've invented, one answer is in language. Both Buddhism and psychoanalysis are eloquent testimony to how we go about describing selves, as they introduce us to a cast of characters, a repertoire of familiar and unfamiliar figures: the Asian self, the familiar self, the no-self, the self-contained, self-reliant, and self-directed Western individual, the Great Self, and selflessness. And of course once you've got a group of characters, there's a drama. What are they *going* to do with each other? What do they believe consciously and unconsciously they're capable of doing together?

One belief they seem to share is that there is something to be done, that there are projects: fulfilling one's role in the social hierarchy, seeking enlightenment or cure, making oneself enviable, going to conferences. Something, in other words, is wanted—even if wanting itself is considered to be part of the problem. Talking about it in this way might make it sound as though we're in a kind of supermarket of cultural forms, where we can simply[y choose whatever sounds best. But the word "we," of course, Is part of the problem here. Who is "we" supposed to refer to? its varied usage presents us with a paradox.

On the one hand, selves are embedded in—that is, made possible by—specific forms of life. To describe a self is to describe a world, a culture that makes a place for such a self. And yet selves, or other versions of selves, might also resemble, or we may wish that they resemble, commodities: transportable, available if we can afford them, something we can try out for a while. In a way, like people, such descriptions of selves can increasingly be seen as socially mobile, or under severe economic constraints. Some might say there are as many selves as we can imagine. And others might say that there is something radically wrong with a culture that produces a self that can believe such a thing.

The history of psychoanalysis has, to some extent, reflected this dilemma of whether the solution is the problem or the problem the solution. But psychoanalysis has only been alive in its muddles; its clarities have been stultifying. Is the aim of analysis, as some of Freud's work suggests, to strengthen character, making the ego a kind of psychic imperialist? Where Id was there ego shall be, and so on? Or, as the early Freud and Lacan suggest, is it precisely a strong ego, or rather the illusion of a strong ego, that people are suffering from? Is knowing who you are, turning yourself into a quasi-fictional character with so-called insight, the project? Or is the project discovering and learning to tolerate and enjoy the fact that you don't know who you are, and that in fact you have no way of knowing? Is this so called self a kind of continual process of surprise or an idol to be revered and endlessly fashioned?

It was, of course, only analysts after Freud who seemed to need the concept of self. Freud himself leaves us with two instructive possibilities: either implicitly the word "self" can be used to refer to the sum of the parts he's described, a kind of superordinate term for id, ego, and superego; or, because of these parts he described, by their very nature and relationship, there can be no unitary "self" that such a word could refer to. A word like "self," Winnicott wrote, naturally knows more than we do. It uses us and can command us. Freud may have distrusted what the word supposedly knew . . . what some Buddhist critics refer to as the reification and absolutization of the self.

It is, I think, reassuring that psychoanalytic means tend to turn to psychoanalytic ends. The patient is not cured by free association, Ferenczi writes, he is cured when he can free-associate. The patient is not cured because he remembers, Lacan writes, he remembers because he is cured. Both of these statements reveal a commitment to process: to the idea that psychoanalysis makes possible something open-ended. The patient is deemed to be suffering from the fact that he has come to certain conclusions about himself. The self by definition is that which is forever unfinished.

The risk is that psychoanalysis can become subtly and not so subtly conformist; that in its theoretical repertoire of possible and acceptable selves, psychoanalysis offers more of the problem that Buddhism addresses—that is to say, the unconscious compulsion to reify "self," to secure it by making it somehow seem real, substantial, and present. Perhaps an inappropriately pragmatic question in this context might be: What do we want the idea of a self to do for us? How would our lives be better, as William James might have asked, if we had "selves"? It's my impression that any given self, any sense of representations we've collected into a self-image or self-story, Is invented for a project. It intends, as it were, a certain kind of performance, which in turn intends a wishful transition: toward a state of no-self, perhaps, or self-integration or wealth or domination of other people, or whatever. At least in the first instance, the culture provides the individual with the repertoire of possible projects. Thus it is misleading, for example, for Winnicott to distinguish between true and false selves, since the individuals inherit their criteria of authenticity from their culture. It may be more useful to think of a person, at least in psychoanalytic language, as the conscious and unconscious performer of a *preferred* self. Both psychoanalysis and Buddhism offer descriptions of such preferred selves and how they might be fashioned. Ultimately, when we try to define the nature of the self, we are not, I think, talking about who we are, but about who we want to be.

Their approaches to the causes of suffering involve both psychoanalysis and Buddhism in stories about origins and stories about agency: stories about when the pain begins, and what or who has made it happen, And to understand one's life, or the stories about it, is to understand what's wrong with one's life: for living a life entails imagining what one lacks. What we call suffering is the acknowledgment of this insufficiency. Our relationship to suffering, what we make of it, the role we assign it in our psychic economy, is integral to the perplexing logic of life. Psychoanalysis, one could say, is the art of turning pain into meaning: a project that it shares, despite its own disclaimers, with many religions.

When people turn pain into sexual excitement, psychoanalysts call them perverse. When they turn pain into meaning, they call them corrective or insightful or good patients. Psychoanalysts, like Buddhists perhaps, assume that suffering is something we're compelled to work on and with. Our survival, not to mention the very beginnings of our lives, has depended on how we have done this. But where do we get our descriptions from—both of what suffering is and from what it is we are *suffering?* How do we know, at any given moment, that suffering is what we are doing?

Great religious leaders, and secular leaders like Marx and Freud, are people who tell us what we are suffering from. Their conceptions of cure or enlightenment or liberation show us what we lack, they reveal the cause and nature of our suffering. They become, or we make them, the masters of the causes of suffering. What's appealing about figures like Buddha and Freud is not that they attract worshippers, but that both of them have given us good, convincing accounts of the causes of suffering and, of course, of the causes of idolatry. Both of them suggest, from quite different perspectives, that our suffering is the consequence of false belief. The question becomes, then: To what extent are they inviting us, explicitly or implicitly, to believe in them? Are we cured or enlightened by leaning to speak their languages? by attending to those things—grief, desire, delusion—they consider to be important? Their own life stories and work are, perhaps inevitably, and at least in part, a critique of the belief systems they inherited; and both of them, I think, can be described as doing something quite paradoxical: not necessarily, or only, replacing one belief system with another, but making us wonder about belief itself. But if belief is somehow integral to suffering, what can we replace belief—or, for that matter, attachment—with?

Both Freud and Buddha suggest that suffering is a consequence of fixed belief. Idolatry is a form of torture, often socially legitimated. A kind of addiction. The risk, then, is that concepts like causality and suffering become scientific or quasi-religious idols, assumptions we come to worship. Embedded in specific cultural contexts, both imply unquestioned worldviews and ways of life. And though a concern like "the *causes* of suffering" might seem to provide a link between psychoanalysis and Buddhism, it also stands, in point of fact, as a question. In what sense Is the phrase "the causes of suffering" meaningful to both groups? The cause of suffering, one would think, is a universal preoccupation, but on this subject or indeed any other, how will we know if Buddhism and psychoanalysis are similar and/or different? Or to put it another way, who's to say? Especially if we consider that there is not one thing, one social practice, called psychoanalysis, any more than there is one Buddhism. Who, then, is in the position to make the useful or the credible link, and what do we want the links to do for us?

For some people, like Mark Epstein, it's both plausible and necessary to translate the Buddhist explanations of suffering into the language of psychoanalysis. Here Freud's "oceanic feeling" fits neatly into the Buddhist cosmology, as do any number of references from the writings of Guntrip, Eigen, Shaffer, and even Winnicott, who all make Buddhism and psychoanalysis seem both complementary and mutually illuminating. As Michael Robbins explains: "Both conceive of suffering as the product of disharmony or division within the mind." But he also qualifies this by suggesting that "it's certainly worthy of consideration that suffering may actually be experienced differently in each culture." Ultimately, it's the differences, the *obstacles* to translation, that preoccupy such thinkers. In this view, each model may finally be inadequate to describe the other; maybe psychoanalysis and Buddhism cannot be transferred or translated into the culture of the other.

For how can we tell, and who's to say, if one person or culture has understood another person or culture? Our wish to respect difference can be used to avoid contact; our denial of difference can make contact impossible. It will have escaped no one's attention just how interestingly symmetrical the positions of Epstein and Robbins are on the causes of suffering. For Epstein, translation is more than possible; for Michael Robbins, it may be misleading. We all know the political consequences that suffering entails in fantasies of purity. And we now live in patchwork cultures in which such fantasies are both harder to sustain, requiring more and more violence, and always something of a temptation. Personally, I would prefer to live in a world in which people can find and use what moves them, mostly for reasons they don't understand, to take them in directions of which they are unaware. Not a quest for purity, but for enlivening combinations. Perhaps each of us should take whatever appeals to us out of psychoanalysis and Buddhism, and from whatever else, to make something of our own. And if someone were then to object, "But this is really not psychoanalysis you're practicing," or "This is not really Buddhism," we should take it as a compliment. On the causes of suffering we need as many good stories as we can get hold of.

NOTES

1. "Reflections on Buddhism and Psychoanalysis," by Adam Phillips was first published in *The Couch and the Tree: Dialogues in Buddhism and Psychoanalysis* (Anthony Molino, editor), pp. 195–199. Originally published by North Point Press, New York, 1998.

Appendix

Psychoanalysis and Buddhism as Cultural Institutions

Freud and the Dalai Lama

Jeremy D. Safran[1]

Although there was a flurry of interest in Buddhism by psychoanalytic thinkers such as Erich Fromm and Karen Horney in the 1950s and 1960s, this interest to some extent went underground until recent years. Currently, however, there is a marked resurgence of interest in the topic, as reflected in the popularity of books by authors such as Mark Epstein (1995, 1998, 2001), Jeffrey Rubin (1996), John Suler (1993), Anthony Molino (1998), and Barry Magid (2002). Epstein's books in particular seem to have struck a chord with both a nonprofessional audience and the psychoanalytic community. This increased interest parallels the tremendous popularity of Buddhism in popular culture, where, to paraphrase John Lennon's quip about the Beatles being more popular than Jesus Christ, the Dalai Lama wins the contest with Sigmund Freud, hands down. While the devout analyst may regard this statement as sacrilegious, like it or not, Buddhism gives every sign of being here to stay within our culture. and its influence on psychoanalytic thinking is growing.

How can we understand the growing interest by psychoanalysts in Buddhism? Psychoanalysis emerged at the beginning of the twentieth century when the secular worldview was ascendant. During this period the modernist worldview and the remarkable achievements of scientific rationalism were making the belief in God increasingly difficult for many people. Freud (1927, 1930) recognized that one of the primary functions of religion is to provide people with comfort in the face of the inevitable cruelties and indignities of life. But he believed that religion is an immature and self-deluding attempt to find comfort in the belief in the existence of an all-powerful and divine father figure. Instead, like many secularly oriented people of his day, he placed his faith in science.

Today, at the beginning of the twenty-first century, people no longer have the faith in science they once had, and the existential vacuum created by the death of God has become more pronounced than ever. It has become clear that psychoanalysis is not a science in the same sense that physics or chemistry are, but rather a secular form of spirituality. In some ways it functions to fill the void that was once filled by religion. But psychoanalysis does not focus extensively on the deeper existential questions that religions ask: What is the meaning of life in the face of our mortality? How do we as individuals fit in with the larger cosmos? How do we find meaning in the midst of the pain, suffering, and loss that are inevitably part of life?

Although many people in our culture experience a spiritual hunger, it is difficult if not impossible for somebody with a secular worldview to return to the religious worldview of premodern times. As the sociologist Philip Reiff (1966) has pointed out, the religious man of premodern times has been replaced by psychological man, and psychoanalysis has played an important role in this transformation. One of the appeals of Buddhism to a secular, psychoanalytic culture is that it is not a religion in the Judeo-Christian model, with belief in God and a theological doctrine demanding a leap of faith. As Stephen Batchelor (1997) puts it, Buddhism is a "religion without beliefs," or in Alan Watts's (1996) words, "a religion of no-religion." This makes Buddhism an appealing religion for the post-religious, postmodern person with a hunger for religion but no stomach for religious belief.

While the assertion that Buddhism does not require any kind of religious faith is true up to a point, the reality is more complex. Buddhism, like psychoanalysis, is a heterogeneous tradition with different schools and conflicting and seemingly contradictory beliefs. Both Buddhism and psychoanalysis are cultural institutions that originally developed as expressions of the values and the complex tensions and contradictions within their cultures of origins. Both are systems of healing that have evolved over time as culture has evolved, as the configuration of the self has evolved, and as new cultures have assimilated them. And both have transformed the cultures in which they have evolved. Today's psychoanalysis is very different from Freud's, and American psychoanalysis is very different from French. The meaning of Buddhism is very different for a contemporary North American or European than for an Indian Buddhist in the Axial Age or for a medieval Chinese Buddhist, and the function that the assimilation of Buddhist ideas into psychoanalytic theory and practice plays can be understood only if we know something about how this process of assimilation expresses contemporary cultural values, tensions, and problems.

In this essay I examine the cultural contexts in which both psychoanalysis and Buddhism emerged and the ways they have evolved. I also examine some of the internal tensions that both psychoanalysis and Buddhism have struggled with over time, as well as the various ways in which these two traditions have reflected these tensions. One source of this struggle in both traditions has been the tension between the poles of agnosticism (or atheism) and faith (or commitment). Another has been tension between the poles of individualistic and communal orientations. Through cross-cultural comparison I begin a dialogue between Buddhism and psychoanalysis, with the objective of exploring various ways in which the two traditions can complement one another.

THE CULTURAL ORIGINS OF PSYCHOANALYSIS

As Reiff (1966) has argued, psychoanalysis developed during a period in which the traditional religious values and symbols that held the community together were breaking down. Religious systems play the dual roles of integrating the individual with the community and of providing a system of communally held symbols and rituals that heal individuals who experience emotional distress. These traditional systems of healing function by giving some sense of meaning to the individual's suffering and by reintegrating the alienated individual into the community. This process of healing involves an act of faith and commitment to the values of the community, and through that commitment, one experiences salvation. For this reason Reiff refers to these traditional systems of healing as commitment therapies. In order for therapies of this sort to work, there has to be an intact, coherent community to which one recommits oneself. When psychoanalysis originated, the religious worldview that had dominated Western culture was no longer functioning in a cohesive and fully viable fashion. The traditional value system was fragmenting. Nietzsche had already proclaimed the death of God, and the secular worldview was securing its hold on the modern mind. Reiff sees psychoanalysis as qualitatively different from traditional systems of healing. From his perspective, psychoanalysis is not a therapy of commitment but rather an approach that liberates people from the type of commitment required by traditional religion and other social institutions.

As he points out, the goal of psychoanalysis for Freud was not to help the individual to recommit himself or herself to the values of the community but rather to learn to manage the strains of living as an individual detached from community. Part of Freud's concern was that the existing cultural value system was repressive, or at least that people responded to the demands of society through harshly or rigidly repressing their instincts, thereby giving rise to psychological symptoms. He emphasized the importance of becoming aware of our underlying instinctual passions and then using our rational capacities to modulate or tame them in a reflective rather than a rigid fashion. In this way, Freud believed, people could develop the ability to choose how to act, rather than be ruled unconsciously by their instinctual passions or by their unconscious, rigid defenses against them. His emphasis was thus on rational renunciation rather than irrational or unconscious suppression.

Thus, as Reiff sees it, the analyst, unlike the priest who speaks for organized religion, "speaks for the individual buried alive, as it were, in the culture. To be thus freed from a tyrannical cultural super-ego is to be properly bedded in the present world. Analysis is not an initiation but a counter-initiation, to end the need for initiations" (1966, p. 77). Freud had no interest in providing people with any form of salvation. In important respects his value system was consistent with the values of science and the modern era. From this perspective, knowledge is power, and self-knowledge allows choice. To Freud's way of thinking, the mature individual is a realist, and the realist does not need the comforts of religion, which he regarded as illusion.

But as Reiff argues, there has always been an ongoing tension within psychoanalysis between Freud's insistence that psychoanalysis not be a therapy of commitment in the traditional religious sense, and the need to find the type of meaning and salvation afforded by more traditional cultural institutions of healing. In contrast to Freud's "hermeneutic of suspicion" (Ricoeur, 1970), Alfred Adler offered a philosophy of social commitment. Jung attempted to breathe new life into religion by relocating the gods inside man as archetypes. Reich developed a psychology of sexual/energetic mysticism. More recently analysts such as Wilfred Bion (1970), Michael Eigen (1998), and James Grotstein (2000) have developed approaches that attempt to reincorporate the spiritual through what can be thought of as a type of psychoanalytic mysticism.

Moreover, what Reiff failed to realize is that in certain respects psychoanalysis itself is a therapy of faith or commitment. Increasingly, analysts are realizing that the analytic process is not free of suggestion and persuasion, and that a certain degree of indoctrination into the analyst's value system is both inevitable and desirable. Irwin Hoffman (1998) has been particularly articulate in his discussion of the role that "analytic authority" plays. He reminds us that Freud (1926) himself thought of the analyst as a "secular pastoral worker" and recognized that he or she plays the role of an intimate, loving authority who has continuity with the kind of authority that parents have. Freud believed that this authority should be used to persuade patients to come to terms with the truth about both their internal and external worlds.

Building on Freud's own conceptualization of psychoanalysis as an "aftereducation," Hoffman borrows the sociological concept of secondary socialization (Berger and Luckmann, 1967) to account for the mechanism through which the analytic relationship influences the change process. He argues that just as the child's initial construction of reality is forged in the crucible of affectively intense human relationships characterized by dependency upon the parent, the change that takes place through psychoanalysis is inevitably dependent upon a new socialization process in which the analyst functions as an intimate and loving authority. Thus in contrast to Reiff, who makes considerable effort to distinguish psychoanalysis from the type of change process that takes place through what he termed therapies of commitment, many contemporary analysts argue that psychoanalysis inevitably involves some degree of socialization into the value system of the analyst and the analytic community (e.g., Hoffman 1998; Renik 1996).[2]

Another way in which psychoanalysis has elements of a therapy of commitment is in its tendency to develop doctrinal positions that the faithful must adhere to in order to be considered "true analysts." As Greenberg and Mitchell (1983) pointed out, for many years Freud's drive theory was the litmus test of whether one was a real analyst, and rejection of drive theory could lead to excommunication from the profession. And even within postmodern and pluralistic circles, the belief in the importance of "throwing away the book" is becoming a new doctrine of sorts (Hoffman 1994; Greenberg 2001).

PSYCHOANALYSIS AND THE CULTURE OF INDIVIDUALISM

Another important shift in psychoanalytic sensibility that has taken place over time has involved an increased emphasis on the importance of the development of an authentic, vital sense of self and on the construction of personal meaning. Freud emphasized the importance of learning to negotiate the tensions between our instincts and civilization in a constructive fashion. As Mitchell has argued, many contemporary analysts are more interested in helping patients construct personal meaning for themselves: "What the patient needs is not a rational reworking of unconscious infantile fantasies; what the patient needs is a revitalization and expansion of his own capacity to generate experience that feels real, meaningful, and valuable. . . . If the goal of psychoanalysis in Freud's day was rational understanding and control (secondary process) over fantasy-driven, conflictual impulses (primary process), the goal of psychoanalysis in our day is most often thought about in terms of the establishment of a richer, more authentic sense of identity" (1993, 24).

This shift in psychoanalytic sensibility corresponds to an important shift in cultural landscape from Freud's time to ours. Psychoanalysis was born during a period when individualism was in the process of becoming more pronounced. In the Victorian culture of Freud's time, the self was viewed as dangerous, and an emphasis was placed on self-mastery or self-control (Cushman, 1995). Over the last century the culture of individualism has continued to evolve, and the individual has become increasingly isolated from the community. This is a double-edged sword. On the one hand, the more individuated person of contemporary culture is freer of the potentially suffocating influence of the community. On the other, he or she is cut off from the sense of meaning and well-being that potentially flows from being integrated with the wider community.

According to Philip Cushman (1995) the disintegration of the unifying web of belief and values that traditionally brought people together and gave life meaning has resulted in the development of what he refers to as the empty self. This empty self-experiences the lack of tradition, community, and shared meaning as an internal hollowness, a lack of personal conviction and worth, and a chronic, undifferentiated emotional hunger.

Christopher Lasch (1979), in a similar vein, argues that the breakdown of traditional cultural values and the fragmentation of societal structures, which traditionally provided a unifying web of meaning, has resulted in the development of a culture of narcissism. The individual in contemporary culture tends to be narcissistic in the sense that he has a grandiose or inflated sense of his own uniqueness and abilities. This grandiose and hyper-individuated sense of self is a defensive attempt to cope with the underlying sense of fragility and isolation resulting from the breakdown of traditional social structures and unifying webs of meaning. As Lasch sees it, the institutions of psychoanalysis and psychotherapy have developed to fill the cultural void left by the breakdown of traditional cultural institutions. The danger, however, is that psychoanalysis and other forms of psychotherapy can perpetuate or exacerbate the pathology that they are attempting to remedy. By focusing on the enrichment of the self they can create pathological individualism. The popularity of theorists such as D. W. Winnicott, with his emphasis on the true self, and Heinz Kohut, with his normalization of narcissism, can be seen as a reflection of the deeply entrenched sense of individualism in contemporary culture.[3]

Whereas people once saw personal contentment as a byproduct of living a good or moral life, in contemporary culture the pursuit of happiness risks becoming a goal in and of itself. There is thus a perpetuation of the narcissistic goal of pursuing self-enhancement or of shoring up the self. Because of the sense of isolation produced by the breakdown of traditional social structures, people become increasingly desperate in their pursuit of intimacy. However, intimacy becomes unobtainable as a result of the same circumstances that lead to the intensified search for intimacy in the first place. True intimacy involves the letting go of rigid self-other boundaries that are necessary in order to maintain narcissistic defenses. Because people are so preoccupied with shoring up their narcissistic defenses, intimacy becomes increasingly elusive. In addition, because of the intense isolation resulting from the breakdown of traditional social structures, people have unrealistic expectations about their intimate relationships or place unrealistic demands upon them, thereby dooming them to failure. People look for the kind of spiritual transcendence in their intimate relationships that traditionally came from religion.

RELATIONAL DEVELOPMENTS AND THE POSTMODERN TURN

One of the more important developments in contemporary psychoanalysis consists of the relational perspective (Aron, 1996; Benjamin, 1988; Ghent, 1989; Mitchell, 1988). This perspective involves a host of related theoretical developments, which share in common an emphasis on the relational field as the basic unit of study, rather than on the individual as a separate entity. Human beings are regarded as being fundamentally interpersonal in nature; mind is regarded as composed of relational configurations; and self is regarded as constructed in a relational context. Although relational theorists trace their roots as far back as Sandor Ferenczi, the growing impact of the relational perspective on the mainstream is, I believe, a reflection of the intensification of the crisis of individualism in contemporary culture. It can be regarded in part as an attempt to remedy the excesses of a more individualistic perspective. It is also interesting to note that although the relational perspective synthesizes theoretical perspectives from both sides of the Atlantic, American culture has played a particularly significant role in its origin and development. This, I believe, is a reflection of the particularly intense sense of individualism and isolation in the United States. While the relational perspective can be seen as a corrective to the excessive individualism of contemporary culture, at another level it represents a further embodiment of that individualism. By emphasizing the mutuality of the analytic relationship and the analyst's embeddedness in the relational field, it challenges the traditional sources of analytic authority. This is consistent with the Western democratic emphasis on the challenge of tradition and the location of authority within the individual rather than the social institution.

Another important trend in contemporary psychoanalytic thinking consists of the postmodern turn. Increasingly analysts are emphasizing the constructed nature of human knowledge and the inherent limits of our understanding as analysts (Hoffman, 1988; Mitchell, 1993; Stern, 1997). Constructivist epistemology asserts that reality is intrinsically ambiguous and is given form only through our interpretation of it. This perspective has profound implications for the nature of analytic authority and goes hand in hand with the increasing democratization of the therapeutic relationship. As we shall see, the shift toward a constructivist epistemology and the recognition that all knowledge is positional is also consistent with developments in traditional Buddhist philosophy.

Associated with the postmodern turn has been a shift toward viewing the self as multiple rather than as unitary (Bromberg, 1998; Mitchell, 1993; Pizer, 1998). This shift reflects a similar shift across a range of different disciplines including philosophy, literary criticism, anthropology, social psychology, cognitive sciences, and neuropsychology. Although it is beyond the scope of this chapter to speculate extensively about the factors underlying this widespread cultural shift, it is worth dwelling for a moment on its meaning within psychoanalytic thinking, given the parallels between the psychoanalytic conceptualization of self as multiple and the Buddhist conception of self.

In postmodern thought, one of the central impulses underlying the deconstruction of the self is to challenge potentially oppressive functions of tradition and authority. Jacques Derrida, for example, "kills" the author of a text, deprives him or her of ultimate authority, by arguing that the final meaning of a text cannot be settled with reference to the author's intentions. Constructing meaning is an endless hermeneutic enterprise, and the notion of truth is replaced by a ceaseless play of infinite meanings. Michel Foucault challenges what he considers the illusion of self as an autonomous free agent by analyzing the way in which intricate decentered networks of power relations within society lead to the construction of the subjective experience of selfhood.

The current psychoanalytic fascination with self-multiplicity has no doubt been influenced by the faddish nature of this type of thinking. But there are other influences. Susan Fairfield (2001) for example, argues that theories of selfhood do not accurately capture some underling reality but are shaped by various intrapsychic needs of the analyst. She draws our attention to the hidden smugness often associated with critiques of monists (believers in a unitary self) who cling to the comforting belief that there is a stable, cohesive, singular self. She also points out the aggressiveness potentially associated with the desire to challenge conventional boundaries. And she suggests that seeing the self as multiple may also be a counter-phobic attempt to master fears of self-fragmentation by arguing that the self really is fragmented. She further adds that North American analysts, consistent with the optimism of their culture, tend to think about self-multiplicity in positive terms. For them, a multiple, contradictory self has more potential than the unitary self. In contrast, European theorists who emphasize multiplicity tend to place more importance on the experience of alienation or loss associated with the lack of a unitary self.

Mitchell (2001), while applauding Fairfield's thoughts about why one might view the self as multiple, also highlights the clinical implications of this view. His central thesis is that the adoption of the perspective of self as multiple helps to liberate us from a view of mental health that emphasizes conformity. In an argument somewhat reminiscent of Jacques Lacan's, he claims that the American ego-analytic emphasis on ego integration tends to value rational analysis and synthesis and to pathologize emotional intensity. In contrast, openness to a range of different states of being is conducive to greater unpredictability and passion in life. It is interesting to note that in some respects Mitchell's understanding of the clinical implications of self-multiplicity is consistent with his earlier emphasis (Mitchell 1993) on the centrality of enriching and revitalizing the self. This sensibility is in keeping with Fairfield's argument that American analysts tend to view the multiple self as a "cornucopia" of possibilities.

ORIGINS OF BUDDHISM

Buddhism originated in what is now northeast India during the fifth century BCE. During this period Indian civilization was undergoing tremendous ferment. The rural society and agricultural economy were gradually being replaced by a market economy and urban centers. A new culturally diverse and sophisticated merchant class was on the rise; traditional cultural values and religious beliefs were being challenged, and a heightened sense of individualism was emerging. Just as present-day individualism is double-edged, the growing individualism in India seems to have been associated with both malaise and exhilaration.

The agricultural society in which Buddhism developed was static and conservative. It divided society into four rigidly hierarchical castes: priests, warriors, farmers, and servants. These castes were hereditary and were thought to mirror the archetypal order of the cosmos. Ethical conduct consisted of performing the duties and responsibilities appropriate to one's caste. This worldview, while providing structure and cohesiveness, left little room for social change or individual conscience. The Brahmans, or priests, were in exclusive possession of the sacred knowledge of the Vedas, which spelled out the responsibilities of the castes and the relationships between them. It was the Brahmans' duty and responsibility to enact various sacred rites including animal sacrifice in order to control the universe.

For some time preceding the emergence of Buddhism, a new religious trend had begun to develop, the Upanishadic tradition. It involved a reinterpretation of the Vedas that emphasized the importance of the internal meaning of things over the external, magical significance of sacred rites. At the same time it enshrined the caste system. Central to Upanishadic philosophy is the concept of atman, which is equivalent in some respects to our concept of soul. The atman is the essence of the person, which transcends phenomenal experience. It is thus the real self in contrast to the experienced self. This atman is conceptualized as identical with the single unified essence behind appearances. The individual experience of self, and all phenomena in the world, are thus illusions, behind which lies a transcendental reality in which all phenomena are one. The failure to see behind this veil of illusion keeps people trapped in the pain of individuation and the suffering of life and death. Those who fail to recognize their true nature as part of the universal essence experience the pain and sorrow of life, and at death are reborn once again into endless rounds of life and death. The goal is to recognize the illusory nature of the self and to unify the true self or atman with the underlying universal essence. As for the historical conditions that led to the perception of life as being so painful, this is a matter of speculation. It may in part have been related to the stress associated with increased urbanization and the breakdown of traditional values. The rapid buildup of urban centers may have led to an increased incidence of plagues (Gombrich, 1988). Regardless of the conditions giving rise to this perspective, however, one of its consequences was a devaluing of sensual and worldly experience in favor of the transcendental.

Two primary practices used for gaining transcendence were meditation and mortification of the flesh. Meditation in this context involved sitting quietly and using a variety of concentrative techniques to focus the mind, thereby stilling discursive thought. Mortification of the flesh involved subjecting oneself to various physical extremes of cold, heat, hunger, and so on as a way of conquering the demands of the body, thereby experiencing transcendence.

Early Buddhism can be understood as a reaction to this worldview in a number of ways. To begin with, the Buddha denied the existence of an atman, or of any transcendental self or soul. At the same time, he never taught that the self does not exist (as he is often interpreted to have done), but rather argued that the self is nonsubstantial, in the sense that it is constructed on a moment-by-moment basis out of a variety of components: memories, physical sensations, emotions, concepts, dispositions (including both unconscious and inherited conditioning), and so on. Furthermore, he argued that the construction of self is always influenced by ever changing causes and conditions. There is some similarity between this teaching of the Buddha's and the Upanishadic formulation of atman. The underlying assumption in both cases is that the experience of the self as a substantial and isolated entity lies at the heart of the problem, and that the modification of that experience is the cure.

The Buddhist perspective is, however, more moderate in some respects. To begin with, it does not conceptualize the individual self as illusory. Again, what is illusory is the experience of self as substantial or unchanging. From a Buddhist perspective, the self, like everything in this world, is transient or impermanent. Death, illness, and loss are unavoidable aspects of life. Suffering arises as a result of attempting to cling to what we desire and to avoid what causes us pain. Liberation emerges as a result of recognizing the impermanent nature of reality and letting go of our self-centered craving. There is no transcendental self to be realized, as is the case in the Upanishadic worldview, and thus no self that is separate from the aggregates of form and psychological or mental experience. In this respect the Buddhist perspective is less dualistic than the Upanishadic worldview and less likely to give rise to extreme forms of asceticism. The Buddha emphatically rejected extreme asceticism as a spiritual practice and instead proposed what is referred to as the Middle Way, that is, a pathway between the extremes of asceticism and hedonism or sensualism. The goal in Buddhism thus becomes not one of transcending worldly experience but rather one of finding a wiser way of living within it.

This difference plays out in the form of the meditation techniques that are used in the two different traditions. In the Upanishadic tradition meditation tends to involve the concentration of attention upon a particular object of focus for purposes of experiencing an absorption. This results in a withdrawal of the senses from worldly experience, a reduction of internal stimulation, and a resulting experience of peace or tranquility, which is believed to be associated with the transcendental reality that one wishes to realize.

This form of meditation, which is sometimes referred to as concentration meditation constitutes one form of Buddhist meditation, but in and of itself it is not considered to be sufficient for liberation. The second form of meditation, which plays a role in most Buddhist traditions, consists of detached observation of one's own mind. Concentration meditation plays an important role in helping the individual develop the attentional skill necessary to observe his or her experience in a mindful fashion, but the experience of meditative absorption is not the goal. The objective of this second form of meditation, which is referred to as insight or mindfulness meditation, is to help the meditator develop a greater awareness of the manifold contents of awareness as they unfold, and an ability over time to develop an attitude of nonjudgmental acceptance of the full range of experience. This objective is in keeping with the Buddhist emphasis on learning to live fully in this world rather than on pursuing otherworldly experiences. Mindfulness meditation leads to a greater appreciation of the impermanent or ever changing nature of all phenomena, including the self. It also leads to an appreciation of the role the mind plays in constructing reality.

Another important characteristic of early Buddhist thinking is the rejection of all metaphysical speculation. In this respect Buddhist thinking, at least in its early form and in some contemporary variants, is essentially pragmatic and agnostic in nature. It is pragmatic in the philosophical sense (e.g., Rorty, 1982) insofar as truth is defined as that which is effective in relieving human suffering. And it is agnostic in the sense that it refuses to engage in metaphysical speculation. There is a story in which the Buddha used the analogy of a man who is shot by an arrow. In a situation of such urgency, questions such as who made the arrow and what type of bow was used are irrelevant. What is critical is the practical affair of removing the arrow. Similarly, argued the Buddha, metaphysical and cosmological speculations are irrelevant to the task of relieving human suffering. Moreover, committing oneself to a metaphysical view or a theological doctrine is a form of enslavement. It interferes with the openness essential to enlightenment or true existential awakening.

One of the implications of this feature of early Buddhist thinking was that it undermined the theological structure supporting the caste system. At a social level, then, early Buddhist thinking was a profoundly democratizing force. It subverted the authority of the priestly class and denied the value of ritual observances of a magical nature. Ethical behavior was no longer defined as performing one's duty as a member of one's caste, and no merit was accrued from observing rituals or depending upon the priestly class. Instead ethical action was defined in terms of acting selflessly, according to the precepts of right action.

In some respects the thrust of the early Buddhist tradition was analogous to the thrust of the Protestant Reformation in Europe. Early Buddhists were interested in purifying the Upanishadic tradition of features that they saw as problematic, just as Luther and Calvin wanted to purify Christianity. They wanted to eradicate the magical or superstitious elements, eliminate empty ritual, and establish a more direct relationship between the individual and the experience of salvation (or what the Buddhists refer to as enlightenment). Just as the Protestant Reformation contained a democratizing element, challenging the role of the clergy as divinely empowered intermediaries between the individual and God, Buddhism eliminated the divinely sanctioned role of the priestly class and emphasized the responsibility of the individual for his or her own spiritual destiny. And just as the attempt to purify Christianity of its magical elements had both desirable and undesirable consequences, so did Buddhism's attempt to purify Indian religion of its magical elements have such consequences. Both developments placed greater emphasis on the inner meaning of spirituality, but both sacrificed some of the magic and mystery that the human heart hungers for.

TENSION AND EVOLUTION WITHIN BUDDHIST THINKING

Since its inception, Buddhism has struggled with the tension between the pragmatic/agnostic perspective at its core and the need for faith and epistemological certainty and metaphysical absolutism. In many ways this parallels the tension in psychoanalysis between Freud's vision of psychoanalysis as a purely rational, scientific, analytic approach and the tendency to develop a new therapy of faith and commitment. One reflection of this tension can be seen in the evolution of Buddhist philosophy. Early Buddhist philosophy and psychology were codified in a body of literature referred to as Abhidharma. This literature emphasizes that the self can be deconstructed into a number of constituent elements. These elements are viewed as arising in dependence upon one another and upon fluctuating causes and conditions. It is on this basis that the self is seen to be lacking in substantiality. In practice, it is held that the meditative process allows one to experience the arising and departing of various constituent elements of the self, and this insight leads to the experience of enlightenment.

Over time, this perspective became reified, and there was a tendency to view the various constituent components of the self as having a fundamental or substantial nature. Various alternative perspectives were offered as to what these fundamental constituents of the self were. Partially in reaction to this trend, the Madhyamika school of philosophy developed. This perspective employed sophisticated linguistic and logical analysis to deconstruct the Abhidharmic analysis of the self into constituent elements and to demonstrate that none of these elements have intrinsic reality. The argument is not that such phenomena are nonexistent, but rather that they are empty of inherent existence. In other words, all phenomena exist in dependence on our construction of them. This perspective anticipated contemporary hermeneutic and constructivist thinking by hundreds of years. The Madhyamika perspective is not a radical constructivism, but rather closer to what Hoffman (1998) refers to as dialectical constructivism. It extends the Buddhist principle of the Middle Way to the epistemological level, by arguing for a position between the extremes of naive realism and radical constructivism. It emphasizes that emptiness itself is only a concept and does not have any intrinsic reality. As Madhyamika philosophers put it, the concept of emptiness is like a medicine—a medicine for the illness of naive realism. But like any medicine, too much of it can make you sick.

Nevertheless, critics of the Madhyamika position interpreted it as a form of radical constructivism, leading to nihilism. The Yogachara school of philosophy attempted to correct what it saw as a tendency toward nihilism in Madhyamika thinking, adopting a position that, in turn, tended toward the metaphysical and transcendental. The Yogachara school holds that both perception and the object of perception spring forth from a single seed, which is contained in a type of substratum consciousness. This substratum consciousness is likened to a river, which is constantly changing and yet remains the same. It has both personal and universal aspects to it.

Then there is what is referred to as Tathagatagarbha tradition in Buddhism, which holds that all sentient beings are endowed with Buddha nature, and thus have the potential for "awakening" and realizing their intrinsic identity as enlightened beings. This Buddha essence, also referred to as suchness, or in Sanskrit as tathata, is often spoken of as equivalent to emptiness, but it has a more positive quality. It is described as beginningless and endless and as pervading everything. In some traditions this concept of Buddha essence or suchness appears to be taken more literally, thus bordering on the type of substantialism that early Buddhism was reacting against. In other traditions, however, the concept is subjected to the type of deconstructive logic characteristic of the Madhyamika approach.

At a more practical level, the tension between the poles of pragmatism/agnosticism and faith/absolutism is reflected in the way in which the Buddha is conceptualized in different Buddhist traditions. In early Buddhism, and in some forms of contemporary Buddhism, the Buddha is emphatically not seen as a divine figure. He is a human being who became enlightened through his own efforts, and who serves as a model for other spiritual seekers. After his death he was seen as no longer directly active in the world. The Buddha is thus not somebody to be prayed to. Over time various doctrines and traditions developed that viewed the historical Buddha as only one embodiment of the principle of enlightenment. In this view, the cosmos is inhabited by an infinite number of Buddhas—past, present, and future, all of whom have an active presence in the world and help sentient beings attain enlightenment. In various Buddhist traditions, practitioners pray to or petition one or another of the Buddhas, just as Catholics pray to the saints. At the level of philosophical doctrine, there is recognition that these Buddhas do not exist in any absolute sense, that like all phenomena they are empty of intrinsic existence. Nevertheless, at a psychological level they function for people in the same way that saints function in the Catholic tradition, or that gods and goddesses function in premodern cultures.

Another example of this tension can be seen in the role that the belief in rebirth plays in various Buddhist traditions. Despite the fact that early Buddhism rejected the notion of an eternal self or atman, it accepted a notion of rebirth. As in the Upanishadic tradition, a formulation of the goal in early Buddhism was (and in some forms of contemporary Buddhism continues to be) obtaining release from samsara, or the cycle of death and rebirth. This state of release, referred to as nirvana, is conceptualized as one in which all self-centered craving ceases. And yet at the level of practice the goal is often regarded as one of achieving a better life at the next cycle of rebirth. My impression is that there has always been a tension between the official Buddhist doctrine of anatman, or no-self, and the belief in rebirth. Buddhist philosophy attempts to reconcile this tension in various ways. For example, it is argued that what continues from life to life is not a substantial self or soul but rather a subtle causal connection. The analogy that is used is that of flame passed from candle to candle. The flame that passes from one candle to a next is not exactly the same, but not exactly different either. But to my mind, this resolution is less than completely satisfying. Some Buddhist traditions downplay the importance of the doctrine of rebirth. The Zen tradition, for example, tends to emphasize that good rebirths and bad rebirths are both states of mind.

On the other hand, Tibetan Buddhism places considerable emphasis on the principle of rebirth. In fact there is a tradition of picking important spiritual leaders at an early age because they are believed to be reincarnations of deceased spiritual leaders. For example, the Dalai Lama, who is the supreme spiritual and temporal leader of Tibet, is viewed as the fourteenth incarnation of the first Dalai Lama.

When Buddhism spread to China, it was transformed by the existing culture and by the Taoist and Confucian philosophies that were dominant at the time. Although a variety of different forms of Buddhism developed in China, Chan Buddhism (more commonly known by its Japanese name, Zen) is perhaps the most distinctively Chinese. Zen is often characterized by its direct and down-to-earth quality. Ancient Indian culture tended to prize abstract philosophical thought and metaphysical speculation. It tended to have a world-weary quality. As we have seen, in Upanishadic thinking, life is suffering, and the goal is to seek liberation from the endless round of rebirth by seeing through the illusion of one's individuality. Ancient Chinese thinking had a more optimistic, humanistic, and earthy flavor to it. In Taoist thinking, liberation is obtained by attuning oneself to the natural, spontaneous harmony of the universe—the Tao. This Tao is not something that can be defined in words or grasped conceptually, and in fact any attempt to do so only interferes with one's ability to function in harmony with it. One can act in accordance with the Tao only when one is able to let go of attempting to grasp it, thereby acting in a spontaneous and unselfconscious fashion. This allows one to be attuned and receptive to the configuration of the moment.

Although the Buddha originally served as a model for the way in which all human beings could become enlightened through their own efforts, subsequent developments in Indian Buddhism tended to present enlightenment as a more and more extraordinary, rarefied, and otherworldly state, available to only the few. Zen tends to bring enlightenment down to earth, as it were, and to demystify and demythologize it.

There is an iconoclastic element to Zen, which was probably influenced by the ancient Taoist image of a sage as somebody who was liberated from convention and from stereotypical thinking. Enlightenment in the Zen tradition tends to be associated with spontaneity and freedom from inhibiting self-consciousness and conformity. Enlightenment is conceptualized as a state in which events are experienced immediately, without the intrusion of reflective self-consciousness. There is a selfless openness to experience.

Buddhism in Tibet took a very different turn from Chinese Buddhism. In Tibet certain developments in Indian Buddhism (referred to as Tantric Buddhism) blended with the indigenous Tibetan tradition of Bon, which had strong magical and shamanistic elements. This resulted in the development of an interesting synthesis of magical and shamanistic practices with Buddhist worldview and epistemology. The Tibetan tradition places great emphasis on the importance of the teacher (referred to as the guru or lama), who is seen as an embodiment of the Buddha and as the gateway to enlightenment. Tibetan Buddhist cosmology is populated by a pantheon of male and female deities, who are invoked during meditation sessions that involve elaborate visualizations. Yet at the same time, these deities are seen as empty of inherent existence and as creations of the meditator's own mind.

In Tibetan Buddhism, one of the foundational meditation practices is what is referred to as guru yoga. The purpose of guru yoga is to facilitate the development of faith and devotion to one's lama. In psychoanalytic terms the Tibetan tradition attempts to cultivate an idealizing transference toward the teacher, and to use that as a vehicle for change. This transference provides an ongoing inspiration for the student to continue on the arduous pathway of spiritual development despite its many difficulties, by helping to generate and maintain faith that change (or relief from suffering) is possible. The lama or guru serves as a living reminder that such change is possible, since he functions as an embodiment of the principles that the student aspires to realize. In addition, being in relationship with a lama who embodies special qualities helps the student feel empowered.

In the Tibetan tradition, the relationship with the lama is never interpreted as it is in psychoanalysis. From the beginning, however, the student is taught to cultivate a paradoxical attitude toward the lama, who is seen, on the one hand, as an embodiment of the highest ideals and values in the Buddhist traditions and, on the other, as a human being with human flaws and failings.

As with so much of the Tibetan tradition, guru yoga is reminiscent of the old Indian rope trick, in which the yogi climbs up a rope suspended in midair, pulls the rope up after him, and disappears. The student is taught to conjure up a world of meditation deities in his imagination, or to imbue the lama with special powers, and then to use the constructed images of his imagination in order to help him to cultivate certain attitudes toward reality. At the end of every meditation session, the meditator dissolves the image back into the nothingness from which it arose. He pulls up the rope.

Although there are many variations of guru yoga, they all involve some combination of visualization practice and prayer or incantation designed to help the student see the lama as an embodiment of the Buddha (and of the qualities a Buddha embodies) and establish a deep connection with him, thereby ultimately internalizing his qualities. For example, the meditator visualizes the lama as manifesting in the form of a Buddha or other deity surrounded by a retinue of important figures in the lineage and by various dakinis (female deities visualized in order to focus the mind). Various colors of light are then visualized as emanating from the dakinis and from the lama, bathing and purifying the meditator of self-centered craving and helping him or her to recognize all phenomena as empty of inherent existence.

This particular practice illustrates two characteristics of Tibetan Buddhist visualization practices. First, the visualization is permeated by a kind of transitional logic or reality, to use Winnicott's term. Although the visualization is intentionally constructed by the meditator, it is also treated as if it had a life of its own (you pray to the visualized lama). At the same time you explicitly remind yourself by means of prescribed incantations that neither the visualization nor even the lama himself has any inherent existence. The meditator thus attempts to enter into a type of transitional space in the sense that the boundaries between subjective and objective reality are intentionally blurred. He or she strives to maintain a type of double vision, on the one hand knowing that the experience is subjective and, on the other, treating it as if it were objective or real.

Second, it involves the imaginary construction of a world in which the normal boundaries of personal identity become permeable. In the visualization the lama becomes identical with the Buddha, and the lama's mind becomes inseparable from that of the meditator. This identification helps to loosen the constraints of ordinary dualistic logic and challenges the conventional self-other distinction. When the meditator conjures up an entire pantheon of lesser and greater deities and, while doing so, recognizes that they both are and are not creations of the mind, the meditator taps into a rich and vast experience that dwarfs conventional reality.

BUDDHISM AND THE CULTURE OF PSYCHOANALYSIS: SECULARIZATION AND THE RETURN OF THE REPRESSED

The trend toward secularization in the modern world, while profoundly liberating in some respects, has also contributed to the experience of the self as empty, and in some more traditional cultures has been seen as a form of oppression and an assault on traditional ways of life. In some cases this has caused a resurgence of religious interest in a variety of different forms, a type of return of the repressed. In the middle of the twentieth century, few would have predicted that religion would once again become an important societal force. And yet, from the dramatic influence of Islamic fundamentalism in the Middle East and internationally, to the growing influence of the Christian Right in North American politics, it is becoming increasingly clear that the trend toward secularism has dramatically reversed. As Karen Armstrong (2000) has pointed out, the rise of religious fundamentalism must be understood, not as a return to an earlier form of religious belief, but as a reaction to the spiritual and cultural crises of modernity. In its extremity and rigidity it involves a brittle and defensive attempt to revitalize a fragmented culture and to shore up a sense of self under assault. Another response has been the emergence of New Age spirituality, which involves a syncretic blend of various traditional Eastern and Western spiritualities with pop psychology. This form of religious expression stems from a thirst for meaning and a genuine spiritual yearning. But in contrast to more mature forms of spirituality, which emphasize balancing the needs of the self with the good of the larger whole, it tends toward strong elements of narcissistic self-absorption and personal omnipotence.

We have seen how both Buddhism and psychoanalysis have struggled over time with the tension between the poles of agnosticism or atheism versus faith and commitment. Within psychoanalysis the tendency to deify Freud and to treat his words as gospel can be seen as another form of the return of the repressed.

From a contemporary psychoanalytic perspective, one of the appeals of Buddhism is the way its agnostic sensibility and its grounding in a constructivist epistemology resonate with the postmodern turn. Certainly Buddhism, like all religions, has gone through various forms of institutionalization and has often lost this agnostic sensibility. It is thus important not to idealize Buddhism, a particular danger for Westerners who have become alienated from their own spiritual traditions and seek spiritual meaning in a foreign tradition uncontaminated by negative associations. The postmodern emphasis on critiquing authority, which plays an important role in contemporary psychoanalytic dialogue, can, however, help challenge the institutionalized aspects of Buddhism that obscure its more emancipatory dimensions. Postmodern critique can help shed light on the various insidious ways in which Buddhism, like all religious traditions can be used to serve the interests of the privileged.

CONSTRUCTIVISM IN BUDDHISM AND PSYCHOANALYSIS

One of the attractions of Buddhist thinking from a psychoanalytic perspective is that the constructivist epistemology that is so prominent in Buddhist philosophy is compatible with the trend toward constructivism in contemporary psychoanalytic thinking. In light of this compatibility it is interesting to think about the impulses behind this trend in the two different traditions. In psychoanalysis an important influence has been the general shift toward constructivism in philosophy and other disciplines. In addition, however, a central impulse has been the desire to democratize the therapeutic relationship, by emphasizing the limits of the analyst's knowledge. Related to this is the emphasis on the mutuality of the analytic relationship and the co-construction of reality by patient and analyst. These emphases are consistent with the Western tradition of democratic individualism and wariness of various forms of authority. The trend toward constructivism in psychoanalysis is also consistent with the growing emphasis on the importance of constructing healing narratives in the context of the postmodern crisis of meaninglessness.

In Buddhist constructivism, the primary thrust is to cultivate a radical sense of openness. The belief is that concepts enslave us and that the tendency toward reification creates suffering. The emphasis is not on constructing adaptive narratives but rather on the radical deconstruction of all narratives. It is interesting to note that this emphasis on radical openness is similar in some respects to the growing awareness in analytic thinking of the importance of the analyst's openness and tolerance of ambiguity (e.g., Bion, 1970; Stern, 1997; Eigen, 1998).

There can be a valuable complementarity between the two traditions here. Analysts, for all of their fascination with constructivist thinking, still tend to have a bias toward wanting to understand and help their patients to understand. There are times when the experience of understanding can be helpful; especially in a more individualistic culture such as ours, the construction of personal meaning (which Buddhism tends to neglect) can be very important. Yet, letting go of the need to understand can lead to the experience of awe, acceptance, and reverence in the face of the mystery of life.

MULTIPLE SELVES AND NO-SELF

The Buddhist emphasis on recognizing the insubstantiality of self offers a possible antidote for the narcissistic or "empty" self-configuration characteristic of our culture. First, however, it is important to bear in mind that, just as the adoption of the view of self as multiple can reflect a counter-phobic attempt to master fears of self-fragmentation (Fairfield, 2001), the adoption of the Buddhist perspective of self as empty can be an attempt to deal with one's subjective sense of self as empty, by normalizing this state.

On the face of it, there are similarities between the Buddhist notion of no-self and contemporary psychoanalytic conceptions of self as multiple. And in fact the growing interest of analysts in self-multiplicity may help create a climate of receptivity to the Buddhist conceptualization of the self. It is important, however, to be aware of the different functions that challenge the conventional conception of self serves in the two traditions. As we have seen, the contemporary psychoanalytic fascination with self-multiplicity appears to stem at least in part from a desire to challenge monolithic views of mental health that are implicitly conformist in nature. The emphasis in the Buddhist conception of no-self is on decreasing the sense of existential isolation, by emphasizing the constructed nature of the boundary between self and others and the interdependence of all living beings. As Francis Cook puts it, in Buddhist thinking: "There is no absolute reality beyond or distinct from this world of interdependent being. It is a place where the individual arises out of an extremely extensive environment of other individuals—parents, grandparents, culture, soil, water, stone, mist, and many, many more—and takes its place as one other individual. Once in the world, the individual is constantly and massively conditioned by the extensive environment of other individuals" (Cook, 1989, p. 24).

It is interesting to note that in some respects this perspective parallels the object relations perspective, in which the self is constructed through the internalization of others. From an object relations perspective, however, the goal is to liberate the self by freeing oneself from one's ties to old internal objects. From a Buddhist perspective, freedom comes from recognizing that there is no self independent of others.[4]

There is a famous passage from Dogen, an influential thirteenth-century Japanese Buddhist teacher that goes as follows:

> To study the Buddha way is to study the self
> To study the self is to forget the self
> To forget the self is to be authenticated by the myriad things

Thus, when we are able to truly see the way in which we construct our experience of self, the barrier between self and other dissolves. An experience of authenticity then emerges, not out of an experience of true self as an individual, but out of an experience of being related to others as one finger of the hand is related to the others. Somewhat parallel to this perspective is Buber's notion of the I–Thou relationship, which emphasizes that relating to the other as a subject (rather than as an object) is associated with an experience of interconnectedness. Further dialogue between the Buddhist and psychoanalytic perspectives on the self can help to recover a mystical dimension to psychoanalysis—mystical in the sense of experiencing a sense of oneness with the cosmos. The danger with any type of spiritual solution, of course, is that it can be used defensively, as a way of avoiding dealing with emotional conflicts, or in an attempt to fill up the empty self or support a narcissistic sense of omnipotence. The Buddhist tradition, while certainly not immune to these temptations, at least attempts to counteract them in various ways. The Zen tradition in particular emphasizes the "this-worldly" or ordinary aspects of Buddhist practice and consistently focuses on undercutting spiritual escapism and poking holes in students' spiritual narcissism.

In a well-known Zen story, for example, a student asks his master, "How do I attain enlightenment?" The master asks, "Have you finished your rice?" "Yes," replies the student. "Then," responds the teacher, "wash your bowl."

As this story illustrates, the emphasis is on the "ordinary magic" of immersing oneself fully in one's everyday life rather than looking for idealized or escapist solutions. In the words of the Zen poet P'ang-yun: "Miraculous power and marvelous activity—Drawing water and hewing wood" (Watts, 1957, p. 133).

There is also an iconoclasm intrinsic to Buddhism that is consistent with some of the more recent developments in psychoanalysis that emphasize the importance of the therapist's spontaneity and personal responsiveness (e.g., Hoffman, 1998; Ringstrom, 2001). The Zen teachers of legend are often distinguished by their spontaneity and unconventionality and their tendency to use unexpected tactics to shock students out of their conventional ways of looking at things, in order to allow them a glimpse of enlightened or unconditioned experience. In Tibetan Buddhism there is a tradition of "crazy wisdom": certain unusual and highly respected teachers act in a way that may look odd or crazy from the perspective of conventional standards, and yet it is believed that their unconventionality, their willingness and ability to transgress conventional standards, is a mark of their enlightenment rather than a sign of psychopathology. So, for example, one of the most beloved folk heroes in Tibet was a character named Drunkpa Kunley, who was notorious for outrageous behaviors such as getting drunk and consorting with prostitutes. At the same time he was seen as an enlightened teacher who guided (or perhaps more accurately provoked) many people to the experience of enlightenment.

Like any religion or established social institution, Buddhism has deeply conservative elements, and there has always been a tension between the more conservative and the more radical elements of Buddhism. But for all of its conservatism, there was something subversive about Buddhism from the beginning. The Buddha himself, very much aware of the limits of words and concepts, reputedly compared his teachings to a raft with which one crosses a river. Just as one leaves the raft behind after one has crossed, one recognizes that the various Buddhist teachings are only a vehicle to transport one along the path to awakening or enlightenment. To cling to these teachings as if they had some intrinsic reality would be counter to the basic thrust of Buddhism. In the Zen tradition they say, "Do not confuse the finger pointing at the moon with the moon," once again emphasizing the pragmatic nature of concepts.

THE RE-ENCHANTMENT OF THE WORLD

Premodern cultures regarded the world as an enchanted place. In these cultures the distinctions between internal and external reality and between subject and object were less clear-cut than in modern culture. The sociologist Morris Berman refers to this as "participating consciousness." As he puts it:

"The view of nature which predominated in the West down to the eve of the Scientific Revolution was that of an enchanted world. Rocks, trees, rivers, and clouds were all seen as wondrous, alive, and human beings felt at home in this environment. The cosmos, in short, was a place of belonging. A member of this cosmos was not an alienated observer in it but a direct participant in its drama. His personal destiny was bound up with its destiny, and this relationship gave meaning to his life" (Berman 1981, p. 16).

In contrast, for modern consciousness the universe is a mechanistic one, operating on the basis of impersonal principles and matter that is inert and devoid of life. Human beings live outside of nature. Modern consciousness is thus fundamentally alienated. There is no ecstatic merger with nature and no sense of belonging to the cosmos.

Ernest Becker makes a similar point: "The characteristic of the modern mind is the banishment of mystery, of naïve belief, of simple-minded hope. We put the accent on the visible, the clear, the cause-and-effect relation, the logical—always the logical. We know the difference between dreams and reality, between facts and fictions, between symbols and bodies. But right away we can see that these characteristics of the modern mind are exactly those of neurosis. What typifies the neurotic is that he 'knows' his situation vis-à-vis reality. He has no doubts; there is nothing you can say to sway him, to give him hope of trust" (Becker, 1973, p. 201).

As Hans Loewald (1980) and more recently Mitchell (2000) have pointed out, psychoanalysis has tended unwittingly to reproduce the values of a culture that experiences the world as disenchanted. By privileging secondary process over primary process, and regarding the triumph of the reality principle over the pleasure principle as the essence of mental health, it has contributed to a loss of meaningfulness.

The move toward a constructivist epistemology within psychoanalysis, however, has opened the doors for a reconsideration of the relationship between reality and fantasy. Traditionally fantasy was viewed as distorting reality, and the analytic task consisted of gaining insight into the nature of this distortion. But as Mitchell puts it in his exegesis of Loewald's perspective: "Separating fantasy and reality is only one way to organize experience. For life to be meaningful, vital, and robust, fantasy and reality cannot be too divorced from each other. Fantasy cut adrift from reality becomes irrelevant and threatening. Reality cut adrift from fantasy becomes vapid and empty. Meaning in human experience is generated in the mutual, dialectically enriching tension between fantasy and reality; each requires the other to come alive" (Mitchell, 2000, p. 29).

It is impossible for us to return to the worldview of our ancestors in a genuine or authentic fashion. We can reject the modern worldview, but we can never completely escape it. It inevitably colors the way we experience reality. Is it possible to achieve some degree of re-enchantment of the world in which we experience a sense of participating consciousness, without an act of denial or self-deception? The Tibetan Buddhist approach to integrating practices and rituals of a more magical nature with a constructivist epistemology may provide some leads. The Tibetan culture in which such practices were originally developed was a prescientific, traditional culture in which magic and supernatural reality existed as a part of everyday experience, just as they did in Western culture prior to the Enlightenment and the dawn of the scientific era. In this culture what was distinctive about Tibetan Buddhism was not the use of practices of a magical nature, but rather the co-option of the rituals and symbols of magic in order to pursue the Buddhist goal of realizing that all phenomena are empty of intrinsic existence. In contrast, in a contemporary Western context, the use of Tibetan Buddhist meditation techniques, or of practices informed by them, can have a different function. It can become a way of participating in the experience of an enchanted reality that is not normative in contemporary culture, while at the same time reminding ourselves of our own role in constructing that reality. A careful scrutiny of the processes through which such practices operate can thus play a role in refining current psychoanalytic thinking of how change can take place.

REDUCTIONISM VERSUS NONDUALISM

As Becker (1973) has emphasized, one of Freud's fundamental insights had to do with the recognition of the irrevocable creatureliness of human beings. Always the iconoclast, realist, and destroyer of illusions, Freud insisted on reminding us that in the end, for all of our noble aspirations and pretensions, we are ultimately animals motivated by sexual and aggressive instincts. Many contemporary analysts are critical of this perspective and view it as reductionistic. And yet it is important to recognize the brilliance of Freud's vision in this respect and his passionate commitment to puncturing our pretensions and revealing our self-deceptions. A problem emerges when the spiritual is seen as something separate from our baser instincts. We imagine that somehow we can be free of our creatureliness, and that there is a clear distinction between the sacred and the profane. The ever present danger is that spirituality can lead to moralism rather than morality, and to dissociation and projection rather than acceptance.

From a Buddhist perspective this attempt to separate the sacred from the profane lies at the heart of the human dilemma. Rather than seeing spirituality as a derivative of baser instincts, however, the emphasis is on helping people recognize that the sacred and profane are one. In the Mahayana Buddhist tradition, for example, it is emphasized that samsara (i.e., conditioned, unenlightened existence, or the wheel of life and death) is no different from nirvana (i.e., the state of enlightenment in which all self-centered craving ceases to exist). In other words, there is no paradise or ideal state to be attained. There is only this world and this present moment, and enlightenment consists of the experiential realization of this. The Zen tradition is notorious for its earthiness. For example, the Zen master Lin-chi said: "There is no place in Buddhism for using effort. Just be ordinary and nothing special. Relieve your bowels, pass water, put on our clothes, and eat your food. When you're tired, go and lie down" (Watts, 1957, p. 101).

In Tibetan Buddhism, some meditation techniques use sexual imagery as a way of expressing the non-dual nature of the relationship between the sacred and the profane. While there is something right about Freud's insistence on seeing our highest sensibilities and accomplishments as derivatives of sexuality and aggression, there is also something off base about it. His reductionism ends up devaluing the worth of our highest achievements and aspirations rather than celebrating the beauty of human nature with all our flaws, imperfections, and self-deceptions. The Buddhist emphasis on nonduality provides a perspective that resonates with Freud's important insights about our baser motivations, yet at the same time provides a corrective to his reductionism.

LOCATING PSYCHOANALYSIS WITHIN LIFE

In a laudatory review of Irwin Hoffman's Ritual and Spontaneity in the Psychoanalytic Process, Donnell Stern states that Hoffman's book is distinguished by the fact that it "locates psychoanalysis within life rather than the other way around" (2001, p. 464). What he is referring to here is Hoffman's commitment to an existential perspective, which emphasizes that the ongoing struggle to create meaning in the face of mortality lies at the heart of the human dilemma. One of the reasons Hoffman's book stands out is that with rare exceptions (most notably Otto Rank) mainstream psychoanalysts have tended to not focus on this dialectic or at least to not place it at center stage.

Traditionally, of course, these existential concerns have been at the heart of all religious systems, and it is understandable that psychoanalysts in their eagerness to distance themselves from their religious predecessors would be reluctant to tread on this territory. And yet we all know at some level that our hearts and souls are left untouched unless we are able to address our fundamental existential concerns about the meaning (or potential meaninglessness) of life in the ever-present shadow of death.

During periods of our lives when things are going well, when both we and our loved ones are healthy, we are able to quickly retreat behind a shield of denial, and death becomes an abstraction rather than something of immediate concern. Like the protagonist in Tolstoy's *Death of Ivan Ilyich* before his illness, we all relate to death as something that happens to others but not to ourselves—or as something that will happen to us someday in the remote future.

Buddhism places the confrontation with death, loss, and suffering at the heart of things. And ultimately it offers refuge, not in the promise of a better afterlife or protection by a divine figure, but in the form of a pathway toward greater acceptance of life as it is, with all its pain and suffering. There are two key features of this pathway. The first is the belief that, paradoxically, the full recognition and acceptance of the impermanence of everything leads to an experience of peace and the ability to truly cherish life. Interestingly, Freud himself expressed a similar sensibility in a short paper written in the shadow of World War I. In this article (Freud, 1915), he recounts a conversation with a young poet who had expressed despondency in contemplating the transient nature of existence. Freud responds that the recognition that all we value and cherish is intrinsically transient can give rise either to despondency or to a greater appreciation of that which we cherish. The determining factor is whether we are able to fully accept this intrinsic transience and not recoil against the mourning that is linked to this acceptance.

The second principle is the recognition that we are all members of the human community, who are linked together by the bond of sharing in the pain and suffering of life. There is an old Buddhist story that captures the importance of this sense of community. A mother whose son had recently died went to the Buddha to ask him to bring him back to life. The Buddha told her that if she would bring him a mustard seed from the home of somebody who had not known loss, he would help her. As the mother went from house to house she came to realize that no such home could be found. She gradually came to feel less separated from others in her grief, and able to find peace in the midst of her pain.

Freud (1927) believed that religion coerces people into renouncing their instincts through promises of illusory salvation and threats of everlasting punishment. He believed it was important for people to have the courage to genuinely acknowledge and accept the hardships, cruelties, and indignities of life, and to relinquish the illusory comforts of religion in order for them to be able to devote their energies to creating a better life here on earth. Given Freud's antipathy to religions of any type, there is an ironic affinity between his worldview and the Buddhist perspective on this issue. Both visions have a stoic, courageous, and uncompromising quality to them. While Freud's vision at times lapses into pessimism and cynicism, however, the Buddhist worldview is a more optimistic one. This optimism is by no means naive or straightforward. As I have elaborated at various points throughout this chapter, the Buddhist vision of what type of change is possible has a subtle and paradoxical flavor. As Ch'ing-yuan famously expressed it: "Before I had studied Zen for thirty years, I saw mountains as mountains, and waters as waters. When I arrived at a more intimate knowledge, I came to the point where I saw that mountains are not mountains, and waters are not waters. But now that I have got its very substance I am at rest. For it's just that I see mountains once again as mountains, and waters once again as waters" (Watts, 1957, p. 126).

If we are going to locate psychoanalysis within life rather than the other way around, it will be necessary to take up the challenge of confronting what Hoffman (1989) refers to as the dialectic of meaning and mortality in a more sustained and systematic fashion. The dialogue between Buddhism and psychoanalysis can play a valuable role in facilitating this process.

A DIALOGUE

Postmodern thinking has challenged the scientific worldview that was dominant in Freud's day. It has relativized the values of rationality and science and demonstrated the dangers of any type of master narrative—religious or scientific—that marginalizes or excludes the values of the other. Freud saw religion as an illusion. But from a postmodern perspective, Freud's faith in the scientific worldview is itself a form of religion. The dialogue between Buddhism and psychoanalysis provides a confrontation between two divergent pathways to liberation. Contemporary psychoanalytic practice in many respects embodies the Western values of democratic individualism. On the one hand, the growing emphasis on the relational nature of all human experience can be seen as a corrective to Western culture's excessive individualism. On the other hand, the growing emphasis on the mutuality of the analytic relationship and the positional nature of all knowledge is consistent with this emphasis on the value of the individual and the challenge of traditional sources of authority. The contemporary emphases on the construction of personal meaning and the enrichment and vitalization of the self are also consistent with those values. Liberation in this model tends to be associated with personal freedom.

The Buddhist model of liberation emphasizes freedom from self-centered craving. In this perspective the experience of the self as masterful and bounded lies at the heart of the human dilemma. In certain respects the Buddhist perspective can serve as a corrective to the excesses of Western individualism that are reflected in the psychoanalytic perspective. It can also help to recapture the missing spiritual dimension in a fashion that is in tune with a contemporary postmodern sensibility. In other respects psychoanalysis can provide an important counterpoint to certain Buddhist perspectives. The value of democratic individualism can provide a corrective to the tendency that Buddhism shares with all religions to crystallize into religious orthodoxy. Moreover, the psychoanalytic emphasis on unconscious motivation can reduce the risk of using spirituality in a defensive fashion. The dialogue between Buddhism and psychoanalysis thus holds a potential for enriching both traditions. Through this encounter, Buddhism will inevitably be transformed, just as it was when it spread beyond India to other Asian cultures. And psychoanalysis will inevitably be transformed, just as it was when it spread beyond its culture of origin in fin-de-siècle Vienna. While it is impossible to predict what new therapeutic and spiritual forms will ultimately emerge out of the encounter, the contributions to this book provide an important glimpse of an ongoing evolutionary process.

NOTES

1.

2. Of course this is an oversimplification. It is probably more accurate to conceptualize psychoanalysis as a process through which values are negotiated by patient and analyst (e.g., Mitchell 1993; Pizer 1998). Moreover, as Lewis Aron (1999) points out, it is important to distinguish between the values of the analytic community and the values of a specific analyst. As Aron suggests, the analytic community can be conceptualized as a "third" that mediates the dyadic relationship between the patient and the analyst. It is critical for the analyst to recognize the way in which personal and community values interpenetrate and influence one another, and to negotiate tensions between them in a reflective fashion when they emerge. Even given these qualifying factors, however, it is still important to recognize that the analytic process inevitably involves social influence.

3. I recognize that Winnicott's conceptualization of the "true self" includes a recognition that it consists of an ongoing evolving process—a "going on being"—rather than a static entity. Nevertheless, I would still argue that the popularity of this aspect of his thinking reflects a culturally entrenched sense of the importance of the individual.

4. Of course, one can argue that the goal of being liberated from one's ties to old objects is not necessarily incompatible with the goal of recognizing that that there is no self independent of others. For example, W. R. D. Fairbairn would argue that freeing oneself from one's attachment to bad internal objects allows one to be open to new relationships. This is still different, however, from the experience of interdependency valued in Buddhist thinking.

REFERENCES

Armstrong, K. 2000. *The Battle for God*. New York: Ballantine Books.

Aron, L. 1996. *A Meeting of Minds: Mutuality in Psychoanalysis*. Hillsdale, NJ: Analytic Press.

———. 1999. "Clinical Choices and the Relational Matrix." *Psychoanalytic Dialogues* 9: 1–29.

Batchelor, S. 1997. *Buddhism without Beliefs*. New York: Riverhead Books.

Becker, E. 1973. *The Denial of Death*. New York: Free Press.

Benjamin, J. 1988. *The Bonds of Love: Psychoanalysis, Feminism, and the Problem of Domination*. New York: Pantheon Books.

Berger, P., and Luckmann, T. 1967. *The Social Construction of Reality*. Garden City, N.Y.: Anchor Books.

Berman, M. 1981. *The Reenchantment of the World*. Ithaca, N.Y.: Cornell University Press.

Bion, W. R. 1970. *Attention and Interpretation*. London: Heinemann.

Bromberg, P. M. 1998. *Standing in the Spaces: Essays on Clinical Process, Trauma, and Dissociation*. Hillsdale, NJ: Analytic Press.

Cook, F. H. 1989. *Sounds of Valley Streams*. Albany: State University of New York Press.

Cushman, P. 1995. *Constructing the Self, Constructing America: A Cultural History of Psychotherapy*. Reading, Mass.: Addison-Wesley.

Eigen, M. 1998. *The Psychoanalytic Mystic*. London: Free Association Books.

Epstein, M. 1995. *Thoughts without a Thinker: Psychotherapy from a Buddhist Perspective*. New York: Basic Books.

———. 1998. *Going to Pieces without Falling Apart: A Buddhist Perspective on Wholeness*. New York: Broadway Books.

———. 2001. *Going On Being: Buddhism and the Way of Change*. New York: Broadway Books.

Fairfield, S. 2001. "Analyzing Multiplicity: A Postmodern Perspective on Some Current Psychoanalytic Theories of Subjectivity." *Psychoanalytic Dialogues* 11: 221–251.

Freud, S. 1915. *On Transience*. In Standard Edition, 14: 303–307. London: Hogarth Press, 1957.

———. 1926. *The Question of Lay Analysis*. In Standard Edition, 20: 179–258. London: Hogarth Press, 1959.

———. 1927. *The Future of an Illusion*. In Standard Edition, 21: 3–56. London: Hogarth Press, 1961.

———. 1930. *Civilization and Its Discontents*. In Standard Edition, 21: 64–145. London: Hogarth Press, 1961.

Ghent, E. 1989. Credo: "The Dialectics of One-Person and Two-Person Psychologies." *Contemporary Psychoanalysis* 25: 169–211.

Gombrich, R. F. 1988. *Theravada Buddhism: A Social History from Ancient Benares to Modern Colombo*. London: Routledge.

Greenberg, J. 2001. "The Analyst's Participation: A New Look." *Journal of the American Psychoanalytic Association* 49: 359–381.

Greenberg, J., and Mitchell, S. 1983. *Object Relations in Psychoanalytic Theory*. Cambridge, Mass.: Harvard University Press.

Grotstein, J. S. 2000. *Who Is the Dreamer Who Dreams the Dream? A Study of Psychic Processes*. Hillsdale, N.J.: Analytic Press.

Hoffman, I. Z. 1994. "Dialectical Thinking and Therapeutic Action in the Psychoanalytic Process." *Psychoanalytic Quarterly* 63: 187–218.

———. 1998. *Ritual and Spontaneity in the Psychoanalytic Process: A Dialectical-Constructivist View*. Hillsdale, N.J.: Analytic Press.

Lasch, C. 1979. *The Culture of Narcissism: American Life in an Age of Diminishing Expectations*. New York: W.W. Norton.

Loewald, H. 1980. *Papers on Psychoanalysis*. New Haven, Conn.: Yale University Press.

Magid, B. 2002. *Ordinary Mind: Exploring the Common Ground of Zen and Psychotherapy*. Boston: Wisdom Publications.

Mitchell, S. A. 1988. *Relational Concepts in Psychoanalysis: An Integration*. Cambridge, Mass.: Harvard University Press.

———. 1993. *Hope and Dread in Psychoanalysis*. New York: Basic Books.

———. 2000. *Relationality: From Attachment to Intersubjectivity*. Hillsdale, N.J.: Analytic Press.

———. 2001. "The Treatment of Choice: Commentary on Paper by Susan Fairfield." *Psychoanalytic Dialogues* 11: 283–291.

Molino, A. 1998. *The Couch and the Tree*. New York: North Point Press.

Pizer, S. 1998. *Building Bridges: The Negotiation of Paradox in Psychoanalysis*. Hillsdale, N.J.: Analytic Press.

Reiff, P. 1966. *The Triumph of the Therapeutic: Uses of Faith after Freud*. Chicago: University of Chicago Press.

Renik, O. 1996. "The Perils of Neutrality." *Psychoanalytic Quarterly* 65: 495–517.

Ricoeur, P. 1970. *Freud and Philosophy*. New Haven, Conn.: Yale University Press.

Ringstrom, P. A. 2001. "Cultivating the Improvisational in Psychoanalytic Treatment." *Psychoanalytic Dialogues* 11: 727–754.

Rorty, R. 1982. *Consequences of Pragmatism*. Minneapolis: University of Minnesota Press.

Rubin, J. B. 1996. *Psychotherapy and Buddhism: Toward an Integration*. New York: Plenum Press.

Stern, D. B. 1997. *Unformulated Experience: From Dissociation to Imagination in Psychoanalysis*. Hillsdale, N.J.: Analytic Press.

———. 2001. "Constructivism, Dialectic, and Mortality." *Psychoanalytic Dialogues* 11: 451–468.

Suler, J. R. 1993. *Contemporary Psychoanalysis and Eastern Thought*. Albany: State University of New York Press.

Watts, A. 1957. *The Way of Zen*. New York: Vintage Books.

———. 1996. *Buddhism: The Religion of No-Religion*. Boston, Mass.: Charles E. Tuttle.

About the Editors

Roberto Carnevali is a psychoanalytically trained psychotherapist who works both privately and in institutional psychiatry. A graduate of the Italian Group-Analytic Society, he is a training analyst for both the Association for Psychoanalytic Studies and the Confederation of Italian Organizations for Analytical Research on Groups. He is director of the Italian online magazine *Pratica Psicoterapeutica* (www.praticapsicoterapeutica.com), the author of several books, and a frequent contributor to some of Italy's foremost professional journals.

Alessandro Giannandrea, PhD, is a clinical psychologist and mindfulness meditation instructor trained in both Italy and the United States. A graduate of the Social Dreaming Institute (London), his ongoing research focuses on the connections among psychotherapy, mindfulness, Buddhism, and the philosophy of mind. As the author of several articles on these topics, he collaborates with the University of California, San Diego Center for Mindfulness and Rome's Sapienza University. In addition to his clinical practice he also teaches mindfulness in prisons and hospitals.

Anthony Molino is a practicing psychoanalyst, PhD anthropologist, and literary translator. Based in Italy, he is best known for his award-winning book *The Couch and the Tree: Dialogues in Psychoanalysis and Buddhism*, as well as for his highly praised book *Freely Associated: Encounters in Psychoanalysis with C. Bollas, N. Coltart, M. Eigen, J. McDougall, and A. Phillips*. Other works include: *Where Id Was: Challenging Normalization in Psychoanalysis* and *Culture, Subject, Psyche: Dialogues in Psychoanalysis and Anthropology*. His most recent book, co-edited with S. Benvenuto, is *In*

Freud's Tracks: Conversations from the Journal of European Psychoanalysis (2009).

About the Contributors

Gherardo Amadei, MD, is a psychiatrist and psychoanalyst affiliated with the International Association for Relational Psychoanalysis and Psychotherapy. He is associate professor of psychodynamic psychology at Milan's Bicocca University, the author of several acclaimed books, and works in private practice as a psychotherapist and teacher of mindfulness.

Joseph Bobrow is a Zen master and founder of Deep Streams Zen Institute in San Francisco, where continuing education in Zen Buddhist practice is provided for mental health professionals, alongside programs to help Iraq and Afghanistan veterans and their families transform the unseen injuries of war. He is also a psychologist–psychoanalyst and author whose first book, *Zen and Psychotherapy: Partners in Liberation*, examines the interplay of Buddhism and psychotherapy. He teaches widely throughout the United States and abroad.

Katie Ferrell earned her Bachelor of Arts in psychotherapy, mindfulness and creative expression from the University of Redlands in Southern California. She collaborates with the University of California, San Diego Center for Mindfulness on a variety of projects, including teaching mindfulness in schools and studying the effects of meditation on mind wandering.

Graziano Graziani is a full member of the Italian Psychoanalytic Society. A psychiatrist and neuropsychiatrist, he has worked since 1977 for Tuscany's Regional Mental Health Services. Formerly a professor of the history of psychology at the University of Florence, he is the author of more than eighty scientific publications.

Thich Nhat Hanh is a Vietnamese Zen Buddhist monk, teacher, author, poet, and peace activist. He is the author of over one hundred books, and he has worked to combine traditional Zen teachings with insights from both Mahayana and Theravada Buddhism as well from Western psychology. He has dedicated much of his life to the practice of "engaged Buddhism" and its mindfulness-based philosophy of "interbeing."

Pilar Jennings, PhD, is a psychoanalyst practicing in New York City. She holds degrees in both medical anthropology and in psychiatry and religion, is a lecturer in the graduate Department of Psychiatry and Religion at Union Theological Seminary, and a researcher at the Columbia University Center for Study of Science and Religion. Her most recent book is *Mixing Minds: The Power of Relationship in Psychoanalysis and Buddhism.*

Michela Morgana works in Milan as a psychologist and psychoanalytically trained psychotherapist, specializing in forensic psychiatry of the child and adolescent. Formerly Honorary Judge of the Court of Surveillance in Milan, for years she has written on the dialogue between scientific knowledge and artistic, humanistic, and religious learning. She is the author of two books of poetry as well as a practicing Buddhist. She is a teacher of the Dharma ordained in the Shinnyo Buddhist tradition. Her chapter in this book is excerpted from her own book *Il fango e il loto* ("The Mud and the Lotus Flower") published in Italy in 2010.

Katriona Munthe is a Jungian psychoanalyst and documentary filmmaker. Her longstanding interest in Buddhism began when, as a student at Rome University in 1979, she helped introduce the practice of meditation to faculty in the Department of Psychology. Founder of the Biodrama School in San Francisco, she now works with the terminally ill in Tuscany, teaches Mindfulness meditation, and trains and supervises hospital personnel. She has written and published extensively, mostly in Italian, on the science of symbols, the study of personality, and psychological types.

Adam Phillips is a British psychotherapist and essayist, and is generally regarded as one of today's foremost psychoanalytic writers. General Editor of the Penguin "Modern Classics" translations of Freud, he is also a regular contributor to *The London Review of Books*. His most recent book is *Missing Out: In Praise of the Unlived Life*.

Antonino Raffone, PhD, is associate professor of psychology at Rome's Sapienza University. After completing his doctorate in cognitive psychology, he later took lay vows as a bodhisattva in the Zen Soto tradition. His research has focused on neural integration processes related to perception, short-term and working memory and, more recently, on the neuronal correlates of consciousness and meditation.

Jeremy D. Safran, PhD, is co-chair and professor of psychology at the New School for Social Research, and former director of The New School Clinical Psychology Program. Past-president of the International Association of Relational Psychoanalysis and Psychotherapy, he is on the faculty of both the New York University Postdoctoral Program in Psychotherapy and Psychoanalysis and the Stephen A. Mitchell Center for Relational Studies. His books include: *Emotion in Psychotherapy*, *Negotiating the Therapeutic Alliance*, *Psychoanalysis and Buddhism: An Unfolding Dialogue*, and *Psychoanalytic and Psychoanalytic Therapies*.

Jeff Shore is a professor of Zen in the modern world at the Rinzai Zen-affiliated Hanazono University in Kyoto, where he has taught since 1987. His writings include the books *Zen Classics for the Modern World* and *Being Without Self*. As an undergraduate at Temple University in Philadelphia in the early 1970s, he was first inspired by Richard De Martino. He trained for over twenty-five years at the Rinzai monastery of Tôfukuji in Kyoto.

Nigel Wellings is a psychoanalytic psychotherapist who works within a contemplative perspective. Based in Bath (England), he is registered with the Council for Psychoanalysis and Jungian Analysis (CPJA) section of the United Kingdom Council for Psychotherapy. He has been a director of training of London's Centre for Transpersonal Psychology and is presently a facilitator on the Bath and Bristol Mindfulness Courses. With Elizabeth McCormick he has written several books including *Nothing To Lose: Psychotherapy, Buddhism and Living Life*, and the recently completed *Why Can't I Meditate? Befriending Our Obstacles To Mindfulness*.

Dorothy Yang is a Mandarin Chinese-speaking psychoanalyst born in China and raised in Taiwan. She has worked extensively with Asians in her private practice in Manhattan, and has used her background in Buddhism and the fine arts to facilitate a creative integration of mindfulness and psychoanalytic psychotherapy. A student of Buddhism for over thirty years, she has more recently focused increasingly on zazen practice.

Polly Young-Eisendrath, PhD, is a Jungian analyst based in Vermont, where she is affiliated with both Norwich University and the University of Vermont. A long-time practitioner of both Zen Buddhism and Vipassana, she is chairperson of the non-profit "Enlightening Conversations: Buddhism and Psychoanalysis Meeting in Person" that hosts conferences in cities across the United States. Dr. Young-Eisendrath is the author of fourteen books, of which the most recent is *The Self-Esteem Trap: Raising Confident and Compassionate Kids in an Age of Self-Importance*. Among her noteworthy edited collections are *The Cambridge Companion to Jung: New and Revised* (with T. Dawson) and *Awakening and Insight: Zen Buddhism and Psychotherapy* (with S. Muramoto).

CPSIA information can be obtained at www.ICGtesting.com
Printed in the USA
BVOW08*1545121213

338842BV00002BA/3/P